AF342664

*Shots at
Mule Deer*

Shots at Mule Deer

Rollo S. Robinson

WINCHESTER PRESS

Copyright © 1970, 1972 by Rollo S. Robinson

Library of Congress Catalog Card Number: 70-159429

ISBN: 087691-040-1

Published by Winchester Press
460 Park Avenue, New York 10022

Contents

Introduction

This book was written for many reasons.

First, to inform others (particularly youngsters) and to instill in them a love ánd respect for wild animals. Especially, I want to help them understand mule deer and the terrain they occupy—the streamsides, deserts, hill country and mountains of the American West.

Second, because of my amusement and disgust with much of the writings of the so-called mule deer "experts." Too often these authors have been content merely to rewrite others, thus compounding their errors. Much of this so-called "expert" material is actually mere speculation—"nature faking." Generally, these writers came West, hunted once or twice, and thereafter wrote as though they were experts.

Third, to point out some of the mismanagement of mule deer and public land by the several states and government agencies and to suggest possible solutions to the problems.

Fourth, to make a modest, personal contribution to outdoor literature. I grew up in mule deer country—among the hills and mountains and along the streams of the West, particularly in Utah. However, I've also lived in several other mule deer states: Idaho, Oregon, Washington, Wyoming. Yet, after more than fifty years of studying these animals, I've still got a

lot to learn about them. In fact, I learn something new—something basic
—each time afield.

My way of life has always been close to the natural environment of wild
creatures. I've loved all animals, particularly the wild ones, and especially
the small and large game mammals. To see even the tracks of the wild
creatures has always been a thrill. As a youngster on a poor-soil, boulder-
strewn farm, it was magic for me to find the tracks of quail, snakes, weasels
and the occasional coyote and deer among the ditches, berry tangles,
squaw brush, cottonwoods and oaks along American Fork River.

During the 1920's and 30's my family was still living ("existing" is a
better word) in the pioneer tradition. A portion of our livelihood depended
upon the products of fishing and hunting. We were harshly near to basic,
raw nature. We lived on the edge of a country village, and beyond were
the stark flats, boulders, trees and mountains home of the grouse, badgers,
deer, elk. Occasionally, some of these marvelous creatures even shared the
resources of our farm. And we fed them when they obviously showed a
need. It's been wonderfully rewarding to identify with the soil, the air and
water and the animals they produce and nurture—and write about them.

Fifth, and by no means least importantly: To defend both the right and
the necessity of sportsmen to harvest surplus wild animals. This statement,
in this day and age, perhaps requires some further explanation; and this is
probably as good a place to go into it as any. For today an increasing number of people are proclaiming that hunting is a barbarous practice. In fact,
there are many organizations which, given free rein, would force hunters
to silence their weapons forever. Sportsmen must continue to expect con-
frontation by these groups, and be prepared to come forward and answer
their accusations. The charges usually run something like this:

"The hunter is a coarse and brutal man . . . a man with a lust for blood,
an urge to kill and take life. "Killing builds up the hunter's sagging ego.
. . . In killing wild creatures he finds an illusion of success and power. . . .
This is primitive and unworthy of civilization."

"A hunter will often conceal his basic motive with one or more of these
excuses: Exercise, enjoyment of nature, companionship. . . . He may even
delude himself with rationalizations thrown up to satisfy squeamish con-
science. . . . Hunters do not understand themselves. . . . To kill for the joy
of killing is psychopathic. . . . People who like to hunt are neurotic.

And on and on it goes.

Is is wrong, somehow immoral, that man has a basic instinct to hunt?
Absolutely not! Man's framework of food gathering is based upon hunting.
In fact, every multicellular animal, including man, lives out his span by
consuming other organisms. The "new moralists" condemn hunters for

being cruel, but obviously, most anti-hunters live only because they have delegated their killing to others.

True, in most environments today it is no longer essential for us to kill wild animals to remain alive, but we must kill animals and plants, or we, the human race, will perish. Human existence on this planet is only possible because of a vast food chain: all organisms living on other forms of life. To grow sweet corn, a farmer must destroy a larval moth. The slice of bread one eats to store energy means that a few thousand creatures have been killed. Have you ever speculated, while eating salmon or tuna, how many organisms gave their lives before those beauties were lifted from the ocean? Literally millions!

Much has been spoken and written concerning the cruelty of hunters. But many who weep copiously for Bambi conveniently ignore the alternatives and the realities of their own nutrition.

Do you know how a Black Angus or Hereford is killed? Or how chickens and turkeys meet their death? Game birds and animals are generally accorded a more sudden, much more merciful death than their domestic relatives. A large number of deer, duck and pheasant escape, but only one obvious, determined end remains for cattle, swine and poultry.

Sure, it's true that a percentage of wild birds and mammals are wounded and escape to suffer a lingering death, and all true sportsmen sincerely regret this. However, sportsmen—and they are the majority of those afield —kill their game quickly and cleanly. Certainly man's weapons are more merciful than nature's: a deer toppled by coyotes; a caribou or moose pulled down by wolves—animals which are often fed upon while alive, devoured mouthful by mouthful as they lie struggling. Millions of wild animals are literally eaten alive every year by screwworms and related insect larvae, bacteria, etc. Lovable, considerate Mother Nature! Isn't a bullet more kind?

What is truly cruel is habitat destruction or destroying the ecological balance. Mule deer, elk, pheasants, quail, fish, etc. are now raised as crops by state, federal and private game management groups, to produce food and recreation. Through management errors we humans have sometimes destroyed their natural predators (often contrary to hunters' wishes) and altered their habitat until they would presently increase until their food supply was gone. Then, provident Mother Nature must necessarily kill thousands, millions of them.

This isn't speculation. Anyone with a memory 15 years long recalls the tragic starvation of deer herds in the north midwestern states. And those with a longer memory will recall the many deer which have died in Arizona's Kaibab Forest, Utah's Wasatch Mountains, Idaho's Snake River country, in Oregon and Washington—wherever food and animal numbers were not in balance.

No one who has watched a deer during its final days of starvation would be likely to criticize hunters for harvesting an adequate number of the animals the previous autumn. A concerned hunter is the best friend that game animals have. Few conservation programs would be alive today but for sportsmen. He's led the fight for national parks and preserves, where there would be no opportunity that he would ever again harvest a game animal from these areas. He's spread game species over the face of the earth and carefully nurtured their numbers. He's fought diligently, to prevent the extinction of the pronghorn, bison, key deer, turkey, elk, fur seal, musk ox, and many non-game species as well. In fact, the sportsman-hunter is the most ardent enemy of factors that would destroy all wildlife, even man himself: radiation, pollution and the human population explosion.

Yes, man is a hunter, and in a broad sense always has been and, I hope, always will be. He has great difficulty understanding the machinations and mechanics of an urban society, but wandering occasionally through the woods, marsh and over mountains is something he does comprehend.

Do hunters conceal their basic motives and use the excuse of physical activity, enjoyment of nature, companionship? Undoubtedly, some do. For while we hunt to kill, afield one learns other importances, all of them more meaningful than slaying game animals. In the field, I've discovered the meaning of sportsmanship, a word so overworked and misused, but which has now come to mean, at least to me, the Golden Rule; and it has made my life much more meaningful. The Golden Rule: almost a forgotten term in this jungle we call civilization. I've learned a measure of kindness, humility, patience, brotherhood—all basic values; some weather and health facts; a great deal of biology not found in textbooks and a thousand other important things. I've learned the value of life itself!

No, hunting isn't simple butchery, as some maintain. On the contrary, it can and for many hunters does have dignity and purpose. For when you respect the animal you hunt and kill it cleanly, and as nearly as possible on the animals own terms; and you truly understand the importance of that animal—its function—of the soil, water and wind of which the animal is composed, only then are you a true hunter. But then you are also a better man for being one.

Shots at
Mule Deer

1

Introducing Big Ears

I first saw the buck in a rugged, semi-alpine basin in central Utah while I was making a collection of small birds. The unusual length and number of his antler points and spread would have stiffened the hackles on the neck of the most demanding trophy hunter. From that moment on, I wanted that buck—hungrily. And, because there was a special place on the wall of my trophy-gun room—and surely in the record book—for such a head, I planned a hunt for that buck to the last detail.

Two days before the season opened, I reconnoitered the basin. The muley was still there, alone, feeding peacefully. However, a swirling mountain wind carried my scent to him, and after a quick look around the basin, he sneaked out, low-tailed, into a brushy ravine. A short time later he trotted through a gun-sight pass, about 600 to 700 yards away.

The thought that I had spooked the buck and possibly driven him from the basin haunted me constantly until the moment when I returned. After a long hike which brought me to the lip of the basin, I crawled carefully through a couple of inches of powdery snow to the top of the ridge, using a clump of sagebrush for cover. I quickly looked over the saucer-bottom and sloping sides of the basin, then made a fast search with a binocular. Finally, I located a little forkedhorn that was casually drifting, eating here and there in hip-high chaparral and scrubby conifers. My spirits sagged.

Bending over, I humped across the top of the ridge to the lip of the basin and sat in the early-morning sunshine. The movement was slow, but it alerted the two-pointer. It also caught the eyes of the old patriarch where he lay bedded in the scraggly chaparral. He slammed to his feet and, tailed by the little forky, quickly sneaked into some brushy cover. The distance was too great for a good shot. Certain that Long Ears and his little pal would head for the distant gun-sight pass again, I jogged rapidly through some screening aspens and pines near the north lip of the basin, hoping to intercept them or at least find their tracks in the snow.

I pulled up at the pass exhausted. A binoc bouncing from a pounding heart and heaving lungs, I tried to glass the area. No muleys in sight! But where had they gone? I hadn't crossed their tracks, nor could they have escaped except through steep, broken talus slopes to the south where rolling rocks would have betrayed them. Retracing my footprints in the snow, I found to my chagrin that Old Roman Nose and the little buck had waited in a brushy thicket as I hurried by on my way to the pass. Then they had slipped out of the basin through a hidden, rocky gully to the north.

Thirty-odd years have passed since that old rascal foxed me, but I still remember plunking down on that snowy hillside and cussing my luck. Of course, it wasn't all luck that enabled the buck to escape; he merely instinctively did what a trophy mule deer will often do. The mistakes were mine. What's more, I continued erring until the muley was lost, although he was in sight three additional times during the week-end. A trophy mule deer is a majestic big-game animal—particularly one that has escaped the red-shirted multitudes for a number of years. He's very crafty; and barring ill-fortune—may die not from a bullet but from age and weather atop some sparsely vegetated, snowy, wind-swept ridge.

This, then, is a game animal to test a hunter's ingenuity and patience. This is a trophy which, when killed fairly and cleanly, merits a chosen place on the den wall beside heads of other magnificent game animals: a beautiful white-tail buck that formerly skulked through a dense, North Carolina pine forest; a noisy, pugnacious, Oregon bull elk; a ghost-white mountain goat that once climbed seemingly impossible cliffs in Montana's

LIFE HISTORY

Flathead Alps; a mighty 42-inch bighorn ram that for 12 years faced winds and snows on the slopes of Canada's Storm Mountain. This, gentlemen, is the mule deer.

As with all mammals, a mule deer starts life when an egg is fertilized. First indication of the breeding season is swelling of necks among bucks which, in the middle of the muley geographical distribution, begins in mid-October. During this time, occasionally referred to as the period of the "Mad Moon," bucks behave very differently: generally lose their characteristic alertness; eat little (resulting in considerable weight loss); become pugnacious (almost unmanageable when penned); sometimes travel long distances and expend much energy while searching for receptive females (muleys usually do not gather harems as do elk); become restless and may prod females viciously with their antlers; duel with other males (although few knockdown battles have been observed). This is the time when bucks "lock" antlers. I've never seen bucks vigorously battling; mostly they spar and push. Some bucks travel very little during the rut. They may find one or several receptive does and remain with them, spending much time beating away intruders. During the rut, bucks offer questionable sport; whenever possible, they shouldn't be hunted at this time. After rutting, males are quiet and docile, and eat heavily. If browse has good quality and is plentiful, they gain considerable weight.

Yearling males are capable of serving does, but their necks do not swell to the same extent as older bucks—some apparently not at all. Nor do they seek females as actively as more mature males. Bucks may collect in groups (I've seen as many as 37 of them together) and "socialize" prior to the mating season, but this friendship disappears at breeding time. Their relationship then becomes a "peck order" system.

Almost all females first breed when approximately 1½ years old. A southern Arizona study showed initial mating occurs about December 7, and during the following 10 days all observed females "came in heat." In Utah, breeding begins in early November, peaks in late November and extends into December. One mating was observed in February. Receptiveness by a female lasts for about 24 hours. If not bred, she experiences two to three additional estrous cycles, 21 to 23 days apart. Average gestation period is 200 days. Fawns are generally born in June, with some births occurring in July. In some regions a few youngsters are dropped as early as March, some as late as August (southern New Mexico and Mexico)—one during mid-October. Fawning varies with geographical location, corresponding generally with favorable growth of vegetation.

As birthing approaches, a female becomes rather "nervous" and searches for concealing cover, ranging from thinly vegetated meadows to heavy brush—but generally near water. There she gives birth, usually to twins, although triplets are not uncommon. I've heard of only one case of quads, in Montana. Two-year-old females almost always produce one fawn; but, with all does, quality and quantity of the food supply determines fawn productivity. Deer biologists believe that most adult females start pregnancy with twin embryos.

Immediately prior to birthing, a doe lies down and rises several times but the young are born while the mother is lying on the ground. Almost at once the female begins tonguing her youngsters and may, like a number of other mammals, consume the afterbirth. Within an hour or so the fawns struggle to their feet and stagger about. At this time the mother usually attempts to drive the fawns of the previous year away.

Fawns weigh approximately seven pounds. They walk easily at 24 hours. Although they nurse heavily for 60 days, they begin eating forage plants when only two to three weeks old. Fawns grow rapidly. Weight is doubled during the first two weeks, quadrupled in just 30 to 40 days. On good range in Utah, fawns weigh about 65 pounds by October. Single fawns weigh more than individual twins, and males slightly more than females.

How many years does a female muley remain productive? Captive does have continued bearing young as long as they lived. I know of one female which has given birth to 6 pairs of twins and still remains healthy and active.

Fawns are almost always found lying on the ground in cool, rather shaded locations. However, if an intruder (human, dog or horse) remains near the youngster beyond a minute or two, it may rise, utter a frightened bleat and run. For several weeks fawns do not follow their mothers as they forage, and for this reason humans may believe the youngsters have been abandoned and take them home. Most fawns continue nursing for about four to five months and a number of does, consequently, are killed during the autumn season while still "in milk."

Contrary to general belief, fawns do possess some odor. A male English setter I once owned could easily locate bedding places of fawns and the youngsters themselves. However, fawn odor is probably rather faint—certainly not easily detected by man. Fawns at birth are spotted: two general lines of spots down the back and indiscriminate patches on sides of the body. These grayish splotches remain for about 75 days, but are shed during late summer-early fall. During hunting season in October in Utah, the youngsters resemble adults in coloration. A mother deer, a day or two after birthing, begins lying some distance away from her fawns at resting time—possibly an instinctive protective device, because adults do have odors. Twin fawns do not lie side by side either—usually a few yards apart. When quite young, fawns permit man to pet them and lift them from the ground, without protest. If standing when danger appears (dog or human) a fawn usually drops to the ground, with head and neck extended. Within a week they can outrun a middle-aged man.

Fawns can often be located by watching the mother, for she frequently gazes intently toward where her youngsters are hiding. As she approaches, the little fellows respond immediately to her low bleat. They arise, come to the mother and begin nursing. When very young, fawns generally nurse several times during early morning and afternoon-evening. They may play for a few minutes after nursing, but soon find a place to lie down. The location isn't selected by the mother.

After about two and a half to three months, youngsters nurse only intermittently. Many hunters believe that fawns die if orphaned during the fall hunting season. This is a misconception. By October, youngsters can subsist on browse, although their reduced ability to sense danger and take appropriate action may be a factor in their survival. The story is told of one Utah fawn which, separated from its mother at about one and a half months, lived in a waterless enclosure for three months until killed that autumn by a hunter.

When danger in the form of a coyote, bobcat, dog, etc. threatens her fawn, a mother responds quickly and stubbornly, rushing menacingly, with ears back, toward the intruder and striking effectively with front feet. However, if a man approaches, she usually runs away, stops at 100 to 200 yards, in sight, and watches intently.

Some mothers accept the fawns of other deer, but an occasional mother may attack a strange fawn viciously. When leading her offspring to another location, she may nudge them along with her head.

Antler growth begins about mid-April, depending upon geographical location. New antlers grow quickly, sometimes reaching a length of six to seven inches in just two to three weeks. During summer months antlers are bulbous and covered with "velvet." This moss-like covering becomes dry between late August and early September and is scraped away on small trees (sometimes called "rubbing trees") and shrubs. Older bucks with large racks shed their velvet slightly earlier than more immature companions. Antler shedding varies with latitude. In Utah, peak is at mid-February but ranges from January to March. One buck I know about retained his headgear until mid-April. As a buck grows older, date of antler-drop becomes successively later, extending into March. There is much speculation concerning the fate of shed antlers— and why they are rarely found. Antler shedding occurs on winter range, and this area may be miles away from where these deer are hunted during autumn. A scab-crust forms on the skull pedicle in approximately one to three days after shedding. Emasculated bucks and few others (perhaps those having a hormone imbalance) frequently retain their antlers throughout their lives. And, of course, everyone has seen or read of antlered females. Fawn bucks sometimes develop small nubbin-antlers. Males become docile after shedding their antlers, sometimes secretive; and they eat very heavily as the new antlers develop.

Mule deer molt their hair twice yearly: during spring (April and May) and fall, generally during the last two weeks in September.

Geographical segregation of sexes isn't as wide as generally supposed. However, some mature bucks do gather before and after the rut—and may range in groups high in the mountains. Winter home range is often very limited, considerably more restricted than summer range. Does with fawns have a very narrow summer range. During migration, of course, travel may be very extensive. In Utah and California, deer units may move seasonally as much as 50 to 75 air miles—a few much farther. Longest distance known to the author concerns a buck tagged at 8 months in northern Nevada and killed as a four-year-old near Blackfoot, Idaho—150 air miles away.

Life span is about eight years. Some live beyond 10, and a few as long as 15 to 20, judging from the condition of their teeth when compared with those of known age in captivity. A number of captive deer have lived as long as 20 years. Mortality among mule deer is very high. In Utah only about two-thirds of the fawns survive to the October hunting season. Causes of death are predation, accidents and disease. A Utah study showed that few fawns weighing less than 6 pounds at birth survive to mid-October. Single fawns have a higher survival rate than individual twins.

WHERE TO FIND DEER

Veteran hunters recognize good mule deer country immediately, although sometimes it's difficult for them to describe the characteristics. It's a matter of experience. One learns over the years that muleys prefer certain types of habitat, varying, of course, with seasons. Deer are "edge" creatures. Sure, they occasionally bury themselves in dense, dark conifers. But, generally speaking, they inhabit the "lip" portions of their cover: groves of aspens, oaks, maples, conifers.

Deer know the physical features of the district in which they live and, if you would hunt them successfully, try to learn a little about these characteristics, too. However, don't tramp through the cover until you've frightened them away. Unless you are afield when deer are moving about, you may see few muleys—perhaps none at all. However, don't be discouraged. Finding tracks and droppings is nearly as important, anyway; if there are a reasonable number of fresh signs, you may have found a good place to hunt. Check them closely. If there are numerous fawn tracks, you have obviously located a doe-fawn area. However, if most of the prints are large, in all likelihood some bucks are around. During the rut all types of tracks are found together. Before the rut, mature bucks are not usually found with the females.

Locating a general area which has a reasonable population of mule deer is often simplified if one studies local weather conditions. When Indian Summer prevails, search high in the mountains for muleys, especially for trophies. However, when a foot of snow falls on their summer range, they migrate to the lowlands: cedar, oak and pinon ravines and flats. When weather moderates, deer follow the retreating snowline upward.

A friend and I drew special permits for a post-season hunt on the Birdseye district of central Utah. After heavy snow fell in November, the deer drifted out of the mountains and began staring, the ranchers said, at their haystacks. We hiked over the country the week before opening day and saw considerable "signs." Here was an opportunity, we were sure, to kill two veteran ridge-runners which range so high that regular season hunters rarely see them. However, by noon opening day our eyes were falling out of their sockets from looking at old signs and for trophy deer. There were a number of does, fawns and mediocre bucks on those benches. But no gigantic trophies. Know what those old tricksters had done? A rancher told us that several days before we arrived the weather had warmed and most of the deer had low-tailed for the ridges.

I believed him, and I needed exercise. The following day I took off for the peaks and within two miles of the ranch started jumping some large bucks. You wouldn't believe me if I told you how many exceptional trophies I saw until I ran out of time and sandwiches. When Mr. Big was finally located, I didn't shoot because there wasn't sufficient time to carry that buster out of the hills; I had to be in school the following morning.

Rarely are muleys found in open areas during heavy storms. They move into cover, thicker the better. Trees shelter them from biting winds and precipitation. Deer also seem to sense when a storm has abated and move out almost immediately to browse. One should periodically check a barometer during a long, bitter storm; when the mercury rises abruptly, go hunting. Don't think, however, that muleys won't eat during a light snowfall and rain. After satisfying their appetites, muleys generally retire to thickets where they lie down, regurgitate and chew vegetation they have eaten—most often just inside the lip of the forest: where the air is cool, where there's concealment, where a short run takes them into cover even more dense and from which they can smell, see and hear the approach of enemies.

Almost never are mule deer seen from 9 a.m. to 4 p.m. in open areas, especially during a warm, October-November day. However, a few deer may even bed where they finish eating, on an open hillside, beside a trail or busy highway. Hence, some writers have manufactured a broad, incorrect generalization: "Mule deer are dumb!" During late spring, muleys frequent "parks" and meadows where they consume large quantities of weeds and grasses. While accompanying Forest Service and Utah Game Department personnel as they checked range in southern Utah during the spring of 1954, I clicked off on a counting device during a two-hour period more than 400 muleys on open range and in cattle pastures. But, of course, these animals were still on their winter range. Very few, if any, of them would be there during October.

Mule deer pay little attention to snow until it's six to eight inches deep; usually, they remain high in the mountains until at least a foot of the white stuff has accumulated. The fact that frost has withered leaves and grasses doesn't seem to start deer migrating. As a matter of fact, they appear to like coolish temperatures. From a hunting standpoint, this indicates that a person should look for them in the cool portions of their range—the north slopes—particularly if the hunting season is marked by Indian Summer temperatures. They sometimes bed on snow even though clear areas are available. However, during late winter and cold spring days, they are most often found bedded on south, warm hillsides. For weather to assist a person, one must have a knowledge of local conditions. A particular district may be swarming with muleys during October—but empty in November. Snow may fall on one portion of the range while a neighboring area may receive little or none.

Can one successfully hunt mule deer if he has a knowledge of browse plants they eat? I don't think so. Several years ago an expert wrote an article in which he informed his readers that if they would make a study of deer forage plants, they then had a reasonable chance of killing a muley. On the surface this author's advice sounds plausible, and he probably misled a few people. As pointed out elsewhere, muleys eat a variety of available foods and plants found rather widespread over the flats, hills and mountains of the West.

Sometimes mule deer go deep into conifer forests—not to seek food, for these places are biological deserts—but to rest and hide. Such locations are excellent areas for a still hunter to look for muleys, especially during a storm. Some inexperienced hunters, frustrated in their attempts to find deer in these jungles, hike uphill, above the trees, and roll rocks or fling stones with a slingshot into the cover. Many sportsmen frown on such a practice.

Mule deer don't regularly bed and feed day after day in the same area. They wander rather aimlessly over their home territory, feeding wherever browse is available and bedding in edges of nearby cover. Springs, livestock watertroughs, impoundments and beaver ponds sometimes show considerable use by mule deer. They visit these places usually near dusk and at dawn. In primitive regions friends and I have seen deer drinking during midday, but only rarely in heavily hunted districts. Muleys can regularly be killed while "water watching," but I believe the practice is rather unsporting for riflemen though perhaps all right for bow hunters. There are a number of vast, nearly waterless, areas in the West which now support a reasonable number of mule deer. Thirty years ago very few muleys inhabited these harsh, starkly beautiful desert flats and rolling hills. Sufficient browse has always been available, but for extended periods water might be scarce or absent. Was drinking water the only limiting factor? There are areas in the Southwest and Mexico where mule deer apparently live in the best of health and never drink a drop of water except during intermittent rains.

A general rule to follow when endeavoring to locate mule deer—one that should be obvious to all—is to look for these animals where they are least disturbed. I dearly love to hunt primitive districts, where human footprints and the men who make them are rarely seen. One should hunt the difficult areas, too, where other sportsmen don't like to go— dense coniferous thickets; steep canyons and rocky ravines where travel is hazardous; broken cliffs where amateurs think only sheep or goats dare live. I recall a little patch of thick firs—about four acres—on the side of a rugged canyon where my brother had killed two tremendous bucks. Nearly all hunters shun this place deliberately because they believe it's an excellent place to break a leg.

Mule deer sometimes live near residential areas of large western cities. In fact, near my home in Ogden, Utah, live six to seven muleys, and I've counted as many as 17 during winter months. Our local newspaper carried a story several years ago about a hunter who killed a buck from his kitchen door. Occasionally friends have dropped deer right in camping areas. I have never killed a deer within a hundred yards of camp, but I nearly threw dish water on one in Utah's Taylor Flat, near Flaming Gorge. A friend and I had finished supper dishes and, with the pan in my hands, I pushed the canvas flap open with my head and shoulders and stepped out into a very dark night. While the water was in the air, I was startled to hear the familiar sound of a retreating deer. We checked with a lantern and found that the muley had been standing within three feet of where the water had splashed on the ground. However, these experiences illustrate the exception. Deer are occasionally found anywhere on their range, particularly during the opening morning barrage; but, most muleys are not killed near camp. The farther one hikes from his tent or car, the better his prospects become.

Where you can find deer—and their behavior when you do—cannot be predicted with total certainty, for individual deer, like people, tend not to conform with theories. Most outdoor writers mistakenly place the behavioral patterns of all big-game animals into tight, little categories. Particularly deer. Mule deer, like humans and numerous other animals, do possess characteristics which sometimes can be catalogued into pigeon holes. Still, they all occasionally slide out of the fixed routine and do the unexpected. For example, one deer may not spook from a bit of man-odor that sends another racing out of the area. We hunters should remember that no two deer behave exactly alike. This results in exciting (some call it exasperating) experiences. Certainly there would be little enjoyment if one could always make an easy kill. Don't be disappointed if a muley escapes your bullet. It's comparable to losing a trophy trout after an exciting battle. Often, the most satisfying thrill of muley hunting is not in dropping a deer.

PREDATION AND DISEASES

Sportsmen are often surprised when they learn that predators remove a considerable number of deer from the range each year. A study in Utah's Daggett County showed that predation accounted for 54 per cent of the total losses: 29 per cent by cougars; 19 per cent by coyotes; 3 per cent by bobcats. Mature deer as well as fawns were taken.

Knowledgeable biologists believe that cougars and other predators are beneficial to a deer herd, because they kill winter-weak, diseased animals. Ten thousand lions were killed and bountied between 1907 and 1947, a period of very intensive hunting by state and federal trappers.

As of May, 1969, only Arizona still bountied the cougar ($75). Idaho, Montana, Texas and Wyoming classify this animal as a predator, while California, Oregon, Nevada, Washington, Utah and Colorado protect the cougar as a game animal. A few individuals consider the lion's take of deer excessive and, therefore, intolerable. However, few would advocate his extinction. Our wildlife is our heritage and, where is the hunter who deserves the name, who cannot thrill when by chance he encounters this "villain" of western mountains?

Coyotes are also a factor in predation, for they will eat almost any-, thing, and few biologists deny that they annually account for thousands of mule deer in western North America. A significant percentage of their droppings show deer hair, but it is believed that most of these muleys were starving, diseased, crippled or eaten as carrion. Without doubt, a mature, healthy mule deer has little difficulty handling a coyote. Charles west, trapper for the U.S. Fish & Wildlife Service saw a buck chasing a coyote. The muley knocked the coyote over, jumped on it, whereupon the yipper crawled into some brush. The buck circled the patch of cover but departed when Mr. Vest approached. The near helpless coyote was easily killed. I've never seen a coyote kill a muley, sick or otherwise. However, I've often observed deer and coyotes in immediate proximity, and sometimes the deer were paying no attention to the little dogs.

A California study showed that predation from all sources doesn't limit deer numbers. Quality and quantity of forage is the important factor. Moreover, extensive coyote control appears to have little or no effect on overall deer numbers. Technicians believe that most deer flesh is eaten as carrion and that some predation is probably good for deer.

While hunting the Skintoe area of northern Utah, a friend and I discovered a freshly-dead muley fawn upon which a bobcat had been feeding. Whether the little buck had been killed by the cat will never be known. Perhaps he had died from a gun-shot wound. Bobcat droppings frequently contain deer hair, but it's thought that this animal generally takes deer flesh as carrion, although there is no question that wildcats do kill an occasional fawn, cripple or an adult isolated in deep, crusted snow.

Black bears also kill a few fawns and cripples. Several observers have reported bears cruising fawning areas, apparently searching for newly dropped youngsters. One study of bear droppings showed that 12 per cent contained deer hair. Were the animals utilized as carrion? Probably, for it's well known that bruins prefer their meat on the "high" side.

Eagles? A number of years ago these large birds were commonly included among the important predators of antelope, sheep, goats and deer. Recent studies, however, indicate that only rarely do eagles capture and kill even the young of these mammals. Very few nests show evidence of deer predation.

Crippling Losses

Concerned sportsmen were startled to learn in a Minnesota study that 68 white-tailed deer were wounded or left in the woods (both legal and illegal kills) for every 100 legal bucks harvested. Results of a questionnaire sent to New Mexico sportsmen disclosed that crippling losses ran about 21 per cent, but it was believed by wildlife managers that the percentage ran approximately 30 per cent because many hunters would not admit they had crippled deer. Similar losses on the Kaibab Forest were estimated to be 10 to 15 per cent. Forest Service personnel working Utah's Fishlake district discovered that 2,568 muleys, or 18 per cent had gone down the drain through crippling. Colorado in a similar survey came up with a 15 per cent loss. During a special removal of deer by game wardens in Utah's Twelve-Mile Canyon, crippling losses were found to be 19 per cent.

Obvious errors creep into surveys of wounded-crippled big game. Some deer are knocked down, recover and race away. Others are crippled and then finished off by other hunters. And some cripples survive. During one hunting trip, I killed such a deer. This buck had lost approximately eight inches of his right front leg, but the wound had healed and the animal was fat. I've seen several other deer that had been similarly crippled but had managed to recover.

Some deer are abandoned by hunters: fawns, when larger animals are desired; does (particularly those nursing fawns), when hunters prefer bucks; diseased animals and those in poor flesh; when terrain is difficult or distance to camp considerable; when sportsmen are forced out of the district by storms; when excessive numbers of muleys are killed by party hunting; when meat has been shot-up or spoiled; when hunters were unable to relocate their kills.

Obviously, crippling losses are significant, both to hunters and biologists-technicians—particularly the latter, because they must know the approximate number of deer a herd loses, so they can manage correctly.

Diseases and Parasites of Mule Deer—

Only rarely does a sportsman harvest a deer showing obvious signs of severe disease or parasite infestation. However, all adult deer are affected in one or more ways. In fact, if you can show me a mature muley which doesn't have some disease, or internal or external parasites, I'll eat the critter—skin, tail, antlers—everything.

Mule deer have been found to be infected with brucellosis; rabies (three cases in California); pyobacillosis (pus collects in the body); hoof rot (has killed many deer in California); and tapeworms. A cysticercus of a tape, *Taenia Krabbi,* has been located in muscles and the heart of muleys, an organism which matures in coyotes and dogs. Therefore, don't feed raw deer flesh to Rover. Tapeworms are easily killed by cooking. Mule deer occasionally have eyeworms, footworms, lungworms (have caused important losses in British Columbia), stomach and intestinal worms, and blood, whip and body worms. Ticks are occasionally found on muleys in large numbers, particularly during winter and spring, a time when the animals can least afford the loss of blood. The larvae of the nose bot fly also sometimes parasitize muleys. These organisms, ½-1½ inches in length, yellow in color, generally locate in the throat and nasal passages. The usual effect of the nose bot fly—true of other disease organisms and parasites—is to reduce vitality in the deer, particularly during winter and early spring. Mule deer also suffer from pneumonia, especially when they are starving.

Deer are likewise killed when they fall, drown, fight each other, become entangled in fences and wires, or succumb from exhaustion in fenced fields. Poachers kill a considerable number and ranchers, who suffer depredations during winter, remove some by permit. Occasionally a buck is blinded during a fight. A California muley was destroyed when his bulbous antlers grew so heavy that he could no longer lift his head off the ground. Automobiles kill hundreds of mule deer every year. And sometimes a motorist is killed, too. A Chicago man was fatally injured when his car careened to avoid 5 deer near Eureka, Utah. Mule deer also suffer bone fractures, arthritis and tooth malformation.

Very little scientific research has been done on diseases and parasites of muleys. This is regretable, for undoubtedly thousands of mule deer are weakened or die from infection and infestation—generally when snow is deep, most of the browse gone and predation high. It's comforting, however, to remember that no known disease, organism or parasite can be acquired by man from eating properly cooked venison.

2

Before You Hunt

BE PREPARED

What happened to three of us during a muley safari a number of years ago shouldn't have happened to a mangy, crippled coyote with rabies. After leaving home at Ashton, Idaho, I picked up two friends at Blackfoot. Our destination: Salmon River country. Our intentions: to bag three old Roman-nosed bucks with record-book heads. Rolling carefree across central Idaho, only once did we casually discuss an ominous bank of gray clouds forming in the west. Darkness overtook us just as we reached our turnoff road deep inside Salmon River Canyon. Spotting a lighted tent, we stopped, thinking we would make camp nearby—and, perhaps, obtain information from the campers, for none of us had hunted that specific area before.

We helloed good-naturedly as we approached the tent, but were invited in only after some delay and a bit of commotion inside. Three men were in the process of preparing supper and, as we stood stiffly attempting conversation, suspicion was so thick it couldn't have been cut with a sharp machete. Eventually, one of the stubbly-whiskered men flipped aside the door-flap and strode out into the darkness. A few minutes later he returned.

"Appears to be all right, Sam," he said to an older man tending a pan of cooking meat. "I've checked their car." Then, turning toward us: "We thought you might be game wardens."

The speaker then uncovered the loins and hindquarters of a deer and, taking the meat to a two-foot high section of log, deftly cut, with a double-bladed axe, about a dozen steaks. First time I'd ever seen meat sliced with an axe.

"You lads look hungry," the older man said, as he speared a grease-popping, dark-brown piece of meat and added it to a growing mountain of steaks on a large platter. The men were woodcutters and, exercising the questionable prerogative of their profession, had poached a deer for camp meat. Travelers and woodsmen are invariably hungery and during the next 30 minutes we consumed an unbelievable amount of venison, fried potatoes, sourdough biscuits smothered with strawberry jam, and coffee.

Finally, the time came to broach the question one pre-season deer hunter always asks another: "Where are the muleys?"

"Ain't many deer around," the older man said. "Especially in this here side canyon. But, if you'll go . . ."

The warm tent, the delicious food, had lulled us into a trap. Accepting the advice of the woodcutters, we drove several miles farther down the main canyon and stopped at the edge of a park which appeared to be the place where we had been directed. No one was certain, though, for the night was as dark as the inside of a black bear's stomach.

Sleeping bags which a poor lad could afford in those days were a sorry lot of near nothingness. With such a bag I was probably little better equipped than my two companions who had three homemade quilts and a piece of canvas.

I had been asleep for perhaps an hour when someone woke me by jerking the side of my bag. And I knew the reason immediately upon thrusting my noggin out of the sack. Snow was already an inch deep and falling more rapidly. While my two pals were rearranging their bed with the canvas on top, I transferred my sack to my one-seater coupe. And, though as cramped as a cricket in an empty .38 handgun case, finally went back to sleep. In approximately an hour, more tugging.

"Move over; we're coming inside, too!"

Eventually, I moved my sack to the rear of the Ford after rearranging food boxes, tire chains, etc. At daybreak when I raised the turtle-back of the car, a solid foot of wet snow lay on the ground. However, the sky was mostly clear.

My companions cussed a little when awakened but refused to stir. Worse, every piece of firewood was wet or hidden by snow. After a cold, soggy, skimpy breakfast, I shouldered my rifle and pointed my nose up a draw to the west. After an hour I was nearly exhausted. After two hours of slogging through deep snow, I was wet to the hips and inclined to call it quits. However, I built a fire beside a large rock and sat for several hours on the side of the mountain where I could see into two deep, long ravines. At about noon, several shots echoed from across the canyon. At two o'clock, having seen only six female muleys, I trudged back to the car. My companions had retired from hunting an hour before and had folded their quilts. We ate lunch and headed the car toward home.

Several decades haven't erased the memories of that Salmon River fiasco. But my friends and I profited from the debacle because almost immediately we began acquiring equipment and know-how that have made deer hunts since then golden, satisfying experiences. For example, the Salmon River safari taught us never to head for the hills without first consulting a barometer. Better still, when near an Air Force base or a government weather station, we've tried always to phone for a weather forecast.

We learned never to believe, even 10 per cent of it, the advice of a stranger concerning a place to hunt muleys. Each of us began skimping here and there on nonessentials until we could purchase comfortable sleeping bags, a wall tent, air mattresses, a sheepherder stove, lantern, binoculars—a hundred other items.

BINOCULARS

Hunters using good binoculars don't mistake horses, cattle, elk, moose and humans for deer. And, to my recollection, never have I heard of anyone killing a doe in error while using a glass. However, I'm sure that over the years many females, particularly when found in oak brush, have been killed by hunters who, without binocs or rifle scopes, believed them to be males. Unless moving, a deer is somewhat difficult to find with naked eyes. But on many occasions I've located muleys a half-mile away—a number as far as a mile—with binocs. At one-quarter mile— sometimes farther—a sportsman can also roughly judge a deer's trophy possibilities. Obviously, a person equipped with a good binocular can save himself much hiking or riding when searching for trophies.

Binoculars also have other important uses afield beside finding and judging game. On one occasion it became necessary that we locate a hunting companion. We hiked to a lookout point and within five minutes spotted him in a rock "nest" about a mile away. Without binocs the search might have required several hours.

After having learned the hard way—and wasted a considerable sum of money—perhaps I can assist you in deciding which binocular to purchase.

Price was my first consideration when I bought that first binoc; then magnification. I was wrong on both counts. The cost of owning an excellent glass is not as much as one first believes. Suppose a youngster of 20 invests $200 in a good binocular. At age 60 the monthly cost will have been only about 42 cents, or five dollars each year. Cheap at twice the cost. From a few feet away, cheap and expensive binoculars look very much alike. In fact, an inexpensive, poor binoc magnifies as much as a costly, excellent instrument; but almost always, the image is murky. Occasionally, sporting literature carries advertisements offering binoculars from $3.50 to $10, and in large print compares them to glasses priced at $200. Don't be duped. These binocs are essentially toys.

A cheap binoc may perform quite well for a short time, but an excellent glass, treated with reasonable care, will last a lifetime. An exception may be found, but price usually indicates quality: coated lenses, construction to take rugged use (firm mounting of prisms and lenses), moisture- and dust-proofing, and precision manufacture of lenses and prisms. Whether one purchases shoes, a bottle of booze—or a binocular— a person generally gets what he pays for.

I've never seen a French binoc that I would have as a gift—same with much Japanese junk. However, during my prowling around the hills and while on active duty with the Air Force at home and abroad, I've seen some good Zeiss, Ross, Leinz and Hensoldt binocs, especially Zeiss. An article in a professional optical journal stated that the best binoculars in the world are now being made in the United States. Therefore, purchase a domestic product, such as Bausch and Lomb. The price is competitive and, something that's important, repairs and replacement parts are readily available.

My first binoc was wrong in another way: too much magnification— a 10X glass. While sitting atop a squirming horse, it was nearly impossible to stabilize an image. Even while standing I had difficulty holding the binoc rigidly, and only when seated or braced against a rock or tree could I use the glass satisfactorily. What I failed to understand as a youngster was that as magnification increases, hand tremors likewise cause an image to be more "shaky."

I've seen binoculars advertised from 4X to 12X. Four power magnification is not enough for the average muley hunter, and anything from 10X upward is too much. Seven and 8X are best, although 9X may be all right for a few individuals, particularly those sportsmen who also hunt sheep and goats. A muley hunter who concentrates on still hunting fairly thick cover would be well equipped with a 6X binoc.

Nearly everyone understands that the 8 portion of the 8X30 represents magnification. Obviously, eight magnifications appear to bring a deer eight times nearer. But remember that increased magnification results in more wobble, reduced field of view and a glass that "gathers" less light—therefore, less image. However, many individuals fail to understand that the second figure of 8X30, the 30, is the diameter of the objective lens, the lens most distant from one's eyes. The wider the diameter of this lens, the more light gathered, and the more effective the binoc will be at dawn and dusk—periods when game is usually encountered. But hunters must also realize that large objective lenses add considerable weight and size. These are the glasses we saw naval officers wearing so heavily around their necks during World War II. Average Mr. Deer Hunter wants a binoc with an objective lens of 30 to 35—certainly not 50.

Don't insist on an extremely wide field of view, either, for this feature also adds weight, bulk and expense. Field of view is that portion of the landscape which can be seen without shifting a binoc. Remember: as field of view increases, magnification decreases. Edges of the field often become curved and fuzzy, too. Through a 6X binocular one can see approximately 445 feet at 1,000 yards; through an 8X, 330 feet. This range is fairly wide and about right.

Two types of focusing are available: central and individual. I've owned both types of glasses and prefer central focusing. A binoc seems never to be in sharp adjustment when Mr. Big Ears appears. And, because no one (including the deer) knows how long the animal will remain in place, it's imperative that a person quickly assess the critter's desirable qualities. With central focusing, a quick twist of the wheel is possible, but it may be necessary to move both eyepieces of the other type. However, a glass with a central wheel, manufacturers admit, may leak a little dust and moisture. Individual focusing binocs are a few dollars cheaper.

During and after World War II, big news in the binocular trade was coating of lenses with magnesium fluoride. This reduces light reflection and the result is a brighter and sharper image. This coating, bluish-purple, supposedly increases amount of light passed to about 5 per cent for each glass surface. That adds up to a sizable amount. An expensive binoc carrying the name of a reliable manufacturer has all lenses coated, but a cheap glass may have only external ones so treated.

A word of warning concerning the buying of used binoculars. Sports stores and pawnbrokers offer many kinds: large and small; cheap, expensive; good and worthless. Suspect each one of them, for the simple truth is that someone didn't want that glass. One must know what he's doing, or he may get stung. If possible, obtain permission from the clerk to take the binoc to an expert for evaluation. If he refuses—after you've offered to make a deposit—hurry to the nearest exit. Remember, also, that probably all pre-World War II binocs did not have coated lenses.

When expert advice is unavailable, first note the manufacturer's name. Bausch and Lomb, Zeiss, Hensoldt and Ross—as pointed out previously—are excellent binocs, if they are in good condition. Next, check external lenses (you won't be able to examine those inside) for a fluoride coating. Is there evidence that the glass has been damaged? Do the central wheel and eyepieces adjust easily? Ask to take the binocular outside—preferably into the mountains. But remember that poor binocs often give a passable performance in bright sunshine, but fall down on a dull day, during early morning and late evening. A real test comes in dim light. While looking at a brick building a block away, are the edges of the field of view fuzzy, out of focus or showing a halo of color? The image cloudy and faint? Do the bricks curve away at the edge of the field of view? Compare the binoc alternately with a new Bausch and Lomb. A big game hunter needs "resolving power"—ability to see small objects distinctly, particularly a trophy hunter who wants to inspect a buck for length and number of tines, spread and general overall bulk in antlers.

If, after using a binoc for 10 to 15 minutes, you experience eyestrain —and after a longer period of use, a headache—something is wrong. Your eyes are straining to align two images and alignment is an expensive problem to solve. Return the binoc and walk away fast—before the clerk has time to tempt you by slicing the price down the middle.

How about field glasses? I don't believe you want this type of instrument: a double-barreled telescope. The field of view is rather limited, the sensible maximum magnification about 5X and the overall length with more power objectionable. However, field glasses are cheap to manufacture.

Why not try a one-barreled glass—a monocular? Monoculars are sold in limited numbers, but they aren't stereoscopic—which is very desirable when hunting big game. A number of years ago a man in our town who was about to die willed a binocular to his two sons. They solved the problem with a hack saw and each went his way with a monocular.

Of course, a person can always substitute a riflescope—especially a variable—for a binocular, but it's a sad compromise. Once a muley has been located, it's fairly simple to "look him over" through a scope, but to search a large area of terrain is mighty difficult. Neighboring hunters also complain (and rightly so) when a man covers the countryside with his weapon.

After acquiring a binocular, record the serial number and mark them so that identification is easy. Now learn to use them before going afield. Takes only a few minutes.

If you've purchased a binoc with central focusing, turn the focusing wheel and right eyepiece outward as far as possible. Then, after closing the right eye, place the binoc to your eyes, turn the central wheel until the left eye-image is sharp. Next, after closing the left eye, turn the right eyepiece until the image is clear. Finally, with both eyes open turn the binoc toward the sky and bend the hinge until the two circles of light blend into one. Thereafter, to focus near or far objects merely adjust the central wheel.

To focus a binocular with individual eyepieces, turn each eyepiece out as far as possible. Close one eye and turn the other eyepiece until the image is sharp. Then adjust the second eyepiece. Finally, turn the binoc toward the sky and align the two circles of light.

Marked on the edges of the eyepieces are diopter numbers. Memorize those settings which fit your eyes. Or to keep the eyepieces in place (during warm weather and use they tend to slide around) employ small pieces of surgical tape. Many binocs also have markings on the central hinge for quick adjustment, but I never use them. My hands automatically adjust the two circles of light as I search for game.

All right, you have a good binocular and you're afield, searching for that buckskin. Whether you're riding Old Paint, standing or sitting, a distinct aid in reducing tremors is to hook one's fingers over the bill of a cap or brim of a hat. Another way to dampen wobble is to press one's forefingers against the brow and thumbs upon the cheeks. When you sight deer, take a quick look and, if you like what you see, go into action with your rifle. However, the animals may be some distance away or a selection must be made; so, if time permits, sit and rest the upper arms over the inside of the knees while glassing. This is also a good position to use while searching the far reaches of deep canyons and giant basins.

Occasionally, a log or rock may be available to assist in decreasing wobble—or the side of a convenient tree or hood of a car. Place your back against a log or rock whenever possible for added steadiness.

Western muley country is a vast expanse of canyons, flats, basins, rocks, trees. As you're glassing this area, working in sections from top to bottom, you'll spy a muley—or what looks like one. When you do, mark a nearby object before lowering the binoc.

I've lost a number of muleys for a short time—a few permanently—when I failed to mark them down. A suspicious object can be re-examined from time to time for positive identification. Here is where a spotting scope is valuable. While you locate deer with a binoc, a pal can work with a scope for certain identification or trophy evaluation.

I don't carry a binocular in a case; they're hanging around my neck where I can use the glass quickly. Before going afield, cut the carrying strap just long enough to slip over your head. Modern binocs are a joy to carry when compared with older models—which were a heavy burden. When rain or snow is falling or dust swirling about—when I must crawl, climb over precipitous rocks or gallop a horse—I slide them inside my shirt or jacket. While traveling through country where game is not likely to be encountered, I keep them in a case, on the car seat beside me, or in a saddlebag or cushioned inside a sleeping bag. Even then, I worry about a horse rolling or throwing a pack. At camp, place binocs inside your car, in a pannier or in an out-of-the-way place inside the tent.

Don't carry a cold binocular into a warm, moist tent or room, for water may condense inside and cause them to be temporarily useless. Don't put sweaty fingers on the lenses. Don't clean lenses with a dirty handkerchief. Use a small, special brush, as with a camera, and blow the dust away while you move the brush. Lens tissue is also cheap. A good cleaning at home should last for several days. In an emergency, use a clean handkerchief or a shirttail. Don't attempt home repairs. Return your binoc to the factory for cleaning and adjustments every five years. Most manufacturers perform inspection and minor repairs free.

Approximately 300 years have been devoted to the development of the science of optics. And since one Mr. Porro developed the first binoculars in 1851, "they have come a long way." Size, weight, clearness and brightness of image have changed remarkably. A binoc enables a hunter to stride with seven-league boots cross-country. In my opinion, a good glass is next in importance to one's rifle. I would much rather hunt for trophy deer with a rusty .32-40 and a good binoc than without a binocular and a very excellent rifle. We humans obtain through our eyes many delightful experiences, and a binocular materially increases this pleasure.

Purchase a good one and be amazed at the additional number of deer you find.

KNIVES

Forty years ago we amateur-kid muley hunters in our end of the woods carried long sheath knives. Such weapons bolstered our egos considerably and we wore them in imitation of the buckskin-clad frontiersman. However, then as now, a large knife is an indication of a novice hunter.

My first hunting knife was a real toad sticker: overall length, 12½ inches; blade, 7½; weight with scabbard, excessive. Although this knife was excellent for cutting through a muley's brisket and separating pelvic bones, it was of little value for skinning and butchering. After lugging this heavy monstrosity—actually a mini-machete—around the hills for two years, it was relegated to camp chores: trimming tent pegs, shaving fuzz-sticks, etc. As the years went swiftly by, the blade length of my hunting knives decreased. At the present time my favorite among several sheath knives is one with a 4½-inch blade. This knife has dressed numerous muleys, an elk here and there, and perhaps 10 pronghorns. Weighing only several ounces, it's a joy to carry. I believe most deer hunters would like such a knife. The blade is thin and curved slightly upward to the tip; the handle is plastic but roughened to insure a firm grip. I wouldn't feel too unhappy if the handle were leather, although this material soaks up considerable blood and moisture.

How about a pocketknife? A good choice! However, a large pocketknife eventually wears holes in trouser pockets and may chafe the skin on one's thigh. Best way to carry such a knife is in a belt sheath. There are several types of folding sheath knives on the market and, after using one for three years, I like it very much. When choosing a folding knife, select a fairly large one, certainly with a blade at least two inches long. Three to four inches is even better. Small knives are difficult to hold and manipulate when one's hands are cold. Generally, these knives have blades of different shapes: one sharply pointed for piercing and the other rounded for skinning. Even a Boy Scout combination knife is satisfactory.

Folding knives have a couple of disadvantages. During cold weather, one must remove his gloves to open the blades on most types. And there is always the danger of a blade closing upon one's fingers. But these are minor complaints. The usefulness of two blades far offsets any faults.

Select a good sheath for a sheath knife. There are many poor ones on the market. A sheath should be constructed of thick leather with rivets at top, side and bottom so the blade won't cut its way through the lacing. Moreover, a sheath must house the knife snugly, and it should come equipped with a safety strap at the top. This prevents a knife from falling out when one leans over or sits.

When a person buys a new rifle, he should sight-in the weapon. Likewise, a person must sharpen his new knife. For some inexplicable reason, blades of many new knives have thick shoulders—are wedge shaped. A thick blade offers much resistance, and must be slimmed down. If the shoulders are particularly abrupt, I remove most of the metal on an emery wheel. But one must work slowly and carefully or the metal may "burn." Perhaps a better way would be to remove excess metal with a file or a coarse oilstone. Sharpen with a circular motion and with the rear of your knife raised slightly—about 15 to 20 degrees—above the stone. Work the knife for 15 to 20 seconds on one side, then turn. Remove the bulk of the excess metal on the coarse side of the sharpening stone, then reverse to the fine grit. When a blade has been sufficiently thinned, an "edge" forms. Test it with a piece of newspaper. A sharp blade slices the edge of a sheet nicely. Finish by stropping on leather.

Always sharpen your knife at home—before the hunt. Working over a new knife may require an hour of pleasant work. When bones are carefully avoided, a good knife will dress out your deer—and possibly one belonging to a friend. If you strike a bone here and there—especially if you slash through the brisket and pelvic symphysis, your knife will require sharpening. When you anticipate such harsh usage, carry a small stone.

The price one pays for a knife is an indication of quality—usually. The ultimate test, however, is use. A blade which dulls after a little ordinary work is of limited value. Soft steel forms a prominent burr as it sharpens. Frontiersmen, we're told, checked their blades by whittling hardwood. If dull after a few strokes, they returned their knives to their blacksmiths for additional tempering.

A final word of caution: Don't carry a sheath knife in front of the body. Belted to the rear, over a buttock, a knife rarely causes injury if its owner happens to fall.

CLOTHING

Gradually, over the years a change in economic conditions and American ingenuity have made it possible for nearly everyone to possess good hunting apparel. Consequently, we muley hunters today suffer only rarely from inclement weather. Friends and I have worn many types of hunting clothing—cheap and expensive, the good and nearly worthless. Perhaps, the following suggestions will be helpful.

Shoes

Excepting red or blaze-orange protective clothing, a good pair of shoes is the most important item of clothing. Many trips for muleys have been unpleasant, some occasionally ruined, by foot troubles caused by wearing poorly fitted shoes. So choose them carefully.

Don't purchase moccasin-type shoes—those with the horseshoe welt, or seam, atop the toe portion; for rain and snow puddle in this area and wet the feet. Don't buy cowboy boots, either, if you plan to do considerable walking in muley country. Nor do you want tennis or basketball shoes, except for special occasions. Boots which extend too far upward over the calf of the leg are a poor choice, too—unless you wear them for protection against snakes. High-top boots restrict muscle movement, blood circulation and add considerable weight. Occasionally, hunters are still seen wearing heavy, awkward parachuter and logger boots—both poor choices for men who hike.

My personal choice for an all-around, laced, leather shoe is one measuring 6 to 8 inches high, with corrugated, composition-type sole, smooth, one-piece leather toe—and as lightweight as possible consistent with durable ruggedness. Make certain your shoes are heeled—the only brake a person has when descending slopes. Never, never purchase the heel-less, flat-soled type, the "wedgy."

When buying shoes, make certain they are large enough to accommodate two pairs of socks. This usually means that your hunting footwear will be approximately one size larger in length and width than ordinary street shoes. Then, break the shoes in, which involves wearing them at odd times about the house and yard; or, better still, using them on several short hikes until they are flexible and fit the contours of your feet. Don't believe the merchants who advertise hunting shoes "already broken in."

A mistake made by many deer hunters is lacing their shoes too tightly. Blood circulation is impaired and movement of air in and out of the shoes is restricted. Use a foot powder if your feet perspire excessively or are inclined to become sore after a day in the hills.

Quite often shoes become wet, and they should be dried and redressed with oil or grease before hunting next day. Hang them to dry from the tent ridgepole or ceiling of the camper or trailer. Never place them near strong heat, such as a fire—or even in the sun. Apply only sufficient waterproofing to restore pliability. Remember, leather must breathe. If your shoes have been subjected to numerous wettings and are soiled after several days afield, clean them with saddle soap and warm water, dry and then hand-rub with neat's-foot base oil or grease. However, don't heavily coat your leather shoes with a waterproofing agent. At zero temperature, leather shoes are cold, and heavily greased shoes are very cold.

If you like to hunt during late autumn or early winter, when cold and wet weather can be expected—but when trophy hunting is best— one method that used to be popular among hunters who could afford to buy some pretty good equipment for use in the field was to place sheepskin moccasins inside their leather-rubber pacs—at least felt innersoles. Another combination I once found quite comfortable (but heavy) was overshoes over leather boots. The pac-type boot also insures warm feet while horse-traveling, when foot muscles are inactive; but the excessive width makes extraction from a stirrup somewhat diffcult. Once, after a long, cold ride, we returned to camp just at dark. When my left foot failed to clear the stirrup and I crow-hopped a couple of times on the ground with the other to maintain balance, my otherwise gentle horse became frightened and dragged me, head down, for a couple of rods before a friend could grab the reins.

Best footgear to protect against cold and moisture was developed during the Korean War: insulated rubber shoes. They were a godsend to our GI's, and they have served big game hunters equally well. One disadvantage, true of all rubber footwear, is that they collect perspiration, and at the day's end one's feet are usually quite damp, even on rather cold days. However, no drying is necessary and, if slightly damp feet are bothersome, carry extra socks and change at midday. Even when a person's feet are somewhat wet from perspiration, usually there is no discomforting sensation of coldness, particularly if one wears a pair of woolen socks.

One final suggestion. If possible, take extra leather shoes to deer camp—especially if one pair is new. Experienced muley hunters also include house slippers or moccasins in which to loaf about camp after a tiresome day.

Socks

A distinct aid to foot comfort are socks of good quality and correct size. Friends and I generally wear two pairs with leather shoes: the innermost of nylon or similar material and a fluffy pair (material and thickness depends on temperatures) to cushion the feet. Make certain that socks extend high on the ankles and are snuggly tight; otherwise, after approximately 10 minutes of hiking they may creep down and forward.

Begin each day with clean socks, and at the end of the day wash them. Keep your toenails and callouses trimmed or your socks soon become ventilated. All wool socks wear out rather quickly so I usually choose cotton, synthetics or a combination of these fibers.

During excessively cold weather, a hunter does himself a favor by wearing pacs or insulated leather or rubber. But, don't make the mistake of wearing so many pairs of socks that your feet are crowded, the result of which is impaired circulation, particularly when riding a vehicle or horse. The secret of comfort while wearing rubber insulates is two or three pairs of socks, thick enough to cushion the feet but still permitting air to gently swoosh in and out as one hikes.

Underwear

At the first hint of freezing weather, we Robinson youngsters, living in the gravel-scratching flats of central Utah, were buttoned into long, woolen underwear. (One neighbor mother reportedly sewed her children into these longies and didn't unstitch them until grass greened in the spring.) Thus, we were prepared for those cold October mornings when we went into the mountains to hunt deer. Chief difficulty with woolen underwear was the constant, interminable itching. The spring day when Mom announced that we could shed the longies was indeed emancipation. But the longhandles did keep us warm, just as they do today while we are out muley hunting.

However, a far better choice for underwear is two-piece thermal-insulates. Under the thermals, wear your customary jockey or boxer shorts and T-shirts. I prefer T-shirts because they don't pull up and bunch across the shoulders when hiking or toting a back-pack. When temperatures are extremely low, I slip into thermals at bedtime—plus heavy, fluffy socks. Then, when it's my turn to kindle a flame under the coffee pot at 4 a.m. the following morning, I can tippy-toe about the tent or camper in fair comfort.

Several years ago I purchased a very thick, heavy pair of quilted thermals, and I wouldn't trade them for a year's supply of willow grouse fried tender in bacon drippings and fresh butter. Of course, you'll sweat if you hike in such an outfit, even during very cold weather. But aboard a horse, with temperatures way, way low, and faced with a 10-mile ride to reach that very special place where you know a six-point bull elk, a white goat, or a trophy muley is hiding, you'll arrive warm and eager, in distinct contrast to shivering companions. If your bottom is soft from years of riding a desk, a heavy, quilted thermal also cushions remrakably well against the ravages of a saddle.

Shirts and Trousers

Bow hunting for muleys usually begins in late August—early September, and our clothing then is camouflaged cotton. However, a month later the rifle season finds us in lightweight, red or blaze-orange shirts. As the days shorten and temperatures decrease, we change to flannel or wool shirts, still lightweight. When necessary, we add a second shirt, a size larger—which can be removed later in the warming day. Purchase long-sleeved shirts, and make certain they button completely to the neck. Buttoned breast pockets are almost a necessity, too—to carry items such as an exposure meter, film, etc. No leather shirts, please; either too hot or cold, and unbearable when wet.

Denim trousers are almost universal in muley country. It's unfortunate that denim outfits aren't manufactured in fast-colored blaze-orange. New denim is stiff and noisy, but becomes soft and flexible after several washings. Purchase trousers one size large and of a length which requires no cuff. Ordinary cotton trousers are adequate, and later in the season can be supplemented with thermal underwear. However, they do soak up considerable moisture and, in my humble opinion, the suntans sometimes seen in the hills are a mite risky when a hunter is near trigger-happy warriors. Experts writing for the large outdoor magazines nearly always advise big game sportsmen to purchase woolen trousers. But only rarely does one encounter a muley hunter in wool pants, chiefly, I suppose, because of expense. However, wool moves quietly through the woods, is comparatively warm, even when dripping wet.

Coats and Raingear

Friends and I own several types of hunting coats-jackets, none of which is suitable for all occasions, but each is very necessary for specific circumstances.

Most useful is a hooded sweat shirt. During most of the September and October hunting season, except during inclement weather, such an outfit is adequate. When not worn, it can be rolled and tied around one's midriff, or stuffed into a saddlebag or pack. If insects are troublesome (and they can be during September) or a cold wind is driving rain or sleet, the hood makes the difference between comfort and misery. All sweat shirts seem to soak up quarts of water; so, of course, during periods of wet weather they must be worn inside water-resistant clothing. I prefer a zippered sweat shirt with pockets. In fact, you should choose zippers for all types of hunting coats and jackets, since there are no gaps to admit chilling winds and rain. A strong wind quickly removes the warm layer of air surrounding the body—and we freeze.

Sweaters worn outside other clothing are troublesome, for they seem to catch a million snags each day and are of little value in cutting wind and driving rain.

The canvas-type hunting jacket is a distinct liability to a still hunter (too noisy). For horse travel such an outfit is adequate because this material sheds wind, water and branches very well. However, when riding a horse during inclement weather, I prefer a parka. Buy one a size or two large, so it can be worn over other bulky clothing. Make certain it has a capacious hood and is scarlet red or blaze-orange.

Quilted, down jackets are extremely popular with muley hunters, and I own one. But I seldom wear it when hiking, for it's too heavy (therefore, too warm) and bulky. Quilted jackets deflect wind, but most soak up considerable moisture and require a day or so to dry.

Best all-around hunting coat I've owned was a checkered wool. It was warm, surprisingly so even when saturated with rain. While still hunting, one could steal as silently as a white-footed mouse through the forest. However, the black-red coloration bothered me and I never felt completely safe.

For two decades I've worn army surplus raingear manufactured from rubber-covered, tough cloth. The coat consists of a hooded parka and the trousers, a suspendered overall. This outfit has shed downpours of rain and snow, afoot and in the saddle and air gently swooshes around the body to carry sweat away. When bad weather is expected, this outfit is always tucked into a back-pack or saddlebag. Unfortunately, this outfit is a drab, rubber-grey color, and it's necessary to wear a red or blaze-orange shirt or homemade smock over the parka. Recently I've seen catalogs which advertise red raingear manufactured from a tough nylon base fabric.

When you purchase raingear (and I strongly advise it), make certain that the trousers and coat do not fit tightly around the belt; otherwise, you will become quiet damp on the inside from perspiration.

Gloves, Hats, Handkerchiefs and Belts

For most early-season hunting, gloves are unnecessary, although you may want a light pair for mid-October mornings. However, during post-season safaris, when temperatures are often way, way low, a muley huntsman needs mittens, perhaps, even a hand-warmer. Good choice for lightweight gloves is a leather-palm knit or unlined goatskin. However, my favorite is thin deerskin, from muleys which my sons and I have collected. One's grip on his weapon is sure with buckskin and trigger release isn't too bad, either. For extremely cold weather, mittens and wool liners insure good protection. Although some hunters complain that mitts delay shooting time somewhat, almost everyone can remove them with his teeth in short order. I've also used mittens with a slit palm and found them quite satisfactory.

Knowledgeable muley hunters are seldom found afield wearing cowboy-type hats, except when horse-hunting or nest watching. Such headgear is quite bothersome when still hunting or stalking. Many hunters wear a hard-finish cap, equipped with ear muffs which is a mistake, as it causes one's head to sweat excessively even in fairly coolish weather. A better choice is a lightweight hat, ventilated, medium-brimmed to fend sunshine and rain and, of course, in scarlet red or blaze-orange. When temperatures skid below zero, one requires a down-insulated or an Alaskan sourdough cap. I've used such a brimmed, down cap for approximately 10 years; and with the dyed mouton flaps turned downward, over the ears and back of neck, never has a severe freeze been the least troublesome.

Some years ago, in southern Utah, while a fuzzy-chinned lad, I yanked out a white handkerchief to wipe my snozzola. Immediately a stranger, who was sharing a rocky nest overlooking a shallow canyon, barked a warning: "Jesus, yawanna git us killed!" For several minutes I sat miffed and silent. But, of course, the man was 100 per cent correct, for it's quite probable that a few hunters have been blasted at, possibly even killed here and there, when their white hankies were mistaken for a deer's rear end. Another use for a soft, red bandanna is prevention of chafing from a shirt or jacket collar when a hunter turns his head 19,000 times each day while searching for deer.

Selection of a belt depends entirely on the number and weight of items one carries: knife, ammo, canteen, etc. When a person totes a back-pack or rides a horse, a one-inch, pliable, leather belt is adequate. Otherwise, a hiking muley hunter wisely chooses a much wider belt, such as the two-inch web-military.

A few general statements concerning hunting clothing. Quality is exceedingly important so purchase the best you can afford. Some garments shrink; so wear, wash and check for fit while sitting, kneeling and bending, especially when you have planned a long pack trip and clothing may be soaked with rain and snow or laundered several times. Take a change of clothing, even on an overnight hunt.

As discussed previously, weather is quite unpredictable in muley country during autumn and early winter; so go prepared for all types. General pattern is coldish at dawn, warmish at midday. An Indian Summer day may be followed by a raging blizzard. Seek advice of outfitters or experienced sportsmen in the district you plan to hunt. However, remember that mountain-bred fellas are somewhat inured to cold, and that you, a city cousin, may need warmer clothing.

Pay attention to small details. A shiny object on your jacket may frighten deer. Don't hike so fast while bundled in thermal-insulates that you perspire.

Having correct, moisture-resistant and low-temperature clothing may enhance your chances of killing a deer; for the best hunting, as we have seen, is often found during so-called bad weather.

SLEEPING BAGS

I've slept in many improvised beds in the mountains—once on the ground, cushioned by a mattress of pine boughs and warmed only by an ever-dying fire. However, I've never experienced a night quite like a man who once rode into our camp just at dark. Strangely, he accepted our food and drink, but refused to occupy a spare sleeping bag or even come inside the tent. Instead, he placed his saddle near the campfire (which he failed to replenish during the night), spread two saddle blankets on the earth and settled a third across his chest. At dawn when I walked outside with a steaming cup of coffee for him, he was still asleep, although frost covered the saddle pads and his exposed clothing. We learned later that he had swallowed a huge belt of Old Grandma when he turned in the night before, which may explain why he slept so well.

Because one spends approximately one-third of his time in bed, he should have a good one, especially during a big game hunt. He must be warm and cushioned from the earth. In a poor, uncomfortable sack one remains awake during a considerable portion of the night, is tired next day.

A great deal of advertising emphasis is given to selling sleeping bags filled with dacron, polyester or similar insulating materials. But, without question, waterfowl down is unequaled. My sack was purchased under a guarantee that it was 100 per cent down, but occasionally it sheds a feather, so, obviously, it is a combination down and feather bag. This bag weighs approximately 11 pounds and is 36 by 76 inches when zippered closed. For warm weather I line the bag with a very thin, cotton blanket, chiefly to keep the sack clean. During cold weather, a medium-weight, fluffy, wool blanket is inserted. In addition, I completely enclose the bag in fairly heavy moisture-resistant canvas. While sleeping, I wear some type of underwear or flannel pajamas. When temperatures are extremely low, I also slide into thermals and thick, fluffy socks. Cushioned with an air mattress, this sack is adequate even when placed on a snowbank—in a blizzard.

Select a sleeping bag that will be comfortable during lowest expected temperatures, and one sufficiently long and wide that the occupant can extend his legs and turn freely during the night. Some bags are lined with slick, hard cloth which is cold to touch, but a liner corrects this fault. Pay no attention to salesmen who point out that a particular sack has a "head canopy." Generally, you'll occupy a shelter and, when necessary to bed-down in the open during rough weather, you'll be protected by some sort of canvas or plastic tarp. Don't believe the merchant who argues that your sack must have a waterproof cover. Water resistant, yes, but not waterproof. Your sack must breathe.

When buying a sleeping bag, read the fine print which describes the amount of down in pounds, not the weight of the entire sack. Two pounds may be all right for August-September camping, but four is necessary when temperatures drop near zero. For late autumn-winter camping, the bag should be stuffed with 5-7 pounds of down. A bag doesn't manufacture heat; warmth comes from body metabolism. Price usually indicates the amount of down and its quality. Expect to pay about $200 for an excellent down bag. However, a good sack is a wise investment if you plan to spend considerable time in the game fields during a lifetime. And, properly cared for, a sack will last a lifetime.

Two general types of sleeping bags are available: rectangular and mummy. Mummies have been available for many years, but were popularized during World War II when GI's used millions of them. I dislike a mummy because in close quarters I develop a mild case of claustrophobia. Movement is restricted and it's difficult to turn without moving the entire sack or to exit the bag quickly.

A sleeping bag, undoubtedly, is the best type of bedding for a big game hunter. It can be readied in a minute or so: merely unrolled and shaken to fluff the insulating material. Quilts and blankets are heavy, cumbersome and require considerably more time to prepare. And they always seem to leak canyon breezes to one's feet and back. No matter how a person may toss and turn during the night, he nearly always remains under cover in a bag. When the night is warmish, sleep on top of your sack, covered only with a liner.

Never pull the top portion of the sack completely over your head—unless a grizzly bear is about to begin chewing on your hide. Even when weather is extremely cold, keep your nose and mouth exposed—or arrange a "breathing hole" in the covers. Cloth surrounding this opening will be covered with condensed moisture, perhaps frost, at dawn but the moisture won't be trapped inside.

A soft, fluffy pillow is a distinct aid to comfortable sleeping, too. If in the past you've slept cold in muley camp, wear fluffy, wool socks because when one's feet are warm, his entire body is generally warm. You'll want an air mattress. Don't be impressed with the cheapness and advertising mishmash which describe the plastic ones. Purchase a good, combination cloth-rubber mattress. Friends and I have slept many times on conifer branches, but such a mattress doesn't compare with a cushion of air. Besides, unnecessary cutting of tree branches is unlawful in most localities. Choose a full-sized mattress, at least 30 by 72 inches. However, if your big game safaris are generally the horse- or back-pack variety, a three-quarter length is a good compromise. Inflate a mattress only to the extent that hips and shoulders remain off the ground, for a breath-tight mattress is difficult to ride during the night. If you're a restless sleeper, place a head-size rock or similar object on each side of your sack.

Make certain that you learn to operate the zipper system of your sleeping bag during daylight. During darkness it may be necessary to exit from the bag quickly: to visit the toilet, pursue stampeding horses, etc.

Open the bag each day (turn mummies inside out), shake a few times and place outside the tent or camper to air in the breeze for 20 minutes or so. Same for the pillow, liner or blanket. Use a tough, water-repellent tarp to cover your sack when horse-packing into the big game camp. This same tarp should be placed between the earth and the sack to further insulate the sleeper.

ON THE TRAIL AND AT YOUR HUNTING CAMP

Time was predawn and late November, and a foot of snow covered the ground. Inside our tent, a half-inch of hoarfrost clung to the canvas.

I touched a match to the fuzz-stick in the wood-burning stove and was reaching for a coffee pot, when a flash lighted our tent, followed by a loud, alarming ka-whoomp. Two other muley hunters, camped approximately 50 yards away, had thrown a quantity of gasoline on their camp-fire "to liven it up a bit."

They, too, had arrived the previous afternoon, but we had been so engrossed with our own chores that their activities had gone unnoticed. But now, after hurrying across the intervening space to see if they were in trouble, we could see that their camp was indeed a sorry affair. They had no tent; they had slept in their two-seated car. They were trying to build a fire over which to cook breakfast—with the temperature so low that a tiny, nearby creek had frozen solid. When we saddled-up our truck and rolled out onto the dim, mountain road to start hunting, they were still huddled near their too-large fire, cooking pans in their hands. We felt sorry for the two lads; for years earlier we, too, had camped several times under identical conditions, sans the gasoline fire.

By way of contrast, our camp was ideal. We had shoveled the snow away, erected a large wall tent and banked the sides with snow. Then, over the rear half of the floor, we spread straw, covered the mass with a tarp and unrolled our sleeping bags. The front portion, except near and under the stoves, was covered with a heavy carpet. We had brought two stoves: a propane for cooking and a wood-burner for heating the tent. Not once on this safari was anyone uncomfortable.

Tents and Shelters

A Whelen tent is good, a tepee sheds water and wind adequately, and an umbrella is convenient to erect. But a wall tent is best although it, first, requires considerable time to erect; and secondly, can be smashed by high winds and heavy snow. However, this type utilizes space well for sleeping, cooking, drying clothing, etc. During pleasant weather, the bottom can also be tied up for ventilation, and it accepts a stove conveniently. It's the hunter's traditional shelter and, whenever you see a well-used wall tent, you can wager your share of fried Rocky Mountain oysters that a well-seasoned muley hunter is the happy occupant. Tent-camping gives one the feeling of really living in the out-of-doors.

Whatever kind of tent you select, choose one which can withstand ordinary abuse from wind, water, snow and usage. The flimflams often seen may be all right for summer camping, but are of little value to mule deer hunters. Don't consider a pup tent, except for one-night jaunts away from base camp. Prior to the deer season, erect the tent on your backyard and check it with a garden hose, particularly if the canvas is five to six years old and has had considerable use.

Purchase a fairly large tent. Mine is 12 by 14 feet, and during inclement weather four hunters are easily accommodated, six in a pinch. One man can erect such a tent, but two simplify the task. When possible, we carry specially fitted sections of one-half inch water pipe for supports. On the pack-trail we cut supports from lodgepole pines and aspens. A stout rope is adequate in an emergency, but the result is a sloppy, saggy monstrosity.

A number of deer hunters have abandoned their tents for campers and house trailers. Even remodeled transit and school busses are occaionally seen. Convenient and solid comfort is the fashion today. Campers and trailers are restricted to roads. For a big game safari into the hinterlands a tent is almost a necessity. However, during extremely pleasant weather, particularly when pausing for a one-night stop, we don't pitch a tent. We sleep under the stars. When there's a little night dew, we pull a tarp over our sacks, saddles, food boxes, etc. Occasionally, abandoned mining and lumbering shacks are available. Members of our family used such a shack for several years until a burden of heavy snow crushed it.

Selecting a Campsite

When possible, choose a campsite on a gentle, grassy slope, near water but at least a foot above the highest flood plain, as indicated by driftwood and other debris. Never locate in the bottom of a ravine, or near dusty roads where noise and people may be a nuisance. Nor over sand which invariably contaminates food and fouls sleeping bags. Nor right smack in the area where you intend to hunt.

Never place your tent under dead trees or near burned snags. When a storm is imminent, pitch inside the forest fringe, preferably among young trees. Never beneath a tall tree which could attract lightning or fall in a high wind. Trench the ground around the tent even though the sun is shining and a forecast doesn't predict rain for a month. Place the rear of the tent into the face of prevailing winds, if this can be determined, and at the edge of the forest for viewing scenery and sighting game. Sunshine during the morning and shade in the afternoon are desirable. Sunshine lifts a hunter's spirits; constant shade is depressing.

After erecting the tent, set the stove in place. Always use a fireproof, chimney-ring and guy the pipe with wire to prevent collapse in a wind. Don't forget to screen the top of the stovepipe to trap wood sparks. Next, remove all rocks and snags inside the tent and bring in the supplies and equipment. Each man's duffel is placed at the head of his bed, and nails or wires are rigged on the ridgepole and rear supports for the lantern, clothing, etc. Equipment needed infrequently remains in the truck or is stowed in a small tepee tent which we erect nearby. Although some meals can be served outside the tent, prepare to cook inside, for temperatures during autumn are usually rather low at dawn and dusk. When our group is large, we erect two wall tents, one strictly for sleeping.

Although a tent is generally well ventilated, we extinguish all flames before retiring. Wood and coal stoves can exhaust oxygen in a tightly closed tent, particularly one covered with snow, and gas lanterns and stoves may emit carbon monoxide. Tie securely both door flaps so occupants won't be kept awake in event of a wind. Place a mat of long, tough grass or reeds near the doorway—for scraping dirty shoes. Finally, clear all grass, brush and pine needles in a 10-foot circle and arrange some wood blocks or camp chairs around the area where the evening campfire will be constructed.

Water

Availability of water, firewood and horse feed (number one priority when horse traveling) are generally first considerations when selecting a muley camp. Once, nearly all water in the West was safe to drink. That's no more—too many people in the mountains. Suspect all water when camps or dwellings dot the waterway. Dysentery is a probability; typhoid and other things are possibilities. So, boil all questionable water for 10 to 15 minutes or add purification tablets. Boiled water tastes terrible. So aerate and add fruit juice to improve the flavor. Or prepare coffee or Postum. Plan to treat water with tablets overnight following package directions. No one can taste disease microbes but foul-tasting water usually indicates pollution. Avoid using water from a source where plants are obviously absent; the water is probably mineralized and may cause the Rocky Mountain quick-step. Strain muddy water through a cloth, but such filtering doesn't remove disease organisms. Nor does freezing kill them. Permanent springs are usually safe; but suspect those which produce water only after a storm. Rain collected from a clean tent or tarpaulin is all right. Don't believe the hokum that running water purifies itself. During early autumn many state parks and forest campgrounds still provide piped water, but such systems in the freezing zone are generally drained by November 1.

Always water horses downstream from where camp water is dipped. And, of course, the latrine should be located where drainage is away from camp, and a considerable distance from the spring or stream. A shovel is necessary in the proper construction and maintenance of an outdoor toilet.

A canteen is probably the best method to carry water while hunting. On horse-pack safaris use a collapsible canvas bucket to carry water from the river. A plastic or metal bucket serves best as an established campground. When water is nonexistent, uncertain or suspect, we transport water from home. An advantage is that one's stomach is accustomed to the mineral and chlorine content of the home supply. For years we used 10-gallon milk cans to transport water. Then we switched to five-gallon "jerry" cans. A particularly sentimental favorite is a German aluminum water can, capacity 10 liters, which I picked out of the sand in North Africa in 1943.

Firewood

Firewood at or near established camping areas is generally non-existent, although some forest supervisors graciously maintain a supply. When planning a muley hunt to an unknown area, we visit a local lumbermill and sack a supply of waste odds and ends. Fires made from western lumber, because of coniferous resin, blacken pots and pans. But this wood does burn with a distinctive, pleasant odor.

When firewood is unavailable at your chosen camp, it's often possible to locate a supply nearby, within a quarter-mile or so. We carry a two-foot bucksaw in the car. It's handy for several reasons, and with it a man can work up as much wood as several axe-men, with considerably less noise, which is important when camp is located near game. A bucksaw is much safer than an axe, and only a little skill is involved. Mine has large teeth, considerable "set," enabling it to cut 8-inch logs rather easily.

Deep in wilderness territory, firewood is generally no problem. Often, a supply for a one-night stand can be worked up with one's hands and feet. At base camp cut a supply three times as high as the cook believes adequate. Then place and anchor a tarp over the pile. Two final tips: First, when it's your turn in the morning to start the fire, prepare previously a fuzz-stick and kindling; and second, upon leaving camp make certain that fires, both inside and out, are dead out.

Camp Lights

Years ago at our muley camps, deep in the heart of the Wasatch Mountains, we depended on a campfire and an unsatisfactory kerosene lantern for light. There was only one advantage: no one could possibly see well enough to identify ashes, small animals and sundry debris in his food!

By way of contrast, some contemporary hunting campgrounds at night resemble a small city. Trailers and campers have electrical or propane lights; most hunters nearly always own a Coleman lantern. Several acquaintances even have small gasoline-electrical generators. Of course, no one should neglect to bring along a flashlight to guide his way to the toilet, check the horses before retiring, etc.

Electrical lanterns are superior to the gasoline types in several ways and, although a little more expensive to operate, should be carried on horse-pack trips. However, some people still prefer the gas type—I suppose, because they also tote a gasoline cookstove, and the fuel serves both appliances. If you choose this type of light-heat source, two gallons of fuel is sufficient for a pack trip lasting one week.

Foods and Cooking Utensils

Don't skimp on quality and quantity of food. More food is required when strenuously hunting, especially during cold weather. It's a good plan to include a number of fatty foods in the diet: bacon, butter, etc. But, remember, a steady diet of fried foods may upset your stomach.

Plan each meal in advance and consult each hunter concerning types of food he prefers. However, on longer safaris carry a surplus in the event it's necessary to extend the days afield because of inclement weather, absence of game animals whose meat was to be included in the diet, etc. Generally choose items which can be opened and cooked immediately. Have you tried the new instant drinks? For years we've been using many dehydrates which are lightweight, convenient to pack and easy to prepare.

All food on horse safaris should be transported in panniers, or, when stowed into convenient boxes, in packsacks (we use surplus cargo parachute bags measuring 24x15x18 inches) or mantas. When traveling to muley camp in the carryall or truck, we stow food in surplus footlockers and ammo boxes. During early fall, when temperatures frequently are still high, we take an ice chest for perishables. Most campers and trailers have built-in refrigerators or iceboxes. If cans of food freeze, thaw slowly. Bury those which burst.

Purchase good cooking utensils; don't depend on your wife's castoffs. Aluminum is best (except for cups) because it doesn't rust, chip or break, is lightweight and cleans fairly easily. Nesting cooking kits are available and the one I bought 15 years ago is still in good condition.

On the trail a compact kitchen outfit is particularly convenient; in a semi-permanent camp, trailer or camper, one can be more elaborate.

If one member of the party prefers to cook, and he's satisfactory, by all means award him a permanent appointment. No one likes to wash dishes; so rotate this chore. Regardless of assignments, first man to camp builds a fire and starts cooking.

Packing the Gear

Equipment which you include on your own private safari is your business; but that which you ask an outfitter to lug along is his. Nearly all mountain packers are extremely reasonable, but I've never seen one yet who wouldn't fight if you insisted that he pack a suitcase on a mule. Arrive at his end-of-the-road, jumping-off-place with your rifle in a scabbard, your bulk clothing, etc. in a duffle bag (some surplus, military ones are excellent), and your sleeping bag tightly rolled in a tough, waterproof tarp.

You'll really make him smile when you show him a pair of panniers; about 22 inches long, 15 inches high, and about 9 inches from front to rear and a pair of saddlebags into which you have stowed such items as camera equipment and other personal items.

When the responsibility is yours to place food and other gear into panniers or packbags, number the packs and stow items by groups as nearly as possible—at least, arrange them for convenient unpacking. No one can remember what items are in what pack, so make a list and keep it handy.

Selecting a Guide-Packer-Outfitter

During the late 1950's a hunting crony and I planned a safari for mule deer, bear, elk and goats in Montana. After securing a list of outfitters-packers from the state fish and game department, we wrote to eleven in the general area we had chosen to hunt. Nine replied.

Final selection was based upon the fact that (1) we weren't promised the moon in the way of trophies; (2) the packer didn't endeavor to sell us a bargain hunt; and (3) he enclosed references without our asking. We were also impressed that the packer, himself, would be in the hunting party—that we weren't to be "farmed out."

Start early to find a packer; certainly six to 12 months should be a minimum time. Some excellent and widely publicized outfitters are booked as much as two years in advance. In addition to state and provincial fish and game departments, the Forest Service and chambers of commerce in some localities maintain lists of packers. Outdoor magazines frequently carry outfitter advertisements, too. Several Indian tribes, although they don't advertise widely, sponsor all-expense hunts for mule deer. A number of ranchers also use their facilities during hunting season to attract sportsmen, but local inquiry is often required to locate these people.

Friends who have had considerable experience report that all kinds of packers and guides are available: excellent, good, fair and the crooks. Big game hunts are very expensive; so endeavor to obtain the best outfitter possible. Certainly one has the right to efficient service, clean food and courteous treatment—and a reasonable opportunity for shots at game. Obtain from the packer the names of hunters he's guided—recently. But remember that such references will be men who've had exceptional success. Write to these sportsmen; and, if possible, talk with those who live in your locality. Ask questions: "Were the guides safety conscious?" "How was the chow?" "How many animals were seen and types of trophies secured?" "Were you treated kindly, courteously?" Ask the references, also, about the liquor situation and gambling in the packer's camp. Some guides are lazy, too. A friend found that his guide was extremely lackadaisical about searching for game, and he finished the hunt with only an immature bull moose, even though he had reason to believe that trophy moose, deer and elk were rather abundant, along with a fair number of sheep. Most states license packers-guides-outfitters, but this alone doesn't always insure excellent service.

You will be furnished a cost figure for the safari, but also inquire concerning possible extra charges such as transportation from end-of-the-road into base camp, use of aircraft, packing out game carcasses, etc. Obtain a list of such fees—in writing. How much to pay depends on a number of factors—services rendered. Endeavor to make a "package" deal. Total expenses for yourself and a friend are usually less than were each to make separate arrangements. Most guides-packers require an advance deposit—usually 25% of the total cost, and this is lost if the hunter doesn't appear. The remainder of the fee is paid when the hunt is concluded. Be certain that you know when the hunt begins. A 10-day safari may turn out to be somewhat less, if two days are required to reach and depart base camp, or if you hunt in a Canadian province where Sunday hunting is forbidden.

Dissatisfied clients usually file their complaints with the local fish and game department. In your letter to the game officials also inquire concerning best period to hunt the particular area you have chosen. Inquire of the packer how many additional dudes will be at his hunting camp. Some outfitters contract with too many sportsmen, and you could be shunted around. Good trophies are far from abundant, and excessive hunting in an area soon depletes them. One guide for three to four hunters is no-go. One guide for two sportsmen may be all right in some situations, but a one to one ratio is best—and more costly.

Ask where you will stay: at his ranch, a motel in town, in tents deep in the remote hinterlands? You might also inquire how long he's been in the guiding business and the percentage of his clients who secure game. Most of them will disclose their success-ratio during the previous two years. Beware of the packer who guarantees shots. Few of the excellent, reliable outfitters do this. Deer are sometimes unpredictable; weather can drive them out of an area overnight. The average dude should be taken within 100 yards of game, yet don't be surprised when this distance becomes 200 yards in the field. Many guides ask hunters to take shots at this distance.

Don't be discouraged if a man replies in a nongrammatical style. Usually his forthrightness shows through his penmanship and syntax. By all means, inform the packer of your age, physical condition, amount of hunting experience, etc. And obtain from him a list of equipment he expects you to bring.

Various types of safaris are possible. A hunt for mule deer is often a part of a longer hunt for other big game and some Canadian horse-trips may extend as long as 45 days. During these full-course safaris large numbers of horses and mules move a mountain of equipment into base camps. All gear is furnished on such a safari except personal items: rifle, binocular, sleeping bag, etc. Or you may contract with a man for a week-end hunt. I know of one individual who flies out from an Eastern state and hunts from a jeep for only two to three days. His guide, however, has previously located concentrations of deer.

The guides-packers-outfitters I know are excellent, dedicated to insuring the dude a successful, memorable hunt. They work hard; they can't afford to do otherwise because their livelihood often depends on that very fact. You, the dude, must cooperate, too. You have employed the guide; so, generally permit him to direct the safari. Don't instruct him when to move camp. He's acquainted with the area and knows where the trophy animals are found. When still hunting or stalking, cooperate by moving as noiselessly as possible. And don't be a loud-mouth or brag about your skill as a marksman or hunter. The crowning insult is a bribe—an offer of money for permission to kill animals on his license or in excess of your own. Don't complain unnecessarily about the weather or demand unreasonable services. Clean your own rifle; pour your own cup of pre-breakfast coffee. He also appreciates the absence of horseplay near horses and with firearms. It's not difficult, when the hunt is completed, to determine that a dude has pleased the packer-guide. He'll offer to ship your trophies to a taxidermist and invite you for a repeat performance the following autumn.

A MASTER LIST OF SUPPLIES AND EQUIPMENT

Friends and I have endured some miserable days and nights in hunting camps. The difficulty, almost always, was lack of sufficient preparation, resulting in our "roughing it"—experiences which discouraged a friend here and there from further hunting. However, a person shouldn't make a ritual of preparations for a hunt nor permit camp chores to become a disagreeable burden. Certainly, one should derive pleasure from the experience.

Many years ago I learned that a successful big game hunt began with a master equipment-supply list. Thereafter, it became a simple matter to check off the items, pack them and load the packsack, the horses or the car. In camp, correct equipment insures that everyone remains healthy, enjoys a wonderful experience and returns safely.

Following is my equipment-supply list; you may wish to add additional items for special occasions.

A. Weapons and Associated Equipment:
   1. Rifles
   2. Handguns
   3. Carrying cases
   4. Scabbards
   5. Ammo
   6. Gunslings
   7. Cleaning equipment
   8. Cartridge carrying case
   9. Broken case remover

B. Personal Hunting Equipment:
   1. Pocketknife
   2. Sheath knife
   3. Sharpening stone
   4. Binocular
   5. Spotting scope
   6. Sun glasses
   7. Spectacles
   8. Pencil and paper
   9. Hunting license and game tags
  10. Canteen
  11. Packrack
  12. Varmint call
  13. Tape measure
  14. Maps
  15. Survival kit
  16. Deer cart
  17. Tire repair kit
  18. Snake bite kit
  19. Pedometer
  20. Wrist watch
  21. Rope and game hoist
  22. Red plastic bags
  23. Game regulations
  24. Insect dope
  25. Carcass cleaning cloth

C. Camera Equipment and Supplies:
   1. Cameras
   2. Film
   3. Exposure meter
   4. Self-timer
   5. Cable release
   6. Filters
   7. Flash unit
   8. Tripod

D. Personal Gear:
   1. Toilet kit
   2. Duffle bag
   3. Washcloth
   4. Towels
   5. Sleeping bag
   6. Pillow
   7. Air mattress
   8. Lip dope

E. Clothing:
   1. Shirts
   2. Trousers
   3. Underwear
   4. Socks
   5. Shoes
   6. Thermal boots
   7. Red handkerchiefs
   8. Coat
   9. Hooded sweatshirt
  10. Raingear
  11. Gloves
  12. Hat

F. Equipment for Horses:
   1. Blankets
   2. Saddles
   3. Packsaddles
   4. Saddle pads
   5. Bridles
   6. Halters
   7. Tether ropes and hobbles
   8. Hay and oats
   9. Panniers
  10. Currycomb and brush
  11. Shoes and repair equipment

G. Automobile Equipment:
   1. Tire chains
   2. Tire pump
   3. Spare tire
   4. Gasoline cans

H. Camp Equipment:
   1. Axe
   2. Bucksaw
   3. Medical kit
   4. Tool kit
   5. Tents
   6. Tent poles
   7. Tent pegs
   8. Coleman stove
   9. Lantern
  10. Table, chairs
  11. Ice chest
  12. Shovel
  13. Flashlight
  14. Canvas tarps
  15. Wire
  16. Hammer, nails
  17. Toilet paper (colored)
  18. Newspapers
  19. Rugs
  20. Matches
  21. Alarm clock
  22. White gasoline can
  23. Water cans
  24. Bucket
  25. Water purification tablets
  26. Meat saw
  27. Meat sacks

I. Food and Cooking Equipment:
   1. Aluminum foil
   2. Paper towels
   3. Lunch paper
   4. Fry pans
   5. Coffee pot
   6. Pancake grill
   7. Dishpans
   8. Washbasins
   9. Stew pans
  10. Knives, forks, spoons
  11. Plates
  12. Pancake turner
  13. Can opener
  14. Ice
  15. Scouring pads
  16. Dish towels
  17. A food list to satisfy individual needs and appetites

3

Rifles And Ammo For Muleys

More nonsense has been written about what constitutes a good deer rifle than any other subject, possibly excepting politics and beauty aids for women. Experts have written that pip-squeak smallbores are perfectly adequate; while, to borrow a sentence from a man whom I admire, "some gun authors advocate that sportsmen use cannons so large that a small terrier could chase a well-fed rat through the barrels." Friends and I have killed mule deer very dead with weapons ranging from .22 to .45-70. But, if I could choose only one caliber from this group to hunt mule bucks the remainder of my life, the rifle would be a .30-06. I'm a reloader, and over four decades I've killed very satisfactorily with this caliber more than a few deer with a number of powder types and bullets, under a variety of situations.

THE .30-06

Through the years I've owned about fifteen .30-06's, but my favorite is a Springfield which is now stocked with Utah walnut, from a tree which I helped topple with a single-bit axe—inletted, finished and checkered myself. Under ideal conditions I've fired several five-shot groups which a quarter would nearly cover.

This '06 weighs 9½ pounds with a 4X Leupold scope, a ¾-inch carrying strap and stuffed with four rounds of ammo. I load 51 gr. of 4895 or 62 gr. of 4831 with 150 gr. bullets; 57 gr. of 4831 with 180 and 54 gr. of 4831 with 220 Hornady bullets. These are mild loads. Immediately before going hunting I target with types of bullets I intend to use. Unfortunately, this rifle (true of most '06's I've owned) does not group all bullets to the same point too well, so I record the results on a small piece of paper and tape it to the wood on the left side of the action. A friend may wish to borrow the weapon.

Deer have succumbed to 130, 150, 172, 180 and 220 gr. projectiles through this rifle. Once I slipped a 130 Speer hollow point between a muley's ribs. He literally fell in his tracks, his heart and lungs a shattered mess. Strike a muley with this same bullet on a shoulder, ham or fringes and you'll have, usually, a crippled, suffering animal. The 150 gr. projectile? An entirely different story, especially when the bullet is properly constructed. This bullet weight, in my humble opinion, is the best in this caliber for mule deer found in the open and at longish distances. It has sufficient speed to deliver a paralyzing shock, knock an animal down and keep him down. However, it destroys much "eating meat" when placed incorrectly. But, doesn't any good bullet? However, if there were only 180 gr. bullets for the '06 on the market, friends and I wouldn't feel too unhappy. For our money, available bullets have good velocity and retained energy, even though they generally zip through a large muley buck. But the animals leave a good blood-trail, and almost always are found within 100 yards.

The 220 Hornady bullet with a muzzle velocity of approximately 2200 fps (feet per second) is a special load for muleys. And in brush and trees it does marvelous work, sometimes killing a deer even after colliding with leaves and small branches. This heavy, round nose bullet comes into its own when still hunting, and I like to carry a few rounds for use in heavy cover. Another bullet which I've found very effective on muleys is the GI 172 gr. Years ago I touched the tips of 100 of these slugs to a grinding wheel and removed about 1/16 inch from the tips. Then, with a small drill I hollow pointed them. Experts have said that this is a dangerous practice, for "obvious reasons." The second largest muley (body weight) that I've ever seen was struck through the ribs with one of these altered bullets. He collapsed in his tracks and, very dead, tumbled down a hill which he had been climbing.

Friends and I like the '06 because of the large number of bullets available: 110, 125, 130, 150, 160, 170, 180, 200 and 220, to list most of them. From this assortment one can experiment and select the most accurate load for his particular weapon.

More hunters use the '06 than any other caliber to hunt muleys—for several reasons. Personally, I like the '06 because I frequently still hunt in dense cover where a heavy bullet is better than those available, say, for the .270, .257 and 7mm. This is especially true when one may encounter larger game, such as elk. The '06 has excellent killing power: a combination of bullet weight, caliber, bullet shape and construction, speed and energy. This caliber is available in most types of actions: bolt, pump and semi-auto. A bolt-action is best choice for long-range shooting—across canyons and open flats. But in heavy cover, perhaps a lever, pump or semi-auto is better for the average sportsman.

THE .270

Under the right conditions the .270 is one of the best calibers ever carried in Western big game country. The realized dream of Winchester's T. C. Johnson, this rifle first appeared in late 1925 in the Model 54. Sportsmen, I'm told, were surprised but pleased with the announced muzzle velocity of 3160 fps with a 130 gr. bullet. The cartridge was the '06 case necked, with minor changes, to .277. It was the first new major cartridge since World War I, and the bullet, 130 gr., by Winchester was called the pointed, soft point expanding. Older friends have told me that it was a good bullet, expanded well and remained in one piece for deep penetration.

The action of my first .270 had its birth in a German factory. I picked the 1942, 8mm Mauser out of a dusty ravine in North Africa, after a German GI had decided that he had business elsewhere. Upon arriving home, I sent the Mauser to a friend in Montana who civilized the action and installed one of his excellent barrels. Before the barrel was somewhat worn, this weapon shot fantastic groups for a hunting weapon, especially with 40 gr. of Hi-Vel No. 2 powder behind 130 gr. Sierra bullets. It will still shoot 3-inch groups most of the day with 4895 and 4831. I also have a Remington 721 which under ideal conditions occasionally prints 1-inch groups.

The .270 pleases me because of its excellent accuracy, flat trajectory and not-too-bad recoil: approximately 14 pounds with 130 gr. bullets. Somehow, the .270 case nearly full of the right powder and wedded to a good bullet gives marvelous performance. Reasonable velocity, also, means less lead on running game and with 130 gr. bullets an explosive effect in tissues. Actually, one doesn't need too much penetration on deer. A 130 gr. bullet easily reaches their boiler room, when heavier muscles or bones are missed. In fact, this bullet sometimes anchors deer even when struck in the paunch or on the fringes. Occasionally, one hears that much meat is ruined by 130 gr. bullets, but most hunting projectiles are designed to do just that. It's understandable that many hunters want a bullet that anchors game on the spot.

Many .270 owners are handloaders and assemble ammo for special situations. They may carry several types of hunting loads: 130 spire points for cross-canyon and open-terrain blasting; 150 or 160 round nose for hunting in brush and trees where a light bullet could be deflected by leaves or twigs. My pet .270 loadings with 130 gr. bullets are: 56 gr. of 4831 or 49 of 4895 with Sierra spitzer boat tails; 54 gr. of 4831 with Speer spitzers. For 150 gr. bullets: 54 gr. of 4831 behind Norma bullets and 57 gr. of 4831 with Speer projectiles. These are mild to slightly hot loads.

The .270 compared with the .30-06? Arguments developed in the outdoor press during the past 30 years have been interesting to read but often have reached the ridiculous. These two calibers are nearly identical when comparable bullets and powders are used. Certainly, a muley would never know which had-done-him-in.

The .270 has less recoil and slightly flatter trajectory than the '06. But, reports from both rifles hurt my ears. I suspect that big-bore author-ities who so disparage the .270 haven't used this caliber enough to know its capabilities. Experience has proved that the .270 delivers very rapid kills on deer. For the gun-nut there is a place in his rack for both cali-bers. However, for the one-rifle, big game hunter, the '06 is the better choice.

Sighting-in the .270? I could be wrong, but I like my .270's to place 130 gr. bullets about 2-3 inches high at 100 yards. The bullets are then 3-4 inches high at 200, on at 260-280 yards and only 10 to 12 inches low at 400. This is flat hunting trajectory and means that a person can aim point-blank out to reasonable ranges.

Several other calibers have been manufactured the past few years to compete with the .270 for the sportsman's dollar. Most of them are excellent deer weapons, but none are appreciably better than Mr. John-son's deer buster. For example, the .264 with same barrel length and bullet with comparable sectional density has nothing over the .270. Same with the .280. The .270 magnums? They have a tiny bit more velocity and energy, but have you experienced the terrific muzzle blast, the recoil? Remember, also, the shorter barrel life and the added cost of purchasing one of these super thunder sticks. All major American rifle manufacturers market the .270 in some type of action, as do many foreign concerns, plus perhaps a hundred small handcrafters.

THE .257 ROBERTS ON MULE DEER

My wife, Ruth, and I were slowly walking through a patch of aspens on the Ute Indian Reservation during October, 1960, when she suddenly stopped and excitedly whispered: "Look at the big buck!" Sure enough, there ahead in a small clearing, in belt-high sage, at about 125 yards stood four does and a wonderfully handsome five-pointer. She raised her rifle, fired and the buck disappeared as abruptly as though Hercules himself had yanked the hillside from under the deer. Because this was the first muley she had killed with a new .257 Roberts, I rushed to the buck, anxious to see the results of the apparent hellfire which this little rifle was shooting that could cause a large muley to expire so quickly. The 100 gr. ABC bullet had sliced into the brain immediately below the right antler. A .22 long rifle would have flattened the muley just as quickly. However, since that happy occasion on the reservation, the little Remington 722 has proved a very satisfactory deer rifle.

The first person to work on the cartridge that eventually became the .257 Roberts was probably Dr. F. W. Mann. About 1900 he began experiments that were completed by A. O. Niedner and Major Roberts. Actually, Roberts was endeavoring to develop a .25 caliber rifle for long-range woodchuck shooting, a weapon that would print 1-inch groups at 100 yards. After approximately 17 years of experimentation, the rifle appeared and was called the .25 Roberts. The case is the 7mm necked down with a 12 degree shoulder. Niedner Rifle Corporation started chambering barrels in 1928. Remington in 1934 became interested but changed the shoulder to 21 degrees. Winchester then chambered its Model 54 for this cartridge. More recently, Remington and Winchester included the .257 in the Model 722 and Model 70. However, at the present time, I believe that a .257 can be obtained only from small handcrafters. Factory loads can still be purchased in 87, 100 and 117 gr. weights. However, handloaders also have 60, 75, 86, 87 and 120 weights available.

Col. Townsend Whelen thought very highly of the .257. In fact, as a friend of Robert's, he assisted with suggestions and testing during its development. "The .257 Roberts," Col. Whelen wrote, "is as good a sheep and deer cartridge as one could wish." It should be remembered, however, that Col. Whelen usually hunted wilderness areas of North and Central America, where it is immaterial that an animal runs some distance before falling. And this, it has been my experience, is what deer and other game animals of comparable size generally do when struck with .257 bullets.

But, the .257 has a very important characteristic: light recoil. Youngsters and women can easily handle the approximate 7 pounds of recoil (with 100 gr. bullets). But the 14 pounds (with 130 gr. bullets) from the .270 and 17 pounds with the '06 (180 gr. bullets) are sometimes discouraging, if not frightening.

The best load in my wife's .257 is 43 gr. of 4831 behind a 117 Sierra bullet (2743 m.v.). Groups are consistently two or three inches, with an occasional five-shot group that the end of thumb covers. Thirty-eight gr. of 4895 pushing a 100 gr. Sierra is quite good, too. Surprisingly, the 75 gr. Hornady generally prints 2-3-inch groups, with 46 gr. of 4831, when wind isn't too blustery.

This Remington .257 I stocked in birds-eye maple. It weighs approximately 9¼ pounds, carrying a 2½X Lyman scope, a three-quarter-inch strap and with four cartridges in the magazine. Sighted-in to strike two inches high at 100 yards, a 117 gr. bullet prints in the black at 200 and about eight inches low at 300 yards. Likewise, it is dead-on at 25 yards, ½ inch low at 15 yards and 1 inch low at 10, data that will interest those who desire to snip off the heads of forest grouse.

The above three calibers are my special favorites for muleys, but a number of others perform as well, or nearly so. On the other hand, there are some weapons used on deer that are inadequate—and several may be excessively powerful.

A number of years ago I read an account about two lads—one Eskimo, the other Canadian Indian—who had slain several white and grizzly bears with firecracker weapons: .25-20's. I've likewise seen several mule deer dispatched neatly with .22 long rifle bullets. Shall we eliminate the .22's? Hear the cries of anguish! True, the Hornet, Zipper, Wasp, .222 Remington, Bee, Fireball, .224 Weatherby, .220 Swift and others have flattened mule deer. I even recall reading years ago that one Jack Holliday put a grizzly's lights out with a .22-250. The .222 magnum, the Swift and the .22-250 will do the job on mule deer *with the right bullet*, but it's a chancy proposition.

THE 6MM's ON MULEYS

Once upon a time I was skeptical of the 6mm's. Then, a .244 on a Mauser action came along. I stocked it in myrtle and gave it to my son. He had dropped a handsome five-pointer the previous fall with an '06, but I suspected that the recoil worried him. The .244 should be about right for a slender teen-ager.

The .243 and .244 were announced in August, 1955. However, the 6mm cartridge is fairly old, having been used during the Spanish-American War under the label "6mm Lee-Navy."

In all fairness, the newly found popularity for this caliber can be attributed to Warren Page, shooting editor of *Field & Stream*. For a number of years he has used this cartridge to kill a variety of animals from woodchucks to elk. In fact, he assembled kill data on 165 medium big-game critters: 66 of which were mule deer; 17 were elk. He reported that 73 per cent of these animals were instant kills (fell on the spot or moved not more than 25 yards). An additional 17 per cent moved only from 26 to 200 yards.

Various comparisons have been made between the Winchester .243 and Remington .244 or 6 mm. The difference is insignificant—nit-picking. True, the Remington 722 was manufactured with a 1-12 twist with varmint sportsmen in mind. This rifle had difficulty handling heavier bullets, those suitable for deer. Consequently, the Model 70, with a 1-10 twist attracted the hunters' dollars. It's been fashionable, also, to point out, using paper bullistics, that the 6mm's are superior to the .257 Roberts. When the two are loaded to potential, not factory data, hunting sidekicks and I prefer the .257.

Recoil from a 6mm, seven-to-eight-pound rifle is approximately 11 pounds, and the report and muzzle blast are hefty. The 6mm's handle deer in most situations, but, without question, there are better rifles for muleys.

THE .250-3000 FOR DEER

My first love affair was with a pretty Savage 99 in .250-3000 caliber. The original owner, a cow hunky on the prod, had stopped in our hometown to gamble a little, drink a lot, and had left his rifle in hock. A month later, the barkeeper sold the Savage to Dad for $20, $5 more than the cowboy's bill. The number of muleys which fell to that little rifle will never be known, but it must have been considerable.

Introduced in March, 1915, the .250-3000 Savage with its 3,000 fps and excellent accuracy with an 87 gr. bullet really intrigued the shooting public. However, Newton (its father) had wanted a 100 gr. bullet at 2,800 fps. The Savage 99 in .250-3000 had a 22-inch barrel and weighed about seven pounds. Winchester also chambered its Model 54 for the .250-3000, but the serious rifleman preferred the .257 Roberts to the

.250-3000 and other .250's because of its longer range capabilities with heavier bullets.

A note of interest: In 1924 a Savage .250-3000, loaded with an 87 gr. bullet, in the hands of Martin Bovey killed the Boone and Crockett number one bighorn sheep, a head that many sportsmen consider the finest North American trophy ever taken.

Other .25 calibers which are good muley rifles when loaded sensibly are the .257 Ackley Improved, .25 Niedner (.25-06) and the .257 Weatherby Magnum.

THE .264

The .264 has been alternately praised and damned. A friend killed several deer with this rifle and then sold it. "Happy to be rid of it," he said. Another thinks it's the greatest.

When the .264 appeared, its announced muzzle velocity of about 3,200 fps with a 140 gr. bullet was electrifying. However, the long barrel (26 inches), heavy recoil and terrific muzzle blast, plus the weight (over nine pounds with full magazine, sling and hunting scope) discouraged many potential buyers who had waited a year or so for this caliber to appear. Winchester manufactured the .264 in Model 70 with a stainless steel barrel. The case is the belted H&H type, fat with a short neck. The barrel has a 1-9 twist, and is overbore with most powders, I'm told. Still, it knocks mule deer askiddle, and a few hunters have told me that they believe it the ultimate deer rifle.

THE 7MM

And then there is that wonderful little 7mm cartridge. No one recalls exactly when this caliber originated, but it is an ancient one. Manufactured first in quantity by Mauser (German) for the Spanish army in 1892, it has been listed as the official military cartridge by about a dozen other countries. Sportsmen and experimenters have been using this cartridge in the United States since about 1896.

Remington early made thousands of rolling-block 7mm's; later, both Remington and Winchester manufactured rifles for this caliber in Models 30, 54 and 70. Many 7mm rifles have also been produced by custom-crafters such as Niedner, Griffin & Howe, Ackley and others. However, I believe that both Winchester and Remington stopped production during the 1940's.

The sporting version of the 7mm is called the 7x57—which hasn't helped its popularity in the United States. It has also appeared as a .275 and .276. Good bullets for this caliber have excellent sectional density; that is, relation of bullet length to diameter.

This rifle has killed game from squirrels to elephants. Once I read an article by a man who had carried this rifle in Africa, Asia, Europe and North America and killed animals from very small antelope to kudu (elk size). Ninety per cent of the critters were dropped with one bullet. Certainly, then, the 7mm should kill mule deer. In fact, this may be the most underrated deer cartridge of all—might even be more effective than the .270 and .30-06 in the hands of women, youths and those sensitive to recoil and muzzle blast. Recoil is only about nine pounds with a sensible load. And the report is not a thunderous roar. A number of bullet weights have appeared over the years: 105, 110, 123, 139, 150, 154, 160, 170, 175, to list most of them. Good bullets from 125 to 175 gr. are still available. Early American sportsmen shot a 139 gr. open point bullet at 2,850 fps and a 175 gr. at 2,550—both excellent.

Thousands of 7mm's are still being carried in this country and Canada for all species of big game and varmints. This cartridge is a reloader's delight, for the brass is durable and the rifle digests a variety of components while giving good accuracy.

THE .280 REMINGTON

Another excellent muley cartridge is the .280 Remington which appeared in 1957 in the Model 740 semi-auto. Actually, it is a 7mm, but is also similar to the .270 and the .30-06. Theoretically, the .280 is a little better than the .270.

Why did Remington produce the .280, a cartridge very similar to several others which have been around for decades? I have no explanation. We've seen so many new calibers fall off the production lines recently that we've about reached the saturation point. However, rifle-nuts hail each new addition with enthusiasm. Certainly, a new rifle provides an excuse to spend long hours at the range.

Other similar cartridges which are effective muley killers, when loaded sensibly, are the .284 Winchester and the 7x61 Sharpe & Hart.

OTHER .30 CALIBER RIFLES FOR DEER

As many as 50 types of .30 caliber rifles—well, maybe 29 or so—have been used to kill mule deer. And probably the most popular of this group has been the "thutty-thutty." In fact, gun editors write that more deer—

hundreds of thousands—have been slain with this cartridge during the past 75 years than with any other caliber. There are reasons for such wide usage. The caliber has been around since 1894 and by 1927 one million Wincester 94's, mostly in .30-30 caliber, had been sold.

The .30-30 was probably the first American smokeless powder cartridge manufactured for big-game hunting. This is the caliber that really put the black powder muskets on the skids. It was very popular because of improved trajectory, not necessarily better accuracy. In addition, .30-30 lever actions were cheap. Report and recoil are mild. And ammo is still available at nearly every crossroad store.

The .30-30 lever action is handy, too; and the rifle weighs just over 6 pounds. The tubular magazine on my '94 holds seven cartridges and can be stuffed with additional rounds without opening the action—a very desirable feature. And the shooter always knows when the weapon is cocked. A rusty, much-abused Winchester or Marlin .30-30 generally still functions. And it's a convenient saddle weapon, one whose bulk doesn't cramp a rider's leg or overbalance a saddle.

A .30-30 bullet doesn't thump deer to the ground as effectively as some better calibers. In fact, even when mortally wounded, a muley generally runs some distance before falling. It's my opinion that more deer are wounded and escape when hit with this bullet than with any other cartridge. The bullet just doesn't have the combination of velocity and weight to drop muleys on the spot. A model '94 in my gun rack (I've loaned it frequently) has killed approximately 15 muleys; and, as I recall, not one succumbed in his tracks. A summary by a game warden showed that under his observations 64 per cent of deer wounded and lost were hit by .30-30's.

I dislike writing this, but most people who regularly use .30-30's aren't knowledgeable concerning guns and hunting. They know little of rifle performance and how to approach deer, but bang away indiscriminately. Much of the blame for poor performance of the .30-30's on game can be laid on the doorsteps of these jaspers.

The open sights on most .30-30's are very poor indeed, and are difficult to adjust satisfactorily. And it's troublesome to scope lever actions, such as the Model '94. But, why place a scope on a rifle not designed to be a long-range outfit?

A lever action weapon with a two-piece stock obviously isn't conducive to gilt-edged accuracy. But, again, Winchester and Marlin didn't intend that their rifles bust muleys much beyond 150 yards. Accuracy, however, is all right for offhand shooting in brush and trees. Still, this caliber won't buck brush as well as the .348, .350 and similar cartridges.

Most .30-30's are manufactured, I believe, with a 1-12 twist, and the 170 gr. round nose bullet at 2,200 fps appears to be the best load.

In addition to Winchester and Marlin rifles, the .30-30 has been produced in the Savage 99, 220 and 340. This caliber is popular in Mexico and Canada. In Europe, GI's found an unusual weapon: a "Drilling," a three-barrel piece. Immediately below the side-by-side shotgun barrels was a rifle tube, often in .30-30.

THE .30-40

This is another cartridge which has accounted for umpteen thousands of mule deer. Numerous older hunters killed their first deer and elk with this caliber in Krag rifles, and not a few have dropped plenty of big game with the Winchester '95, also chambered for the .30-40. A Krag in my gun-rack (a weapon I've loaned many times) has accounted for 12 deer and 2 elk, as I recall.

Although slightly less powerful than the '06, the .30-40 is still a better muley rifle than the .30-30 or the .300 Savage. Recoil isn't bad: approximately 11 pounds with a hunting load. The case is rimmed.

The Krag is an ugly weapon, but it does have a honey-smooth action. The magazine is very functional, although it was cursed by the military. It consists of a horizontal box, capacity five rounds, with a loading gate on the right side. One excellent feature is that it can be filled (even with a gloved hand) while the bolt is either open or closed, ideal for hunting conditions.

The Krag was developed in Norway, not in Denmark, as many believe. Adopted in 1892 by the U.S. Army, it replaced the single-shot .45-70 Springfield. Although this rifle proved satisfactory during the Spanish-American War, the Philippine fracas and the Boxer Rebellion, the Army yearned for something better and found it in the '03 Springfield. However, before production was discontinued, approximately 506,000 rifles and carbines had been manufactured. Many of these were later sold to sportsmen for $1.50. That's not bad for a weapon that cost Uncle Sam only $25.

One distinct fault with the Krag is the single locking lug—forces reloaders to keep pressure and, thus, velocity down. Nevertheless, some handloaders like the .30-40 and have concocted a considerable number of loads. A maximum charge of powder will drive a full jacketed bullet through five feet of pine boards. The rifle is also difficult to scope; a side mount must be used.

Commercial ammo has been produced in 150, 180 and 220 gr. weights. Friends and I have found the 180 projectile a good cross-canyon bullet; but in brush and trees the 220 gr. is better.

THE .308

A cartridge which should become a favorite with many muley hunters is the one U.S. Army Ordnance first called the T-65. It was then adopted by NATO as the 7.62mm, but is better known among sportsmen as the .308 Winchester.

During World War II, research produced an improved small rifle propellant: "ball" powder. The result was equal ballistic efficiency with reduced bulk in the case, a shorter action, and a lighter weapon. Winchester quickly saw the possibilities and manufactured a lightweight Model 70: 1-12 twist, 22-inch barrel, weight approximately 6½ pounds. At present, weapons—both foreign and domestic—to handle this cartridge can also be purchased in semi-auto, slide and lever actions.

This cartridge, with a case one-half inch shorter than the '06, was labeled "critical" by early handloaders because of erratic pressures. Although not as powerful as the venerable '06, but appreciably more than the .300 Savage, this cartridge gives good performance on deer with 150, 165 and 180 gr. bullets. A number of other .30 caliber cartridges, both factory and wildcat, are fair to excellent deer killers. Among these are the .300 Savage, .303 British, .30-06 Improved, .30 Remington, .30 Newton and 8mm Mauser.

THE .348 WINCHESTER FOR MULEYS

Here is a cartridge that will knock a muley askiddle! Need verification? Two friends have jointly used this caliber for more than 50 years and are enthusiastic about its capabilities as a muley rifle. Once, one of them ambushed a handsome, running buck. When hit, the rascal flipped into a somersault and struck his head so hard on the ground that the skull was split.

Manufactured commercially since 1936 only in Winchester's lever action Model 71, this cartridge may be a little powerful for deer. However, as a woods weapon, it's excellent when firing 200 to 250 gr. soft point or round nose bullets. Velocity with these projectiles is about right for least amount of deflection by small branches and leaves.

The action of the Model 71 is fur-smooth and quick. One can keep this rifle, true of all lever actions and pumps, against his shoulder and work the action to prepare for a second shot if necessary—as he watches the game. Trigger pull is adjustable; weight and balance are good; and the outside hammer enables a hunter to react quickly.

Critics have occasionally maligned this rifle with complaints of inaccuracy. However, while still hunting, who is concerned with better accuracy than four-inch groups at 100 yards? Winchester never intended that this cartridge qualify as a long-range demon. But, when sighted-in to strike dead-on at 150 yards, it kills well out to 200. The Model 71 doesn't take a scope too well; but, again, who needs a scope on a woods rifle?

.35 CALIBERS FOR MULEYS

Four additional rifles that fire hefty bullets which will go through—end to end—the largest muley that ever lived are the .35 Whelen, .35 Remington, .358 Winchester and the .350 Remington Magnum. All are a mite powerful for deer but function admirably in trees and brush.

The .35 Whelen, which some erroneously believe was developed by Col. Townsend Whelen, was introduced in 1922. This cartridge is the '06 case necked up to .35 caliber. It fires a 250 gr. bullet at about 2,400 fps.

Another good brush bucker is the .35 Remington. And, like the .35 Whelen, it doesn't destroy a large amount of meat. Originally, this cartridge appeared in the Remington Model 8 self-loading rifle. Then followed the Remington Model 760 and Marlin 336. This is a much better woods rifle than the .30-30 and similar cartridges. The 200 gr. Hornady bullet is an excellent projectile and, when sighted-in for 150 yards, is only 5 inches low at 200 yards.

The .358 Winchester was announced in 1955, and has appeared in Models 70 and 88. I have never carried either of these rifles into muley mountains, but friends tell me that they "tear through a lot of stuff (leaves, small branches) and still bring down a deer."

As I recall, the .350 Remington Magnum was introduced in 1964, in the Model 600 carbine which carries an 18½-inch barrel. Obviously designed to be used in brush, this cartridge has killed a long list of North American game, from mule deer to brown bears.

HIGH-VELOCITY AND MAGNUM CARTRIDGES

Most old-timers considered the flat-shooting .30-30 cartridge a most distinct boon. By comparison, the 400-plus gr. bullets in great-grandfather's .45-70 burst out of the barrel at approximately 1,300 fps. To hit a muley at around 200 yards he had to hold a foot or so high. Then followed a short period of rifle history when we had placed into our hands such additional wonders as the .280 Ross, .275 British, .250-3000 Savage, .270 Winchester and .300 H&H, to list some of them. In reality—certainly at the time of their introduction—these were all magnums, or "great" rifles.

After World War II the high-velocity and magnum advocates really went to town. Roy Weatherby came riding out of his California corral with fire in his eyes and thunder in his fists. His films and advertisements showed game from small jackrabbit-like antelope to elephants dying in their spoor without a preliminary cough. He started with the .300 and followed with the .257, .270, 7mm, .375, .460 and several others. Remington, Winchester and assorted other domestic and foreign manufacturers then jumped on the magnum wagon and a constant stream of super-rifles has since been rolling off assembly lines.

Consequently, we entered a period of hunting history when a number of citizens started throwing extremely tiny, high-speed bullets at many kinds of game animals—some of them capable of biting, goring and trampling back. Results at odd times were more than sensational. But, generally, something was askew. Maybe poor bullets were to blame. These small projectiles at tremendous speeds often "blew up," even on the surface of thin-skinned, normally easy-to-kill creatures, such as mule deer. Better bullets were then made; still, there were problems with small, fast-stepping bullets.

No one knows how far the magnums will travel. Startling different powders, new metal alloys—and the moon is within reach. Politicians have boasted that we're living in the atomic-space age. Certainly riflemen-hunters are living in the magnum age.

Where do magnums fit into the mule deer hunting panorama? I've been accused of being too conservative (meaning a stick in the mud), but I have found only limited application for magnums—the extremely souped-up cartridges—for shooting muleys. As a matter of fact, I believe the average sportsman is handicapped with a magnum. Pressured by advertisements and stories in the rifle and sporting magazines, he's been so brainwashed that he now believes that all he must do is buy a magnum to become a sure, deadly killer of deer. He's been told that in spite of his poor skill he can collect a deer by placing a bullet into its guts or on the fringes.

An acquaintance, believing such intriguing nonsense, purchased a .300 Weatherby. Invited to a sighting-in, I was amazed at the amount of body movement—the man weighs about 180 pounds—that occurred at moment of recoil as he lay at prone. Close observation of his face showed after the first shot that he was closing both eyes so tightly that the crow's-feet at the corners of his eyes turned upward and bulged. This rifle was just too much gun for this man. He was flinching badly; was visibly frightened by the recoil, muzzle blast and report. And the bullet strikes on the target were so scattered they appeared to have been made by a curious, pecking bird.

Magnums can be criticized on several counts: First, advertised sensational velocities. Oftentimes, these figures are "paper" ballistics, having been taken in 26-inch, or longer, test barrels. A hunter then finds that the 22- to 24-inch job he has bought checks out at 100-300 fps less—little better than the standard caliber, but still retaining excessive recoil, muzzle blast and report.

Second: most magnums are overbore capacity. Which means to you and me that a portion of the powder isn't burned in the barrel. Consequently, muzzle blast and report are terrific—frightening to the average individual. Try shooting your .264 or 7mm magnum at night. Did the ball of flame spewing from the muzzle scare a year off your life?

Third: magnum rifles and ammo are comparatively expensive.

Fourth: recoil is punishing. I have two magnums but rarely shoot them. The 35 to 40 pounds of recoil from a .338 gives me flinchitis, a headache and blackens a shoulder. Recoil over 20 pounds cannot be handled comfortably by most hunters, especially women and youngsters.

Fifth: loss of accuracy. Friends and I have rarely owned a rifle that would print groups as tightly when loaded to maximum as with medium, sensible loads.

Sixth: barrel life (good accuracy) is often gone at 500 to 800 rounds.

A very distinct advantage which some magnums possess is extremely flat trajectory. When sighted-in to place a bullet 3-4 inches high at 100 yards, a hunter has a weapon with point-blank range out to 300 or 400 yards.

High-velocity advocates firmly believe that increased speed in their rifles increases "killing power" and "shock," whatever these words mean. With a slide rule they point out that the faster a projectile is humping along, the more energy—thus, more tissue damage and probability of instant death. And bullets that zip along at 3,000-4,000 fps sometimes do spectacular magical things to tissues of game animals. On the Snowville Flats I saw Jim McClure clip a black-tail jackrabbit with a Swift so slightly that only the incisor teeth were sliced away. Yet, that long-eared varmint died as quickly as though struck by Thor. Likewise, I've seen a couple of deer killed almost instantly when smacked on the fringes, such as the fleshy part of a leg, with a speedy magnum bullet. Can you explain it?

The following magnums are excessively powerful for mule deer: 7mm, .300 H&H, .300 Weatherby, .308 Norma, .300 Winchester, .338 Winchester, .375 H&H—to name some of them. A needlessly large amount of tissue is often destroyed. I owned, probably, the first .338 Winchester Model 70 in Utah. An Eastern friend sent one before they were released in the West. It not only kills muleys; it rips huge chunks out of their bodies. Three deer have fallen to my 7mm magnum. The first was standing, looking back over its shoulder, at about 125 yards. The 160 gr. Sierra spitzer B. T. sliced through the top of the shoulder and into the neck. Devastation is a mild word to describe tissue destruction. The second, a long yearling buck, took the same bullet in the heart and lungs, and these organs were transformed into a red, soupy mixture. The third, in an ideal situation at about 75 yards, had his head nearly ripped off at the first neck vertebra by the same 160 gr. bullet.

THE OLD-TIMERS

Besides being a stick-in-the-mud, I'm occasionally labeled as old-fashioned, because I sometimes recommend .45-90's, .45-70's, .32-40's, .25-20's, etc.—even large caliber handguns, flintlocks, percussion rifles and arrows to experienced, skilled muley hunters. With increasing emphasis by today's people-warren civilization on super-this, magnum-that, I find myself turning nostalgically to the good-old-days when activities and possessions were far less complicated.

In fact, to witness the grim, relentless behavior of many moderns afield is frightening. I rarely go fishing or hunting opening day anymore. To return to the black powder era, or even to conditions of the early 1900's is impossible, of course. But, I have found that to hunt big game with one of the older weapons—especially, arrows—is tremendously refreshing, satisfying. Particularly, now that the number of mule deer has alarmingly decreased—and will likely continue downhill—why not hunt them, at least part of the time, with the so-called antiquated weapons?

Bow hunting has lent a new zest to my deer hunting. And, even though I may travel several days afield and never loose an arrow, I return home refreshed, with new enthusiasm for the out-of-doors.

In my gun-rack is a scarred, 38-inch barrel rifle, a black powder, ball weapon. How many deer, turkeys—perhaps even Indians, for this rifle is an ancient one—this weapon killed before it left the Appalachian

Mountains no one will ever know. To "test" this weapon and to step into the moccasins of the unknown frontiersman who once used this rifle, I used it on a 200-pound muley. When the approximately .40 caliber lead ball took him in the ribs, he sprinted only about 50 yards and died. Just as dead as though hit with a .40 caliber super magnum. Not an ounce of eatable meat was destroyed.

If you own an 1881 Marlin or an 1886 Winchester in good condition, take it off the wall and try it on deer. Leave the 1873 trap-door home—action too weak for modern powders. Or a .45-90 will do as well—as will a number of other cartridges fired from the John Browning designed 1886 lever action: .33, .38-56, .38-70, .40-65, .40-70 and .40-82. Believe it or not, the '86 Winchester which appeared in light and heavy models, with solid and takedown frames and with barrels of various lengths, was manufactured until 1936. I wish I had a .32-40 in good condition. This cartridge has killed plenty of muleys and still functions very effectively when loaded with a mild charge of smokeless powder and a good bullet. A man who lived alongside us in the gravel-scratching flats of central Utah during the 1930's brought home many a deer with a .25-35. Introduced in 1895 by Winchester for use in the Model 1894—and later by Savage in the 99—this cartridge is quite accurate but is by no means a long-range miracle. However, in the hands of a good hunter, with the right bullet, as a Remington Core-Lokt, at about 2,200 fps, it will do the job. Perhaps, the minimum among the old-timers for deer is the .25-20. More than a few muleys have met their end with this cartridge, but I'm acquainted with no one who is presently using it. Certainly, one should approach to close range in order to place a bullet accurately. This is no beginner's weapon. Accuracy is good to 100 yards.

Handguns on deer? Powerful weapons such as the .357, .41 and .44 magnums will kill muleys. All handguns are illegal for big game in Utah, but a certain percentage of Utah's hunters have killed deer with these weapons. A growing segment of hunters in Montana, Idaho and other Western states regularly tote them on deer safaris. Sure, they'll drop deer—more dead and at a greater distance than, say, with an arrow. And I have a great deal of respect for a good arrow.

At the risk of writing monotonously, may I say again that almost always the killing of big game depends more on the placement of a good bullet rather than speed of the bullet or caliber in which it's fired. For general usage, select a sensible weapon. Don't be an extremist with either too fast or too slow bullets, too large or too small a caliber. Use a rifle which you can handle, one which in your honest opinion, can kill a muley under fair, perhaps even adverse, conditions. Confidence in one's ability and equipment is more important than caliber, type and speed of bullets.

AMMO AND WEAPON CARE

Purchase cartridges in your hometown; don't wait until on the highway. Special brands and types are occasionally scarce, and a dealer may require several weeks to obtain them. Store ammo where it won't be soiled or lost. To toss the containers on the car seat or with other paraphernalia is lazy, haphazard. I transport my cartridges in a metal, .50-caliber ammunition box. Perhaps the most bothersome single item to stow on one's person is the ammo. Most hunters carry their shells in awkward belts or in bulging pockets. A much more convenient method is a leather case, into which the cartridges, or the box itself—minus top or cover, can be slipped. How much ammo should one carry? For years I've packed a box of 20, plus a full magazine. However, I've rarely used more than 5 rounds. But, I still believe a muley hunter should have at least 20 rounds—an extra few to blast at a coyote, a grouse or for signaling when lost.

If you're a handloader, check all ammo through the action on the range at home. Occasionally, a bullet is seated incorrectly and may lodge in the lands and spill powder into the action. Solution: remove the bullet from another case and with the muzzle pointed skyward, chamber the case and fire.

Don't use old brass for hunting loads. Run new cases with normal loads through the rifle and reload. I carry a broken-shell extractor—takes very little space in a pocket or pack. Weapons care in muley camp is simple—if one remembers to include screwdrivers for scope mounts and action screws; a cleaning rod, patches and a rust-inhibitor.

SIGHTING-IN

Most deer rifles are incorrectly sighted which results in numerous missed and crippled muleys. Each hunter should sight in his own weapon. Some factory and custom rifles place their bullets fairly accurately, but most need additional tuning up. Don't trust this responsibility (I find it a pleasant experience) to a friend or gunsmith. Each individual holds a weapon differently, especially one with iron sights, and no one except you can tune a rifle until it satisfies 100 per cent. Only when bullets print correctly should you be contented; for then you will have confidence in your weapon, which is very important. A few hunters are so lackadaisical about sighting-in that after blasting at distant rocks or tin cans they believe that their rifles are shipshape to hunt deer.

To sight in a rifle isn't difficult, nor does it involve secret or mystical details. First, check the bore. A new weapon may have a glob of grease blocking the barrel; the tube of the family deerslayer may have been stuffed with an object by tiny, busy fingers. Next, if the outfit is new, remove the barrel and action from the stock and coat the barrel channel with a thin layer of waterproofing shellac and the barrel and action with a rust-inhibiting grease. Reassemble and tighten the action screws.

Because associates and I shoot rifles fairly frequently from a bench, we've purchased an adjustable forearm rest and made a bench and target holder which assemble in about one minute. Improvise if you don't have these items. A car hood, a folded jacket or sleeping bag on the ground, target stapled to a foodbox, etc. serve quite well.

Now, we shall bore-sight. This preliminary is unnecessary if you're certain that bullets will print on a target at 100 yards. But, if your weapon is new, or you have recently installed a scope, start with this simple step. To do otherwise usually means wasted ammunition and time. In all probability, after bore-sighting, bullets will strike a target at 25 yards, although they may not be in the black. Barrels differ remarkably because of vibrations.

Next, after tightening the scope mount screws, prop the weapon into a steady position on the car hood, into notches cut into a cardboard box, or on the bench. Remove the bolt (with bolt-action rifles) or thrust into place one of the so-called barrel mirrors (for lever and other actions). While looking through the barrel, locate the target bull, that white stone or shiny tin can which you've placed at approximately 50 yards. Without touching the rifle, find the same object through the sights. They don't lineup? Adjust the sights until they do. When considerable side-to-side adjustment is necessary with a scoped rifle, make it in the mount.

Next, walk the target-holder out to 25 yards, if your weapon has a telescopic sight; or, to 12½ yards with iron sights. We've chosen 25 yards because with scoped rifles your bullets first cross the "line of sight" at or near this point. But, of course, this distance depends upon bullet velocity. A bullet then rises and again passes through the "line of sight" at a considerable distance from the muzzle. The 25-yard distance has also been selected because errors here are multiplied by four at 100 yards. Thus, if bullet strikes are, let's assume, 3 inches from center of bull, they will be 12 inches away at 100 yards—may even miss the paper.

Now, over the hood of a car or from the bench, with the forearm padded with hand, coat, foam rubber or any other nonsolid object, squeeze off two rounds. Let's assume that these bullet strikes, nearly in one hole are approximately 2 inches low and 3 inches to left of center of bull, or whatever type of target is being used. To return the bullet strikes to center of target, turn the scope knobs an appropriate number of clicks. Assuming your scope has ½ minute clicks, turn the right-left knob 12 clicks right and the up-down knob 8 up.

Almost everyone understands that a minute-of-angle equals one inch at 100 yards. Thus, one minute also equals 1/8 inch at 12½ yards; one-quarter at 25 yards; a half at 50; 2 inches at 200, etc. Most receiver and scope sights have either one-half or one-quarter minute-of-angle clicks. It should be apparent now that you must move the rear sight in the direction you desire bullet strikes to move. Front sight? Just the opposite.

Older weapons having sights in semi-permanent slots are somewhat more difficult to adjust. But same general principles as outlined above also apply. Don't use a hard-faced steel hammer to move them.

After correcting the sights, fire two more rounds. If additional corrections are necessary, make them, and follow each change with at least two rounds. Now walk the target out to 100 yards and continue firing corrections until strikes are where you want them. Follow with at least one five-shot group, from a cold barrel. Now your rifle has been sighted-in for that muley hunt!

If you hunt in a portion of muley country where shooting may be longish, fire a group or two at 200 yards. Don't be surprised when your bullets don't all fall into one hole. Be happy if the group is a 6-8-inch cluster because you have a reasonably accurate rifle and your trigger release is good.

When firing for groups, determine the center of the bullet prints to make adjustments in the sights. And don't fire all of the commercial ammo in a particular box; keep enough rounds for the hunt. A box from a different lot or brand may not print the same as those used to sight-in. However, never hesitate to use sufficient ammo. Personally, I'd rather expend 18 rounds to sight-in and carry only the remaining two, than go afield with a questionable weapon. Friends and I use .270's, .30-06's, .257's, etc. for muleys. We sight-in to place bullets 2-3 inches high at 100 yards. This means that a .270, 130 gr. bullet is on at about 260 to 280 yards and only 2-3 inches low at 300 yards. The '06 is on target at approximately 250 yards with 150 gr. projectiles. A 170 gr. .30-30 bullet, when targeted 2 inches high at 100 yards, again passes through the line of sight at 150 yards. Try always to sight-in so you can hold dead-on up to a reasonable distance. Several arms manufacturers sell or give away charts and tables which show where bullets impact when sights are adjusted for given distances.

It should be apparent now that each individual should sight-in his rifle because of conditions he, himself, has imposed: distance he expects to kill deer; type of bullet—weight, brand, etc.; various kinds of weights of powders, if handloaded. One's rifle should be sighted-in immediately before the hunting season. Humidity may warp a stock; the weapon could have been dropped; youngsters sometimes fiddle with sights. Don't encourage others to handle your rifle once it's been correctly sighted, for a semi-alert individual may twiddle with the adjustment knobs. When, during a hunt, your rifle goes out of kilter, because of rough treatment in a saddle scabbard, etc., re-sight. Do this near camp, away from the hunting area. Even then, neighboring sportsmen may be piqued. Buy or make targets so that at 100 yards the bull is the same size as the scope dot; or with cross lines which match the cross wires in the scope. Then, any deviation from correct sighting is easily observed. A 6-8-inch bull is best for open sights at 100 yards.

May I repeat—briefly? Always sight-in that smoke-stick before hunting deer—even though you have recently returned from a pronghorn hunt in Wyoming. In fact, correct sighting-in is probably the most important thing to do *before you hunt!*

4

Letting the Deer Come to You

Basically, there are two methods of hunting mule deer. In one, the hunter takes a position overlooking a basin, canyon, pass or stands, or hides beside a game trail and waits for deer to come to him. In the second, the hunter hikes or rides and looks for deer. Which method is best? Which provides the most venison and sport? Arguments for and against any particular hunting technique seem to go on endlessly. In this chapter, let's consider some of the pros and cons of watching, pass hunting and driving in detail. In the next chapter, we'll consider still hunting and stalking.

NEST WATCHING

Through the years I have found that to sit or stand on a hillside, or atop a ridge or cliff where an extensive area can be watched, is a very effective way to kill mule deer. Especially on opening day when thousands of persons are hiking the hills, muleys move constantly about their home territory. Almost anyone can drop a deer at this time if he has the patience to wait at a good location for a few hours.

Because most men make considerable noise while hiking, some hunters think it wise to let deer come to them. Good reasoning, for the average person probably sees only one out of five deer that he encounters while hiking cross-country. Also, a hunter who sits has most of his neighbors who are prowling the countryside working for him. In the West, where terrain is rather open as compared to north Midwestern and Eastern deer cover, a person from a nest can see many of the deer that move within a quarter-mile, and frequently at greater distances.

Many Western sportsmen prefer to nest hunt. They realize that it is convenient and simple, yet very productive. Primitive country isn't required, either. In fact, one would handicap himself were he to hunt wilderness areas in this way. Mule deer sometimes use trails, but they prefer to wander rather aimlessly around their mountain-forest-desert home. When surprised or pursued, they may run in any direction. Frantically they want to put distance between themselves and danger. And, if they chance to run your way, you'll have some shooting.

Nest watching, I believe, requires very little know-how skill. It's a lazy way to kill deer. However, this is a technique that older hunters, the handicapped, and women can use effectively. Sportsmen who refer to themselves as "nervous" hunters will have no part of nest watching. It's virtually impossible for these persons to remain stationary for an hour or two. They're restless and must constantly fight an urge to keep moving continuously. Like many outdoorsmen, they have an exploring trait—always wanting to see what is on the other side of the mountain. If you are a nervous hunter, choose another method to hunt mule deer.

Best time for nest hunting? The first day, particularly the first few hours after daylight, is worth more than the remainder of the season. The multitude of hunters now roaming western forests during opening morning puts most deer on the move, and one's chances of seeing animals during this brief period are very good. This is the time to be in a nest— when deer are traveling. Moreover, when noisy leaves or crusty snow make still hunting impractical, it's wise to let deer come to the hunter.

You've chosen an area somewhere in the Western United States to hunt mule deer, to try for a trophy buck from a nest? Arrive on the scene a day or two before the season opens, particularly if unfamiliar with the area. Even though you may be a native of the district, it's still a good plan to make camp early, for mule deer sometimes change their routines from year to year, week to week—yes, even day to day. A heavy snowstorm often moves deer out of a local area overnight. After camp has been made orderly, become acquainted with the countryside. A map helps, but isn't all important. Hike through the district and search for deer tracks, fresh droppings, muleys, and, of course, a nest from which deer can be seen moving about. If on your own, hike into the hinterlands

—away from the immediate camping area from which kids, dogs, noisy men and vehicles have frightened most of the deer. Look for a spot where you can stand or sit and see in several directions. Such an ideal location isn't always easy to find, but in typical muley habitat of rolling hills and mountains a hunter can nearly always locate a nest which overlooks the surrounding countryside.

The nest may be a spot on an open hillside or astride a rocky spur overlooking a basin, ravine or canyon. The top of a ridge is also a good place from which to watch. From such a spot a hunter by moving only a few yards can alternately look for moving deer in two ravines or canyons. It isn't necessary always to select a nest where a hunter will be hidden. In fact, many western hunters stand clearly in the open, often silhouetted against rocks and sky. But the chances of deer approaching near enough to kill are somewhat improved if you scrunch down into rocks or brush. Then, too, if one is hidden, the possibility of being struck by a stray bullet or mistaken for a deer are materially reduced.

It's quite vital that a hunter be comfortable in his nest. When chilled, he becomes less alert. He may even approach the point where his desire to become warm is stronger than his desire to kill a deer. Best insurance against freezing is warm clothing. Modern thermals keep almost everyone comfortable. However, if you just can't remain a minute longer in the nest without icicles forming on your nose, build a fire. Many muley hunters do, and, if the wind isn't blowing down into the basin or canyon where you expect to see deer, chances of making a kill may still remain quite good. However, mule deer sometimes approach a nest from almost any direction; and, because I believe that tobacco and fire alert deer, for years I've never smoked while hunting and rarely built a fire. Other distinct aids to comfort while nest hunting are sandwiches and a canteen. Even a box of raisins or a candy bar helps.

What should a hunter do while waiting in his nest? Obviously, he's there to look for deer, and should avoid doing anything which frightens them away. Watching from a nest, however, is somewhat different from stand-watching beside a deer trail: one doesn't need to be as constantly alert, absolutely quiet and motionless, generally speaking. Ordinarily, deer are first seen some distance away and aren't near enough to see a man occasionally moving about. Therefore, a hunter can stand, s t r e t c h and walk about to keep his blood circulating. However, one shouldn't carry a paper-back to his nest nor stare at the ground or into space. Nor are small man-noises too important. Sneezing and coughing may make the difference in bagging a deer while sitting beside a deer path, but in a lofty nest, unless deer are near, these sounds are of little importance.

Low talk with a companion won't, generally, drive them away, either. Nor is the rustling of sandwich papers, etc., crucial.

Even man-odor, which many wild animals, including mule deer, dislike so much, may not spoil your chances. During opening day, particularly until about ten o'clock—when you will probably be nest hunting—there are so many persons in the woods that human odor may saturate the area anyway.

Ordinarily, a nest hunter sees most of the deer that approach his station. But, occasionally a deer moves cautiously and slowly into a basin or along the slope of a canyon, stopping here and there, and approaches quite near before being sighted. Remember, mule deer often stop at the edge of a clearing, a road or slash cut through timber for electric or telephone lines and check for danger. Then, they'll hustle across to adjacent cover where they again slow their pace, sometimes even pausing to feed. Therefore, an alert nest hunter frequently uses binoculars to scan the bank of trees surrounding the area he is watching. Occasionally, he may catch the quarry pausing at the lip of the cover and have an opportunity for a standing shot, certainly better than a wild chance at a running, bouncing target.

Often a person hears deer before he sees them. Rocks tumbling down a slope, disturbances in dry leaves or on hard snow obviously should alert a hunter. And it goes without saying that if a person hears a deer snort or stomp his foot, a muley is nearby. Shooting in the distance should alert a hunter, too. Shots usually indicate that a deer has been sighted. When a hunter hears someone blasting over yonder ridge, he should twist his alert button full up and watch for deer.

Sometimes a person sees only part of a deer's body. Sun reflecting from a buck's antlers or a whitish rump patch. Now is the time to use those binoculars. In fact, while nest hunting, binocs may be almost as valuable an aid as one's rifle toward hanging a carcass on the meat pole!

Many western hunters ride horses to locations from which they wish to nest hunt. Horses have excellent hearing, sight and smell. On numerous occasions I've seen them locate deer. It's a good practice to tie Old Red where he can see the same area you plan to watch. Turn and check him occasionally. If he is intently looking at a particular place, with his ears cranked full forward, he may have located a real granddaddy buckskin.

Finally, the big moment arrives! A tremendous trophy has sneaked into the little basin you are watching. But he is still a quarter-mile away—too far to kill cleanly. Now is the time to prepare for the shot you will make when the buck has worked his way up the shallow ravine, through the stunted patch of quaking aspens, and onto the tiny flat about 100 yards away.

Take a sitting or kneeling position! Better still, if you are in a rock nest, place your rifle over a boulder, cushion the forearm with your hand or jacket and find the muley in the scope. Now follow the buck up the gully, and, just as he sneaks out of the quakers into the open, ease off the safety and squeeze the trigger!

PASS HUNTING

A variation of "nest" watching that an increasing number of muley hunters have found very effective is "pass" watching. When thousands of citizens begin tramping the hills on opening day, deer—after some preliminary racing around—start moving to areas of their range where man-odors and bullets can be avoided. A considerable percentage of them funnel through depressions at the head of ravines and canyons. Again, it's very important that a hunter hikes over the district prior to the opening of the season to select a pass. Almost always in good muley country one can locate active deer trails winding through several of these passes.

Where to locate—your position in the pass from which to watch—is important. Some areas are choked with aspens, wild cherries, conifers. Then, it's necessary to sit or stand near the trail. However, don't locate right smack in, or within a few feet of a trail. Deer look ahead and check their pathway and surroundings. Don't move too far away, either. You must be in a reasonably clear spot to see deer and near enough to shoot at them. Passes at high elevations may contain only sagebrush or other chaparral-type vegetation. A hunter can scrunch down in such cover and be well concealed.

Winds also funnel through these passes, especially at high altitudes. Almost always the breezes are fairly strong and direction of flow is obvious. Pay attention to wind direction; unless muleys are all-out scared, man-odor will turn them back. But if you sit on the adjacent hillside, away from the bottom of the depression, your odor may not smack approaching deer in the face. Don't locate so far up on the side of the mountain, though, that you can't make a killing shot.

Generally speaking, information concerning hunter noise, movement, shooting, etc., are applicable to both nest and pass watching.

One additional word of advice: Arrive at the pass before daylight— at least by the time migrating hunters burst from their camps in the bottoms of the canyons and start their noisy cross-country hiking—before they loose the opening barrage from their blasting rifles.

TRAIL OR STAND WATCHING

Another method to bag a mule deer—one not generally used by Western hunters—is trail watching, or "stand watching." Eastern and Midwestern sportsmen employ this technique a great deal. One reason that Western hunters neglect this kind of hunting is that many mule deer don't regularly travel trails or pathways. Western flats and mountains are generally sparsely covered with trees and brush. Hence, mule deer are free to travel haphazardly. This is not true of the white-tail habitat I've seen in Michigan, Pennsylvania and North Carolina where deer follow rather well-defined routes. In such dog-hair thickets, they have no choice. The type of vegetation cover makes the difference, along with the varying instinctive pattern-habits of the two species of deer.

There are a number of locations in the West, however, where cover and other conditions are such that some muleys do follow well defined trails to feed and water, somewhat like white-tails. In addition, hordes of plodding hunters moving noisily over the terrain opening day eventually chase most deer into brush and trees. In these thickets deer move around in front of hunters and, if a person quietly sits a short distance from a game trail showing a reasonable amount of recent use, his chances of eventually killing a muley are very good, close to 99 per cent.

When should you watch one of these trails? From daylight until 10 o'clock opening morning you'll probably want to sit in a nest or watch a pass. Then, if the fates and noisy nimrods haven't driven a deer your way, find a game trail and locate at a spot where you can see at least 25 yards in one or several directions. Or, you may choose to go a few minutes before daylight to such a location you have selected in advance.

Probably the chief clue in selecting a trail is knowing the direction the foot-sloggers walk opening morning. A local resident can be very helpful at this point. However, a survey of camping sites in the area usually supplies the answer. Most hunters walk directly from camp, up canyon trails and roads and along ridges toward higher country the first morning. In flat cedar-piñon terrain, a majority of nimrods have sketchy plans and wander aimlessly.

Watching trails to water—streams, springs and livestock ponds—isn't too productive the first two to three days of the season. Later, when the woods—and the deer—have quieted down, paths to water, and the water itself, can be profitably watched, particularly when the season is hot and dry. How about watching trails to feeding areas? Generally, mule deer feed in almost all locations where browse is available and then bed during mid-day in adjacent cover. However, there are local situations throughout the West where muleys daily move back and forth from protective-rest cover to feeding areas. To wait beside these pathways—or, during early morning or late afternoon, to hike, ride a horse or jeep through the general area of travel—can be very productive.

If you've chosen to watch a game path, find a pile of stones, the base of a tree or clump of brush, a short distance from the trail where you are reasonably concealed. Usually it's not necessary to further camouflage the position with rocks and branches, unless you are fidgety. As a general rule, don't locate right beside the trail, even when bow hunting. A deer watches his path for enemies, so back away into the cover a few yards. By all means, don't select a spot where you are silhouetted against rocks, snow or the sky, for deer discover a man more easily in such locations. It's also rather important to have a clear view of the trail where you expect Mr. Antlers to appear. Although a few deer have been killed by bullets passing through brush and even small trees (the experts tell us), such obstructions deflect most bullets.

While on a stand, remember to pay attention to wind, even though you can do nothing about its intensity or direction. It may change direction a hundred times during the morning's wait. Then, too, the area may be saturated with man-odor, in which case deer may approach your position without much hesitation. A hard running, very spooked muley sometimes disregards human-odor, but a deer that is casually or intently mooching along a trail will run or sneak away when he smells a hunter.

I've seen a few of the stands that hunters build in other sections of the country. They vary from utilization of corn shocks in open fields to elaborate, comfortable apartments. Buck Daley, a friend who lives and hunts near Dallas, Texas, annually rents a small shack built on stilts from which he watches for white-tails. Perhaps the most unique blind I ever saw pictured was a stump-like cylinder, shingled with tree bark, with double doors at the top which folded outward for shooting. This Maginot Line-like structure also had knotholes in the sides for observation ports, seats and electric lights. Such a deluxe structure may be all right for the aged, women, and others, but my friends and I want no part of such an elaborate contraption. There is a point beyond which an activity ceases to be sporting. To accord the hunter too many advantages destroys quality hunting and labels it slaughter. Certainly this can't be called hunting in my book. A certain amount of frosting on a cake is all right, but too much fluff is sickening.

Eastern hunters, particularly bowmen, more and more are building platforms in trees along game trails. This is an effective way to kill white-tails. In special situations, it also works with mule deer in the West.

Muleys don't often look upward. In addition, a station above ground may tend to keep man-odors off the earth, but this depends on weather. To build a platform in aspens and conifers would be fairly simple. Some trees can be climbed, and a person sits astride a branch and waits for game. However, it's nearly impossible to be comfortable while sitting in a tree, and to assume a good shooting position is most difficult. Waiting in such a hide also requires infinite patience. In addition, there is another important consideration: the desecration of an otherwise beautiful forest when a number of ugly platforms are built among the trees.

A hunter certainly deserves to be reasonably comfortable at his stand. He must be warm, but this is not difficult with the array of products now on the market. If one's legs are inclined to cramp or circulation is impaired when sitting or kneeling, build an old-fashioned folding milking stool. Or sit on a log or stone. Scrunching on snow or rain-soaked earth, even bare ground, may slowly paralyze. So, you may wisely choose to carry a small square of canvas to keep a little life in your rumpus. Obviously, the color should blend into dead leaves, grass, rocks or snow. Here is another hint: Don't try to be a spry spartan. Carry a canteen of water or coffee and sandwiches to the stand. You may be there a few hours before Mr. Bucko comes along.

While trail watching, a person should obviously be alert for approaching deer. After all, the chief reason most hunters are in the mountains is to see and kill deer. Yet, it's surprising the number who do otherwise: stare at the sky, go to sleep, watch ants, daydream, read books.

Waiting for muleys in a stand differs from nest watching in several respects. One doesn't see deer a quarter-mile away in semi-thick pines and aspens—usually not farther than 50 yards, sometimes much nearer. From a nest overlooking a canyon or basin a hunter sees walking, trotting or running deer. In the trees, muleys usually mooch along slowly. Therefore, because deer approach quite near before being sighted by a stand hunter, it's imperative that small noises—sneezing, coughing, spitting—be eliminated or minimized. One should also move his hands very slowly, as when scratching an itch or using a handkerchief. Fidgety hunters are poor stand watchers. It's nearly impossible for restless persons to remain reasonably quiet and motionless near a deer trail. I, too, find it difficult to sit absolutely quiet, without moving, for longer than five minutes. This time is considerably shortened when the day is cold.

ODORS

If you have the smoking habit, nothing written here will probably stop you from puffing a pipe or using cigarettes while stand watching.

But you will certainly have fewer deer approach your position. Yes, you may see some deer in good muley country: animals spooked by neighboring hunters and perhaps deer that are foolishly curious. Tobacco smoke is a foreign odor in a deer's environment, and I've proved to my satisfaction that it alerts and frightens most deer. In addition, a person who smokes moves his hands considerably. I believe that experienced deer associate tobacco with men—and danger. It's a conditioned response. Friends and I believe that many deer remain alive because of tobacco odor. However, one expert advises hunters to smoke—that deer pay absolutely no attention to tobacco. Another writer has also said that tobacco odor probably has little or no effect on deer because man-odor is likely stronger in the area and more frightening. Such may be the case, but I don't think so. Certainly it would take several deer biologists, plus a little equipment and time to prove this point. Once a friend and I were watching a canyon from the top of a cliff, at the bottom of which ran a game trail. A fairly strong wind was sneaking up-canyon, and I'm sure that this doe had neither seen nor smelled us. But, when she came to the spot where my pal had been flipping cigarette butts down into the rocks, she stopped abruptly, squirmed as though jabbed with an electric cattle prod and back-tailed as though the devil himself had her by the tail.

However, human and tobacco odors don't always scare mule deer. In fact, just the opposite may occasionally happen. Young muleys, particularly in primitive country, are sometimes exceedingly curious. Although experienced deer generally hasten away when man and his odors appear, I've seen fawns, does and small bucks approach within "talking distance."

In my opinion, man-odor is the number one problem to solve before one can slide a muley into the family wagon. Scientifically, very little is known concerning the effects of man-odor on mule deer. Biologists have found, however, that the olfactory lobes of deer, elephants, dogs, bears, horses and elk are comparatively large, enabling these animals to detect odors of which man is unaware. Apparently these creatures live in a world of smells. There are exceptions, but man's odors generally cause deer to vamoose; to quietly sneak away or clamor out of the area like the clatter wheels of hell. Therefore, the successful stand watcher endeavors to learn as much as possible about how deer react to his odors and ways to prevent or reduce the effects of the odors. Because the average hunter spends only two to three days each year hunting deer, he obviously doesn't have time to study these animals very thoroughly and must depend, therefore, upon others to keep him informed.

Experts tell us that the problem—frightening game by man-odors—

isn't new. In fact, these writers (although they don't reveal the sources of their information) report that American and African aborigines have been keenly aware of the situation for centuries. While hunting, these primitive people wore little or no clothing and generously rubbed their bodies with concoctions manufactured from bark and animal scents. What can a modern hunter do about his odor problem? For one thing, he can bathe before heading for hunting camp, making certain that all perfumed soap is washed away. No perfumed hair oils or shaving lotions, either. This particularly applies to women whose clothing and hair often reek of exotic perfumes and hair sprays. New clothing, shoe oils and polishes have distinctive smells, too. How about the eating of certain foods: onions, garlic and highly seasoned delicacies? Maybe, as the experts report, odors emitted by a person having eaten such foods may be the cause of keeping some deer away from a stand hunter. Man-odors may rise under certain weather conditions and cause no difficulty. But odors, even though there is no apparent wind, generally seep out into the surrounding area a short distance and warn deer as they approach a stand. If odors appear to be keeping deer from your stand, change the location every hour or so.

Scientists may soon develop a scent that not only cancels man-odor, but will actually lure deer to the hunter. As a matter of fact, several products now on the market are "guaranteed to attract deer." I've tested a couple of them, but they weren't successful. I hope that such attraction-devices never prove reliable. Perhaps a concoction to cancel man-odor would be all right for wildlife photographers and bow hunters. But to attract deer to a hidden rifleman for an easy kill would be adding some of that well-known fluff to the already too sweet pie. Don't fret and worry yourself into a dither about the fact that, as far as deer are concerned, you stink. Don't become so involved in nit-picking details that you don't enjoy yourself. Keep hunting anyway. Who knows, the buck of your dreams may be unable to smell an excited skunk two feet in front of his nose.

ATTRACTING AND SPOTTING DEER

Gimmick makers are also trying to develop noise-makers that will attract deer to a hidden man. The one I experimented with alerted several deer as they approached my stand but failed to bring them near enough for me to slip an arrow to their ribs. Perhaps, the deer smelled me, the odor cancelling the lure qualities of the device.

Don't build a fire while stand watching. If you become so uncomfortable that a blaze is required, try another method of hunting or return to camp. Unless a muley is hell-fired scared, he will not approach near enough to be killed from a stand where there is a fire.

To watch deer migration routes is very productive. Heavy storms during late fall move muleys toward winter range. To wait beside traditional trails at this time is deadly for mule deer. So deadly that some persons consider it unsporting. Thousands of deer summer high in Utah's Uinta Mountains, but they start hiking toward lowland cedar and oak forests when snow begins to accumulate during late October and November. Once a group of friends and I obtained permits for a post-season hunt on a portion of the Ute Indian Reservation. More than a foot of snow fell one night. This amount was sufficient to move the deer, and their obvious migration trails were very evident in the canyon the following morning. Here was a situation that would cause the most calloused trophy hunter to drool, for we saw more than 25 trophy bucks that day.

A Texas friend has told me that hunters in the Longhorn State attract white-tails to stands by rattling antlers. The tips of two antlers are first brushed as though two bucks were sparring. Then the tines are brought together with a loud smack, followed by much twisting and scraping. I know only one hunter who has tried to attract mule deer by this method, and I feel a surge of adrenalin every time I recall the incident.

Time was mid-November. I had started at daylight to hunt coyotes. But then I saw some deer. Among the group was a large, nervous buck who kept forking his younger fellows away from the females. Finally, one of them turned on the herd master, and they clapped antlers several times. Immediately two other large bucks, out of sight of the two battlers but certainly within hearing, came rushing into the arena. I returned the following Saturday with a pair of antlers. After selecting a spot near several deer, one of which was a pretty fair buck, I started banging the antlers together. Unfortunately, a horseman came over the ridge just as I had reached the climax of the antler-rattling act. The expression on his face was one I'd never before seen on a human's face. As geese fly, the state mental hospital is only 16 miles from where I was beating those antlers in an oak clearing on the rolling slopes of Mt. Timpanogos. Whether that rider phoned the superintendent of the hospital I don't know, but I'm happy that he didn't recognize me.

From a stand in thick cover one sometimes hears muleys before seeing them, especially when deer are frightened and running hard. Their hoofs break sticks, strike stones, rustle leaves and pound the frozen earth. Likewise, they brush against trees and branches, pull their feet out of mud and splash water. Have you also heard their desperate, panting breathing when they've stopped in cover after a long-exhausting run? You may even hear the ruckus when a buck forks a small aspen or maple viciously with his antlers, a noise clearly audible for a hundred yards when wind is favorable. Some hunters have told me with a sober face that they can smell nearby deer. Yes, I can smell an old bull elk when he's rutting, even when suffering from a cold—but not deer, although they may be standing upwind, within a few yards from my hide.

About half of the deer that approach a stand are never heard by a hunter before he sees them. This results when a person isn't completely alert. Suddenly the muley is there, stopped, sniffing the air, rotating his huge, antenna-like ears. If a hunter is 100 per cent alert—which is impossible 100 per cent of the time—he often spots part of a deer before seeing the complete animal—reflected sunlight from an antler, a twisting ear, a moving leg. Whatever the situation, keep looking, remain as alert as possible—until you are tired. Look for the unusual in the tree-brush cover; objects that don't appear quite right because of their shape or color. Some people locate deer right away, without difficulty. Usually, these persons are experienced hunters, but not always. The first time my wife hunted she spotted four animals that had escaped my attention. One's inability to see deer may be caused by various eye problems, but generally it's laziness, disinterest. Eager, attentive hunters have little trouble locating deer. If an individual trains himself to be alert, to keep looking for muleys, he usually finds them. Even in the limiting confines of a stand, where visibility is sometimes restricted to 25 to 50 yards, a binocular is worth its weight in pure platinum. Especially to identify 'pieces' of deer. Even though you may have no reason to suspect that a muley is near, occasionally raise the binoc very slowly and scan the bank of cover in front of your stand. Very slowly does the job.

Before shooting, always make certain that the object you've seen is a deer, not a cow, elk or man. Don't make "sound" or "flash" shots. Such is the mark of an idiot—or a murderer. Don't blast at a portion of a deer, either, unless you are absolutely sure that you would shoot at that same piece of deer were it standing in the open. It's far better to wait until the muley is clear of trees and brush, stopped and near. Not too near, though, if you're using a scoped rifle. When a muley is within a few yards of a scope, the image may be fuzzy, or you may see only patches of deer hair and be unable to place a bullet in a vital area.

All right, you've done everything the experts have said you should do, and there is Mr. King Antlers himself standing in the clearing, head up, nibbling leaves. If the deer isn't in front, turn slowly around. Don't jump upright to do your shooting. Remain seated or kneeling. Then slowly, very slowly, raise the rifle and squeeze the trigger.

DRIVING MULEYS

Driving may not be the most sporting way to kill mule deer, but a drive, when properly organized, is very productive—probably the most efficient method of putting carcasses on the meat pole. After all of the foo-foo about techniques of hunting mule deer have been chewed and digested, any shag-toothed, Western muley hunter will confide that organized driving will do most effectively that which we usually go into the hills to do during September, October and November—kill mule deer. In fact, close friends and I have never participated in a drive which failed to produce venison. Make no mistake; this type of hunting can be great fun, too.

Terrain and available man-power dictate the way a drive is organized and executed. A considerable portion of the Mountain States consists of cedar and piñon forests, areas which are mostly flatish, slashed occasionally by ravines and ridges. There are also other areas—islands of aspens; lodgepole, fir and oak thickets; woody stream bottoms; canyons and basins—where muleys bury themselves. It's very difficult for the average person to solo hunt these places, but a drive will push the deer out. These locations are naturals for groups of experienced hunters. In fact, there are districts in the West where deer can be adequately harvested only by driving. The locale you and friends intend to hunt may be extensive—mile after mile of hills, ravines, trees and brush. In such areas muleys may be so widely scattered that a lone nimrod would have difficulty finding them. Believe it or not, there are also a few locations in the Rockies where there aren't enough hunters to keep muleys on the move, or to make nest watching and pass hunting profitable.

Muleys which might never be seen except by chance are flushed from cover and driven before the men. Someone along the line or a watcher will enjoy some shooting. It's also an excellent practice to drive-hunt when conditions are unfavorable for other types of hunting: when the ground is frozen, snow crunchy, dry leaves lying everywhere—conditions which make still hunting impractical if not impossible.

Driving deer is not a new technique—a white man's invention. North American Indians, outdoor writers tell us, employed this method to kill deer centuries ago. I've seen several places where antelope and bison were supposedly driven over cliffs by the Indians.

What is the best time of day or season to drive deer? There are exceptions, but perhaps on opening morning the easiest way for the average man to kill a deer, as previously pointed out, is to sit in a nest or pass. Mule deer run wildly for the first few hours opening day but thereafter bury themselves in thick cover. But a drive will dig them out.

Eight or ten drivers, plus three to four watchers, is about the right number of men to conduct a drive in big-country terrain. A greater number becomes unwieldly for several reasons. In larger groups there always seems to be one or more individuals—who invariably foul the operation—someone who walks too fast or too slow, fails to keep his companions in sight, doesn't relay signals, or commits one of a hundred idiotic bungles that seem inherent in some human beings. However, a lesser number can effectively work out smaller pockets of timber, brush and canyons. A group of good friends, men who have been found to be safety-wise, can plan and complete a drive safely, successfully. When one must worry about his neighbors, the hunt isn't worthwhile. For this reason we accept a new member into our group reluctantly.

Selection of a drive leader isn't difficult. Automatically, choice goes to the most experienced and responsible, the most likable man in the group. His task: organize the men, explain the plans, supervise the hunt. He is the person who remembers important details: where deer were found on former drives, where they will probably run when flushed. He's the man who has hunted over the terrain many times; he knows the location of ravines, ridges and deer trails.

If the selected area has been driven during previous years, and if no new hunters are in the group, only a few details need be discussed: weather, exact time to start the hunt, review of whistle signals, whether to post watchers. The following morning the men assemble, wind direction is checked, clocks synchronized, and watchers, if they are to be used, dispatched to their posts. When new members have joined the group, the leader outlines plans in fine detail the day or night before. He may use a map to show newcomers the terrain features: roads, trails, streams, ravines, etc. Yet, a level spot of earth or grimy side of a truck is often employed to indicate the area's general physical features.

Here are some comments taken from a recording of a leader's instructions to such a group:

"All right. Everybody listening? Two and a half miles north of camp is an old cabin. It's in a big sagebrush flat, so none of us should miss it.

"In the morning, about daybreak, we'll form a line. I'll be in the center, and Jim, Ike, Rusty and Stever—you guys will walk due west from here, along the old road. The rest of you will walk straight east, with Paul at the extreme end. Space yourselves about 75 yards.

"We're going to hike to the north first. When we reach the cabin, we'll stop. Then I'll give four blasts on this here whistle; and everyone, except Jim, who is anchor man on the west end, will hike directly to where he is standing—in the open. Then, after we've assembled, we'll space ourselves across new territory to the west and walk south."

The leader outlines other details, too. He explains emphatically and carefully that each hunter must neither lag nor advance beyond his neighbors in the line. Of course, one's neighbors will be out of sight much of the time, but each person will see the two red-shirts adjoining him often enough to adjust his walking speed and maintain position. The leader likewise explains that no one—absolutely nobody—shoots at a flushed deer until the animal has passed at least a 45-degree angle from the line of hunters. Never is a deer fired at when jumped between two men, no matter how wonderful the opportunity. It is very important that each person know his responsibility in keeping the line straight. Never should there be an arc—the ends of the line bent forward—as one expert suggests. When a group arcs the line, soon a driver will be lost either through a man killed or a canceled membership because someone has been frightened by a hot, whiny bullet.

Type of terrain determines spacing between drivers. Twenty-five to 100 yards is about right. The leader and veteran members of the group set the distance, for they have been over the ground a number of times. When spacing is too wide, deer slip unseen through the ranks, and hunters have difficulty spotting their neighbors often enough to keep the line straight. If too near, a drive may be ineffective because insufficient ground is covered.

Many years ago, drives were purposely noisy. Kids were brought along for the express function of noisily beating brush in an effort to frighten deer toward posted watchers. Drivers often yelled, and some-times beat on cans. Such noise did keep hunters in line, since no one had much difficulty following the progress of his neighbors. But I've never believed that a group should turn a drive into a shivaree. In fact, loud-mouths and noisy kids often frighten deer so badly that they behave abnormally—take off cross-country, in any direction, to escape the racket. A clumsy man creates too much noise anyway. Deer generally know he's coming. But why frighten them into bolting wildly? Fact is, if a driver moves cautiously, he may drop Mr. Tangle Horns before he reaches the "guns" stationed ahead. After long years of experience, I believe that silent driving is best.

Some deer quickly move out in front of drivers, despite efforts of everyone to move carefully. But these muleys travel ahead—through the bottom of ravines or along stream beds and ridges—toward the watchers. They don't tend to scatter helter-skelter or spill around the line's ends.

We don't usually station hunters in advance of drivers in piñon-cedar forests. Too dangerous! Bullets zing a mile or more in flat country. Drive hunting is hazardous enough anyway, now that hordes of citizens are in the hills each autumn. One drive may run afoul of another, and solo hunters may be in the area. An exception to this rule is when a ravine crosses the line of drive. In such a situation the "guns" can scrunch down on the side of the gully facing away from the drivers. Unbelievable opportunities for shooting come for these men when spooked deer move across the ravine.

Watchers should be trucked to the ravine, when there are roads. Otherwise, the men must walk; but they should skirt the area to be encompassed by the drive. These men, obviously, must depart an hour or so before daybreak. Upon arrival at the ravine, the "guns" space themselves across the face of the drive according to a pre-arranged plan. It's extremely important that the watchers find cover where they can't be struck with bullets fired by the drivers. Large rocks and the lip of the ravine afford good protection. A person should never stand in the open, nor crouch behind small trees and brush. Watchers must station themselves where they can see a considerable distance—to the sides and in the same direction as the drivers are moving. As pointed out, it's extremely dangerous to watch the area from which the drivers are approaching. Anyway, a watcher can't fire toward the walking men even though he is foolish enough to peek—and see the world's record muley. Watchers must remain at their posts until the drive has been completed. To wander around is to invite death, or at least the criticism of fellow hunters. Certainly such a person could never expect a repeat invitation from that particular group.

Everyone should kill his own muley. For most individuals, dropping a deer is the fun-thrill of hunting. Certainly, there are other pleasures: memorable nights around a campfire, stimulating conversations. But each hunter should bag his own deer, boast to companions two or three times about how Mr. Wily Buck fell to his bullet and take a carcass home which he himself has earned. Nor should a person shoot at a deer that another person has sighted and is attempting to kill. I'll always remember how frothy-mouthed I once became when, after slipping a slug into a buck across a little canyon, three acquaintances ripped him apart with an assortment of .30-06 and .300 magnum bullets as he staggered downhill. I walked away, killed another buck that afternoon, which forced one of those characters to tag that buck's chawed-up carcass. After a person has killed his muley, he still has the responsibility of continuing the hunt by plugging a gap in the line—helping his fellows obtain some shooting. Same is true of a "gun." He relinquishes his place to another and takes his turn as "dog" in the brush.

Wind direction must be considered when planning a drive. Obviously, men moving downwind push deer toward the watchers. On the other hand, while walking upwind (wind in face), drivers quietly approach deer because of decreased sound and absence of man-odor. A cross-wind is best, much better than even a calm. For such a breeze carries away odors of watchers and drivers as well as small hunter noises that otherwise might alert or spook deer. However, winds change directions frequently, but don't become discouraged when they shift. Continue the drive; you'll still have a passel of fun and, in all likelihood, kill a deer.

When the drivers have had sufficient time to reach their stations in the line, the leader whistles one blast. The drive has begun! Following instructions, everyone walks slowly, quietly, sharply alert. Usually, deer aren't encountered for 200 to 300 yards, for they've likely been disturbed by the posting of drivers. However, if there are a reasonable number in the area, several should be spotted within the first half-mile. Occasionally, a muley is seen standing, looking back over his shoulder. But, generally speaking, mule deer are wary creatures, see the drivers first and start to move. Unless badly spooked, muleys are spotted walking or trotting, but not running.

Everyone along the line will hear the blast when a person shoots at a deer. But, usually, no one except the fortunate hunter knows that a deer has been grounded. Therefore, the successful nimrod whistles twice, signal that a kill has been made. An empty cartridge is a good whistle. This signal is then repeated by everyone along the line, including the end men, for an obvious reason. All hunters stop immediately. The two-whistle signal is also an invitation for the neighbors of the lucky hunter to join him, to assist in dressing the carcass. Ten minutes is sufficient time for three experienced men to gut a carcass, hang it in shade, bag it if necessary, and mark the location with a handkerchief or toilet paper. Then the hunters return to their positions and, after a one-whistle signal —blown by the successful hunter—has passed along the lines, the drive continues.

Experienced hunters use whistle signals, for they've learned that a whistle is far less alarming to deer than human voices. Even when a deer is dropped and men assemble to eviscerate the carcass, they keep conversation to a minimum and volume low.

Because hunters can easily move out of position on a turn at the end of a drive—a very dangerous situation—we do not half wagonwheel the men. A piñon-cedar, aspen or lodgepole forest can be rather dense with trees, making it nearly impossible at times for a hunter to see his neighbors often enough to keep in a line while completing a turn. So our driving group always stops at the end of one portion of the hunt and reassembles. The end-point of a drive should always be determined in advance and agreed upon by all party members. A cabin, ravine, prominent ridge, canyon, or a large, conspicuous boulder or tree make good landmarks. In their absence, an elapsed amount of time is used. When the destination is reached or time has elapsed, the leader blows four blasts on his whistle. This signal is repeated down the line. Drivers at distant ends of the line then walk toward the leader, gathering their pals as they come in. This insures that no one is lost. Then the group decides on a new location for a drive—or returns to camp with deer that have been killed. Oftentimes, however, we hike to one end of the line, space ourselves out again and continue driving.

A drive occasionally runs afoul of another group of driving men. Deer—caught between the lines of men—bolt excitedly and bounce off the lines until killed, filter through the ranks or spill out the ends. Such a situation is extremely dangerous if hunters fail to use common sense and keep peppering at the deer. The first hunter to notice that his group is approaching another drive should warn his neighbors. They in turn relay the warning along the line, and all hunters should drop to the ground immediately. When the leader believes that all hunters in both driving groups are aware of the predicament, he whistles four blasts to assemble his men. Often a drive encounters a solo hunter. Again signals are used to warn every man in the line. If the leader believes the situation dangerous, he assembles his men and begins a new drive elsewhere. Usually, however, a solo hunter is quite anxious to clear out, so after he has passed through the line, the drive continues.

Another interesting and very productive driving technique involves two hunters who work opposing sides of ravines or small canyons. Each man drives for the other. As one hunter progresses quietly along his side of the canyon, he pauses frequently to watch the opposite hillside—in front of, behind, above and below his companion. Hundreds of mule deer are killed each autumn by men using this method.

Four friends and I used this buddy-method on a post-season hunt to kill three deer. A friend and I teamed in one canyon. We began seeing deer almost immediately. First, two does and a fawn ran out of the bottom of the canyon before we had gone a hundred yards. Fifteen minutes later my companion spooked a forked-horn from some dense pines. Then an assortment of small bucks, does and fawns sneaked out in front of me, but my friend didn't shoot because he wanted a very excellent trophy or a doe not followed by a fawn.

Because the wind was blowing miserably cold and drifting several inches of snow, we stopped after a mile or so and built fires. After 10 or 15 minutes, we moved down the canyon again. Suddenly a very large five-pointer sneaked out of the dark conifers in front of my friend and crossed a little clearing. I didn't shoot because I thought my companion, who was quite near the buck, would spot him. It was too late when I finally realized that he couldn't see the old deer. Then someone fired six to seven rounds below us in the deep canyon. Thirty or so deer which had been standing on the sides and bottom of the canyon moved when they heard the shooting. It required the rifle blasting or possibly our scent (the wind was twisting) to spook them into moving so that we could find them in the oak-cedar cover below. Most of the deer were too distant for shooting, 400 to 500 yards away.

My friend and I continued down the canyon, meanwhile jumping more muleys. However, we had now hiked so far from the jeep that I had decided that only a very good buck would tempt me. After watching the muleys for a few minutes, we circled out of the canyon and hiked back to the jeep. We spent the remainder of the day trying to move transportation nearer to those deer. A member of the party finally managed somehow to fly the jeep across a creek and through high sagebrush until we were within a mile of where we had seen most of the muleys. Then, the following day we staged a repeat performance. As previously said, three of us killed deer: two eating muleys by my two friends, plus a 15-pointer (all tines counted) by me.

Horsemen can also drive effectively. In fact, mounted men can hunt more efficiently some sections of the piñon-cedar forest and in mountains than foot-sloggers. Hunters on horses are high above the ground; they can more easily scan the countryside; and mounted they can cover an unbelievable amount of terrain from dawn to dark. In addition, when a deer is killed, pack transportation is available. Horsemen, however, handicap themselves in several ways. They must dismount (should, anyway) when blasting at deer. Also, a person may be able to see a deer very clearly from his throne on a horse but, after dismounting, finds that trees and brush screen the muley.

5

Still Hunting And Stalking

STILL HUNTING

Still hunting is the quiet, stealthy search for game—game which has still to be seen by the hunter. He walks as noiselessly as possible through the woods, pausing often, watching carefully, moving slowly, listening constantly. Still hunting is by far the most enjoyable, most sporting method of all to hunt deer. To approach a trophy muley, an animal which is unaware that a person is near, and to kill it cleanly is one of the greatest of all hunting thrills. The experience is comparable to skimming just above the earth in an aircraft at 500 m.p.h.—or seeing that one pretty girl the first time. That is, it is exhilarating and unique. Still hunting ranks as the best, most pleasurable way to hunt mule deer. The hunter pits himself against a quarry whose senses of smell and hearing are superior to his. In fact, in several ways the hunter actually handicaps himself—in all ways except two: he carries a rifle and has a brain that reasons. The hunter leaves his familiar surroundings—his farm, his city streets—and enters a relatively strange environment. And for a few hours or days, he tries to find a deer. Still hunting is a neglected technique. Too bad! One experiences a great deal of satisfaction when he has out-foxed an old codger which has escaped the multitudes while running the ridges for many years. This is the type of hunting that gives the greatest thrill. Alone in the mountains, matching one's wits and abilities against a wild creature satisfies the primal urge which has surged through frontiersmen for centuries. Forgotten are the petty problems which vex a man most of the year. And how can one place a value on the pleasures of filling his lungs with clean, mountain air, watching the explosion of a ruffed grouse, pausing to admire pale, lazy, autumn flowers, or seeing the commencement of day heralded by a breathless dawn?

Most people can't successfully still hunt because they will not or cannot learn to move quietly and remain alert. Therefore, they prefer to sit in a nest or drive-hunt. Most hunters have acquired the habit of knocking about, depending upon luck and the long-range capability of their rifles. Actually, there are very few excellent still hunters at the present time, but the number is slowly increasing, chiefly because of interest in bow-and-arrow hunting.

How can the average person become a successful still hunter? There is no easy, sure way, but attention to a few details and a reasonable amount of practice help. The most important element is hunter attitude. One must really want to walk among rocks, brush and trees with as little disturbance as possible. A man who makes as little noise as necessary—while remaining alert and constantly looking for deer—consistently hangs muleys on the camp meat pole to the surprise of his less skillful companions.

The best piece of advice for beginners is: try to see the deer before the animal spots the hunter. This generally is rather difficult. However, if a person studies the problems carefully, he can develop his skill until he can, occasionally, kill deer in their tracks and beds, the animals unaware that danger is near. Certainly, if one desires to become an expert still hunter, he should go afield frequently and practice moving quietly in the forest, endeavoring to get near enough to deer to kill them. While in the woods a person learns a great deal about mule deer and also becomes acquainted with other animals which may assist or hinder his quest for a trophy.

To wear camouflaged clothing while still hunting certainly gives one a distinct advantage. But, nowadays, only an idiot would hunt deer during the regular rifle season while clad in camouflage. Besides, all western states require the wearing of red, orange or yellow. However, no such requirements apply to bow hunting. In spite of the fact that some experts have said that mule deer are colorblind, I'm on the fence.

I don't know. It's a problem for animal physiologists. I'm certain that bright colors do have a striking attention factor, particularly when coupled with movement. These colors contrast greatly with objects deer see in their environment—except in early autumn. On several occasions, deer have stopped suddenly when they saw my bright red or orange shirt—even when I was motionless—affording the opportunity for a standing shot. In such a predicament be prepared to shoot immediately since such muleys, after a rubber-squealing stop, pause only for a moment.

When to Still Hunt

At daybreak, near sunset, just prior to a storm, while a storm is in progress and immediately after rain or snow has stopped falling are excellent periods to still hunt. My favorite time is at daybreak after a snowstorm, for conditions are then ideal; deer are feeding, and, with several inches of new, soft snow underfoot, one can walk almost noiselessly. Too, snow and rain seem to smother man-odor. Don't neglect the opportunity to hunt during periods of fog and when rain and snow are falling. You'll likely have your favorite cover for yourself, for such weather chases most people into camp. A storm also immobilizes mule deer, keeping them sheltered under trees. Even though they detect a hunter, muleys are quite reluctant to move out rapidly; nor do they travel very far during stormy weather.

One of the easiest kills—but one of the wettest hunts—I ever made was high in Utah's Wasatch Mountains. Rain fell that morning in a steady drizzle, and fog kept visibility at times to near zero yards. We had reconnoitered a little basin the previous week and found deer. Early opening morning, in spite of questioning faces of other hunters camped along the creek, Dad and I hit the trail. Within a half-mile from camp we were skin-wet, but we found our deer. In fact, the hunt was over much too quickly. We spotted a herd of nine deer standing in a sparse grove of aspens. Conveniently, a bank of cloud-fog rolled in, and we quickly sneaked toward the animals until we estimated our distance at 60 to 75 paces. We had to approach very near to those muleys because of the trees. But over the wet grass and soft, moist earth, our stalk was made with a minimum of noise. Then, while waiting for the fog to drift away, we knelt on the ground with rifles ready. Those two bucks never knew what hit them.

When high, noisy winds are screaming across the countryside, a person can also approach close to deer. Several years ago, three friends and I were trying desperately to find a new place to hunt. Our favorite locales were swarming with trigger-happy, shouting, foot-sloggers. On the advice of a conservation officer we reconnoitered a quaking aspen-pine belt paralleling Bear River, near the Utah-Wyoming border. At dawn, winds were sweeping down-canyon at near hurricane force. A friend and I still hunted side by side and had walked perhaps a half-mile when we saw two bucks, a three- and a five-pointer. We easily stalked them until the animals were about 50 yards away. When brush and trees are moving, twisting and the wind howling, a careful person can approach muleys quite easily. In addition, high winds carry man-noise and man-odor out of the immediate area.

Still hunting is rather difficult during midday. The woods are quiet, for most hunters are resting or sacked-out. However, deer haven't relaxed. On the contrary, their ability to detect a person is increased because they are then quiet and motionless, bedded, chewing their cuds. But that's all right. We don't want our quest to be too easy. Only a lazy meat hunter wants the convenient kill.

Where to Still Hunt

Knowing where, or where not, to still hunt is all important. This type of hunting is impossible in districts overrun with red-shirts. In fact, one other person in the immediate area often botches one's plans. Wilderness regions are best but, regretfully, few of these places remain. If your favorite territory is being heavily hunted, go elsewhere. However, the day is rapidly approaching when very few primitive districts will be available. Currently, the mushrooming population is building roads and summer homes in forest areas and noisily banging around in the woods during much of the year.

Deer can be found in sparsely wooded places—often in open parks, meadows and along game trails, especially during early morning and at dusk. But the average person can't go to primitive areas; distance from home-base is a factor, and nonresident fees and general expenses are considerable. Consequently, one goes afield week-ends near where he lives. And if he wishes to still hunt heavily hunted districts, he must wait until the initial week-end surge of humans has dispersed. Novice and casual week-end still hunters are often uncertain where to look for deer when they step out of their urban environment into the mountains. Usually it's a frustrating experience as these individuals try to find an undisturbed animal. Unlike the veteran hunter and the biologist, who know within limits where these creatures are found, the beginner must ask questions and foot-slog many miles.

To successfully still hunt, it's necessary to "know" an area. As indicated previously, one should visit the district prior to opening day, otherwise, considerable time may be wasted. A friend can be the answer to your problems—or a stranger may be encountered who will help. But don't depend on either for much assistance, for ordinarily both want their favorite terrain for themselves. They may, however, suggest another location. As a matter of fact, to "learn" a district—particularly one which is heavily hunted—well enough to have a reasonable chance of killing a deer by still hunting, requires several days of study, spread over a year's time. During this interval learn as much as possible about general flow of winds, location of heavy cover—a hundred and one important details.

How to Find Deer

Finding game easily and quickly seems to be an innate, individual characteristic. True, one's ability can usually be improved by experience. Yet, some western hunters have lived in the hills most of their lives and still can't readily spot game. This is the exception. On the other hand, there are some beginners and city dudes who are adept at finding deer. A hunter sees the quarry because his eyes are open—because he wants to see deer. And, something which is important, a person must know what to look for. Prospective hunters, of course, should know the general physical characteristics of mule deer—clues to identify these animals. No, I'm not trying to be facetious. Why do organized groups of concerned sportsmen display large posters of caricatured deer-, cow- and man-figures at entrances of western canyons? True, many westerners have seen muleys since diaper days—living, breathing specimens or a portion of the thousands of heads hanging in dens, beer-joints and museums. Still, nonresidents and city-reared youngsters haven't been so fortunate.

How does a hunter find a mule deer among billions of rocks, shrubs and trees? When silhouetted against snow or rocks, deer are easily seen. However, one almost never finds them in such exposed situations. Normally, there is no snow during early autumn hunts, and most deer don't pause very long where they are framed against the sky. A person ordinarily finds them in terrain where their coloration and shape blend nicely into rocks, grass, brush and trees.

Most individuals haven't had sufficient still hunting experience to approach deer unseen. Consequently, muleys are found on the move: walking, trotting or running. A person sees "movement," rather than a motionless animal. Only after one has worked hard and become sufficiently skilled to regularly locate unalarmed deer can he be considered an excellent hunter. Until then, he depends chiefly upon luck, and his rifle, to secure deer.

For years, friends and I blundered through the hills, sometimes purposely making noise, hoping to spook deer into moving so that we could see them. Not until we became bow hunters did we really learn to hunt. Rifle hunters should doff their hats to the bow-and-arrow sportsmen, who must necessarily sneak within a few yards of their quarry to make a kill. Riflemen depend far to much on the capabilities of their weapons as a substitute for skill.

A still hunter, like a stand hunter, must look for "parts" of a deer. Branches that don't appear quite right—that suddenly become an antler. A whitish rock that finally moves—and changes into the grey rump of a deer. A bird hopping from one low branch to another—that suddenly defines itself as a muley's ear. Once I located a buck when he raised his hind leg to scratch the side of his face. Another muley caught my eye when he shook his head, perhaps to chase flies away.

While still hunting, kneel occasionally. It's sometimes surprising how much farther one can see from such a position, than when standing—particularly in a cedar-piñon forest. I've spotted a number of deer while on my knees. Once I found a buck, an outstanding trophy, and four does. At first only their legs could be seen, until they moved into a little clearing. Stop frequently and look into the "wall" of cover around you. Mule deer occasionally stand or lie quietly and permit a still hunter to approach very near if he moves quietly, nonchalantly. A muley's coloration blends with boulders and vegetation, and apparently such deer instinctively are under the impression that the hunter hasn't seen them and will pass. Sportsmen fail to find a number of deer in such circumstances. Turn around and look over your back-trail, too.

Use your naked eyes first, then a binocular, to look into brush and trees. If deer are fairly obvious, one's eyes, having a wide field of view, often locate them instantly. But, when animals are partly hidden, only a detailed search with a glass will find them. Even after 30 years of using binocs, I'm still amazed at their ability to penetrate tangles of vegetation and pick up deer which otherwise might go unseen.

After a person learns where muleys are generally found, these "deery" areas can be approached carefully, purposively. Other regions can be covered quickly, with little regard to noise and odor.

When a deer has been found, particularly a female, a hunter should look for other muleys in the immediate area; deer are ordinarily found in groups—family units and herds. Time of year is the determining factor. During early fall, does and fawns, along with young bucks, are grouped;

during the rut and throughout the winter, bucks are usually found in or near the general herd. Males sometimes congregate, especially before rutting.

When a single deer has been sighted, watch it closely. If the animal is a female, she may be looking toward where her fawn is standing. But she may be watching Mr. Tangle Horns to see what interpretation he has made of your sounds and scent. Remember, also, that deer are very alert to the reactions of other muleys—such as the "fittt" snort and stamping of their hoofs. When one animal "signals wolf," others respond very quickly, even though they may not have detected the source of danger.

Traveling muleys customarily move in a column—females in front and the buck, or bucks, at the rear. Still the herd master occasionally takes a station in the middle of the group or lags 10 to 15 yards behind. Badly frightened, alarmed deer often scatter like surprised quail.

Now and then a fellow hunter tells me that he can locate mule deer by smell. This may be true, but I've had no luck finding them by odor. Perhaps, if muleys have been bedded or standing in one place for a long time, and the breeze is right, their odors can be detected by a sensitive human nose. Human odor can sometimes be used to locate deer. Once a friend took me to a place where he was certain we would find a buck. The little basin, perhaps 200 yards in diameter, was a veritable jungle of oaks about 10 feet high. After hiking to the lip of the basin, we checked the wind and then began walking around the bowl so that our odor was wafted down into the trees. We would walk about 25 feet and then stop and look for movement. After making, as I recall, four to five stops, we saw a mossy-horn sneaking out through a little boulder-dotted ravine at the far end. We shot twice but missed. However, my friend killed that buck in the same basin a week later while using the same technique.

I depend on my ears every autumn to find deer. And you do, too. Try pulling a hunting cap over your ears while still hunting. You've very definitely handicapped yourself. No matter how cold the weather becomes in muley country, never completely hide your ears: just the tips to keep them from freezing, leaving the canals clear to pick up sounds. A man with the best ears in the world can't match the hearing of a muley. One November while hunting elk deep in Utah's Salina Canyon, I was invited by another hunter to dismount and warm myself beside his fire. As I tied my horse to a nearby aspen, I saw a doe deer watching us from scrub oaks perhaps 75 yards across a shallow ravine. To stoke the fire, my friend reached for a small, dry branch and, before tossing it into the fire, snapped it into a couple of pieces. That muley had been quietly watching him, the stranger said, for five minutes. But, when the stick was broken, she bounced quickly over the ridge. That deer may have seen and smelled all of the men, smoke and horses she could take for one day and decided to get out of there. And the last stimulus she needed was the sharp crack of that stick. I don't believe the average man could have heard that sound, even on a cold, crisp morning, more than 30 to 40 yards away.

Mule deer and coyotes aren't generally found together, but I recall two instances when I located muleys because coyotes were nearby. One of the mossy horns was a big buck. His left rear leg was broken just below the hip, and he was very sick. The coyote was waiting. Season was closed for deer but not for coyotes. Two winters later in the same area I spotted a coyote trotting through some scrub oaks. I followed him over a ridge and to my surprise found a group of four canine yodelers near about 20 muleys. Most of the deer were pounding their feet and watching the little grey dogs. I couldn't find a sick deer in the herd; but I made two of the coyotes very ill before they could clear the area.

Sportsmen occasionally ask if still hunting downhill is more effective than uphill. Doesn't make much difference. Ordinarily, wind determines the direction a person should hunt. Friends and I usually start out each morning hunting up-slope because we nearly always camp in the bottom of canyons near water. Too, early morning winds generally flow from the peaks downward. Consequently, wind is usually right for upward travel. I sometimes hike during darkness to a favorite location, check the wind and hunt the area with the breeze in my face. Often I wander around the district, taking advantage of wind direction whenever possible, and return to camp just at dark. Everyone knows, however, that a hunter going uphill moves slowly, pauses frequently. Another good reason for hiking up-slope: one is generally moving out of the canyon bottoms, where most men hunt, toward primitive regions where a majority of trophies are killed. Yet, a person sometimes sees plenty of deer while traveling downhill, chiefly because he is hiking toward the lazy hunters who are spooking deer while prowling the bottoms of the canyons.

How many deer should a person see during a day's hunt? Today (1972), with game departments managing the herds—be it good or bad— and with human hunter populations exploding, if one sees 10 to 15 muleys (one or two of which are bucks) during the opener, he's had a very good day.

Tracking and Trail Signs

A number of years ago a pal and I came upon two still hunters mildly debating. They had followed two sets of deer tracks through two to three inches of snow. Suddenly, the animals had separated, and the men were endeavoring to decide which tracks had been made by a buck. Frankly, I can't always separate buck from doe tracks, but I've talked with a few experts and read the accounts of others who insist they can. One expert maintains that bucks drag their feet. I believe that most older deer, regardless of sex, drag their feet and leave trail marks in snow. One of the largest muley prints I ever followed were laid down by a doe—and she dragged her feet. Some so-called experts don't even know that the front hoofs of muleys are larger than the rear ones.

In no other segment of deer hunting lore is experience more important than in reading tracks and trail "signs." I can't remember the day when I couldn't recognize the tracks of a number of common animals: grouse, quail, weasel, coyote, snakes, deer, etc. Such was a part of my education because Dad considered this as important as having verbs agree with subjects, or rising when ladies came into the room. I've made plaster casts of various animal tracks and manufactured others in dust, sand, mud and snow at home with deer and miscellaneous animal feet— even photographed them at successive intervals and studied the changes over days, weeks and months—to educate myself, friends and students in biology classes. One can then compare his homemade tracks with those found in the mountains.

A muley hunter should be sufficiently skilled to know that a particular set of tracks was made by a deer—not by a sheep, cow, elk, or goat. He should likewise be able to determine the approximate age of the tracks. The facts are obvious when one finds tracks in which water is still muddy, or into which snowflakes or pellets have only recently fallen. However, have you tried to estimate the age of tracks in desert portions of Utah or Nevada?

Obviously, a muley hunter hopes to find fresh tracks. But how can a beginner, the inexperienced, determine whether an ordinary track is "smoking hot"—or a week old? Examine the edges of the tracks. Usually a recently made print in soft earth, dust or snow has a well defined, clearly lined rim. Then, remember the weather over the past few minutes, hours or days. Wind, rain and snow can smudge tracks in seconds— nearly obliterate in minutes. Often, old tracks have dull, broken edges— or an icy coating. Fresh tracks possess a smooth glaze, and in good weather may remain in this condition for several hours. However, night frost—even dew—eventually changes them. Particles of earth or ice often rise inside tracks from frost action. Age likewise can be estimated by the amount of leaves, pine needles or snow pellets which have fallen into the prints. Tracks most difficult to age are those found in dust, since, in the absence of wind or precipitation, they appear to remain "fresh" for weeks or months.

Deer move about a great deal at dawn, dusk and sometimes at night —feeding and traveling. Several deer can manufacture hundreds of tracks in a few hours, especially in snow. Obviously, when numerous fresh tracks have been found, deer should be near. On the contrary, when most tracks are oldish, in all probability the animals have migrated. Feeding and walking deer create clearly defined tracks, close together—and the tracks frequently wander. Prints of running deer are not only far apart, but the hoofs frequently open at the front—splay; and often the dew claws print in mud and snow. Moreover, running deer almost always leave deep, rumpled tracks.

A skillful muley hunter also knows something about deer feces. Fresh pellets are soft and greenish. A blackish crust forms in a few hours, and after several days they are difficult to crush between one's fingers. However, remember that rain and snow freshen old pellets, but nearly always they lack the green hue. A final hint to remember: deer sometimes urinate after rising from the ground. Bucks wet the middle of their beds; does at the side.

Move Slowly, Stop Often

While still hunting, a person should walk slowly, stop often. Ninety-nine per cent of today's hunters move too rapidly. It's very important to remember that the number of deer a person sees during a day's travel doesn't necessarily depend on the distance hiked. A hunter goes afield to find deer, and chances are considerably improved if he doesn't hurry. To race the other fellows to the peaks is a poor practice.

How rapidly a person travels depends on type of terrain. Dense cover—in which mule deer are often found after the opening morning barrage—is difficult and time-consuming to hunt. To walk one mile per hour in such a forest is much too fast. Still, there are many districts in the Rocky Mountain states, in which cover is quite sparse, where such a pace, perhaps even faster, is all right. Certainly, a western still hunter can ordinarily walk more rapidly than a person hunting white-tails in the forests of Michigan or North Carolina. After observing other hunters and varying my own individual methods, I've proved to my satisfaction that a man who travels too fast sees only a fraction, perhaps as low as 10 per cent, of the muleys present in good, still hunting cover. Certainly, there is one thing a speedy man will find—fresh tracks.

Man Noises

Most humans are astounding noise makers. Because of centuries of civilized living, it's nearly impossible for most of us to move over rocks and through brush and trees without broadcasting our presence. This, perhaps, has resulted from the fact that our survival no longer depends upon killing wild animals for food and clothing. Deer are generally very alert—with sensory antennae turned full high. Consequently, they have little difficulty sensing most hunters. Their exceptionally large ears are the most active part of the animal's anatomy; rotating this way and that, constantly seeking sounds. Yet, those sportsmen having a sincere desire to become skillful hunters can train themselves until able to approach near enough to muleys—and other big game animals—to kill them, occasionally without the quarry ever aware that danger is near.

An expert on big-game hunting lore has said that a person should, while still hunting, try to create the same amount and types of noises with clothing and feet as a moving deer or elk—no more, no less, no different. Now, any good big-game hunter suspects that this bit of advice is plain horse malarky. A Wyoming moose, a Montana elk, an Oregon black-tail, a North Carolina turkey and a United States taxpayer all create different sounds in the woods. A mule deer manufactures noises peculiar to mule deer, and no sportsman can imitate these sounds sufficiently well to deceive these animals.

True, a skillful still hunter can approach deer near enough to kill them, but he never arrives within "brushing" distance of a muley because the animal believes that those noises were made by another deer. He approaches a deer simply because the animal is unaware that a hunter is in the neighborhood—or is curious enough to want to see what is making that godawful noise or spots the hunter and stands or lies in cover, waiting for the man to pass. Without question, you will kill more deer while still hunting if you approach them as silently as possible.

Incidental noises, such as a rifle striking a dangling binocular or buckle or cartridges clicking against coins, knife, compass, cigarette lighter and other items carried in pockets, can cause one to miss seeing deer. A person attempting to hunt as quietly as possible should muffle all sound made by his equipment, even to the extent of wrapping noisy sling swivels with cloth and easing a safety on or off very carefully to avoid a click against the scope, action or stock. Upon starting to still hunt I chamber a cartridge so that when the opportunity comes to shoot, there is no need to work the action.

Clothing—hats, jackets, shirts, trousers and footwear—should be as noiseless as possible. A cap is far superior to a hat, particularly the cowboy type, because it doesn't scrape against branches nearly as often. Shirts, jackets and trousers should be manufactured from soft materials because, when they scratch obstructions and "talk," one can't hope to approach deer undetected. Many western hunters wear denim trousers and jackets. When new, denim clothes are noisy, but after several months of wear and washing, they become quite soft, almost noiseless.

Selection of footwear is important. Primarily a person thinks of comfort, safety, utility. Rubber footwear is quiet, but a person's feet eventually become wet from perspiration. Hobs are noisy. The so-called crepe and "lug" (Vibram) shoes are best—even more satisfactory than leather. Don't buy the heelless—the 'wedge' type—of shoes. They may be all right for flat, dry conditions but are troublesome, even dangerous, in mud and snow, particularly when hiking downhill. Because most sounds a still hunter creates in the woods arise from placing his feet on the ground, he should choose his shoes with the noise angle in mind.

A few still hunters carry packs of various types in which they stow lunches, extra cartridges, ropes and other equipment. Unfortunately, most of these bags are made from canvas-type materials, and it is almost impossible to keep from broadcasting one's approach when such a pack scrapes brush and trees.

Occasionally, a person may wish to create—deliberately—some noise while still hunting. For instance, he may find a muley moving in cover or in a direction which makes a good, killing shot impossible. Sometimes, a sharp whistle stops such a deer; it may even cause the animal to turn around. A cough or striking the ground or trunk of a tree with a foot often has the same effect. Snapping a twig usually vaults a muley to its feet. However, if an animal is badly spooked and trotting or running, these noises are ineffective. Another fact we still hunters should keep in mind is that moist air decreases the distance that man-sound travels— that in dry air noise seems to travel far.

How to Walk

Veteran, successful still hunters report—without reservation—that quiet hunters see and kill more deer than noisy, bumbling persons. You must, then, learn to walk quietly. And nearly everyone, if he makes a conscious effort, can place each shoe on the ground as though he were walking on ice. No, it isn't necessary to sneak like the picture-book Indian. When cover is fairly open, or if deer aren't momentarily expected, walk leisurely, flat-footed. But, when brush and trees thicken or "signs" indicate that muleys are in the area, slow down, walk several steps, stop and check the surrounding cover. Then, while looking for deer, take a few more steps. A person's peripheral vision, when the ground is fairly level, often enables one simultaneously to search for deer and avoid most obstructions. Yet, rocks and brush tangles sometimes necessitate watching where each foot is placed to move quietly, safely. When this is the case, walk a step or two, then "stop, look and listen."

Suddenly you hear a "deer noise," you place your hand in a muley's recently deserted but warm bed, or find steaming, warm, fecal pellets. Now is the time to proceed carefully: one step, pause, listen, look. I can't overemphasize the necessity of walking slowly, stopping for minutes at a time and looking into the cover. While an individual is moving, his sounds drown "deer noises." Pausing breaks up hunter noise patterns, too. This is the time, also, to put those feet on the ground as though walking on eggs. Tiptoe if you can. This type of hunting is tiring—but very exciting. Here is the thrill you've been waiting months to experience.

A stationary man sees moving objects rather quickly. And while standing still, he isn't easily spotted by muleys, either. A deer is also very adept at sighting moving objects, and this is especially true if the animal has already sensed the hunter by noise or odor. In steep or rough terrain a hunter can't listen and keep his eyes peeled for deer while walking. For safety, he must watch his footing, perhaps every step. In such circumstances, he should climb a short distance, then pause. He then uses these rest intervals to check the surrounding area and regain his breath. Don't wait until you are tired or breathing heavily before pausing. Stop often enough to keep your chest from pounding. A thumping heart and laboring lungs make observation with a binoc and accurate shooting somewhat difficult. A person who hurries has perspiration problems, too. One should carefully avoid dislodging stones that tumble downhill, crash into other rocks and roll through noisy brush and leaves. Sounds made when sliding, while hiking up- or downslope, also alert deer. But, most difficult of all still hunting is over dry leaves and crusted snow. When these conditions exist, plan a drive with friends or sit on a point overlooking a game trail, basin or canyon.

Don't listen to phonies who write that a man can't sneak near deer without their knowing he is there. Friends and I have done it many times —even killed trophy muleys in their beds—deer which never suspected that we were near. True, this type of hunting isn't easy to learn, or carry out; but, because its pleasures are far superior to driving or nest watching, give it a try. Yes, a sneaking man, like any stealthy predator, telegraphs a "danger, look out" message. But a still hunter is trying to approach deer unseen, and this a skillful hunter frequently does. Even though he is detected by the quarry, his silent approach is far less alarming than a noisy, slogging hunter. Noisy men occasionally kill mule deer, but only through luck or when the population of animals is high.

Still Hunt Alone

A skillful hunter still prefers to travel alone. By himself he experiences the ultimate pleasure and has a better opportunity to obtain trophy heads. Alone, a person challenges the cunning of creatures which are his superior in many respects. In addition, he walks where and when he chooses. There are no discussions concerning best localities to hunt; no one to please except the hunter himself. While slowly mooching through the mountains, a lone hunter creates far less noise and odor than two people. There are no alarming human voices, and only two feet to bump stones, break fallen branches and crunch dry leaves. And certainly deer can see two men more quickly than one.

Nevertheless, there are distinct disadvantages in solo hunting. One hunter may fail to see some deer because he has only two eyes. He may become lonesome. However, I consider it a distinct, indescribable pleasure to be alone in a wilderness. Yet, it's best for a beginner to hunt with a friend who has mastered the techniques of still hunting. After a period of training he should then go on his own. My grandfather and father taught me and many other western sportsmen have also been tutored the same way. However, a person can teach himself to walk quietly, to remain alert and, after a reasonable amount of practice, become very skillful in finding deer.

If you are the type of individual who prefers company, yet wishes to still hunt, agree with your companion that both will minimize conversation; human voices seem to strike terror into the hearts of most mule deer. You and your pal should also plan to move slowly and stop at the same time when looking and listening for muleys. Even under the best conditions, though, you will see fewer animals than when hunting alone.

Deer Noises

Mule deer create very few sounds. However, if a hunter can identify their "noises" and make an interpretation, his chances of snapping a tag on a carcass are considerably improved. Deer sounds for which a still hunter should be constantly alert are the snort, the bounce-noise, and the sounds made when deer strike the earth with their hoofs.

When a muley becomes aware, by sight, sound or odor, that a man is near, the animal sometimes "whistles"; and this snort can be described by these letters: fittt. This sound obviously warns a person that a deer is quite near. If one remains motionless and quiet, he may sight the quarry. Often a mule deer in these circumstances, after a few seconds of waiting and watching, takes a step or two forward, twists an ear or raises its nose—to make positive identification. If no additional sounds are heard, the deer may have sneaked away, particularly if it has had considerable man-experience. On the other hand, the muley may still be there, waiting for the hunter to move first. A young, inexperienced animal tries to identify a hunter with more than one of its senses. For instance, a deer may have spotted a man moving stealthily through the woods, but it may hesitate before running until man sounds or odors have also reached him.

Don't be impatient, and don't believe the experts who glibly write that no man has ever lived who can "out stare" a deer. Without moving your head, run your eyeballs around their sockets and look into the cover. Mr. Bucko is probably there, watching you. Your eyes are nearly as good as his, so find him. Don't be in a hurry. Wait two to three minutes, or longer. No luck? Then very, very slowly, almost imperceptibly, move your head—and body if necessary—until you've examined the entire "bank" of brush and trees—all 360 degrees. If the muley remains hidden, it's possible that he hasn't seen you, only picked up your sound or smell. Move slowly a few feet and once more search the cover. A change of viewpoint may now reveal Mr. Big Ears. Keep moving slowly and pausing until you suspect that the deer has sneaked away. If you think he might have scrammed but aren't 100 per cent sure, tap the rifle stock with your knuckles, or utter a sharp, low whistle. A snapped twig brings identical results. Such noises often cause a deer to reveal its location, but then you have a moving rather than a standing target.

The snort is made when a deer blows air through its nose and mouth, and ordinarily indicates that a hunter or another enemy, such as a dog or coyote, has been sighted. A muley may also make this sound when it finds a strange object and can't make an interpretation. Naturally, all deer in the immediate area are alerted by these nasal whistles, and they jerk to full attention, ready to flee.

When a hunter hears the characteristic bounce-sound, the animal is moving rapidly. Stop immediately, with rifle ready. In all probability the animal is moving away; yet another huntsman could have frightened a real granddaddy bucko in your direction. Occasionally, you may hear a deer scraping or thrashing brush or a small tree with his antlers. He is then quite engrossed and can be stalked easily.

Muleys also thump a front hoof against the earth, a noise which, if the earth in frozen, can be heard for a hundred yards or more. Females with fawns so react to coyotes and dogs. This may be a ruse to frighten these enemies away, or a warning not to approach nearer. I have also had deer, both does and bucks, do likewise when they found me partly hidden in brush and trees. Muleys often simultaneously snort and bang a front hoof on the ground.

Mother deer sometimes utter low bleats when near their fawns, and the youngsters may reply with a similar call. Severely wounded bucks, especially those with hind legs paralyzed, often bleat like frightened domestic sheep. And everyone who has hiked the hills during the breeding season has heard the "gr-uh" warning of the herd master when he chases an interloper away from his females.

Unmolested deer create very few sounds—sounds that man can hear, anyway. When feeding or casually moving about deer make noises almost imperceptible to human ears a few yards away. Stampeding deer, though, can be heard for long distances when they crash through brush or race along hillsides or talus slopes where they may dislodge rocks which tumble downhill. Although mule deer immediately become alert when they hear the alarm sounds of other deer, they pay scant attention to usual, ordinary muley noises. I'm sure that they know when other deer are approaching. During the rut, bucks carefully watch each approaching deer.

One expert has suggested that deer sounds, "friendly little noises," can be imitated in such a way that these animals can be lured to a hidden man. Sounds that might be imitated are the snort and hoof pounding—and, of course, the clashing of antlers when bucks spar during the rut. I've tried them all and have found that these sounds nearly always stop and cause muleys to face in my direction, providing they haven't been previously alarmed. Once a deer has seen, heard or smelled a man, to use these imitative sounds is a waste of time.

A successful still hunter has a knowledge of the noises which deer manufacture, and he seldom confuses them with other wilderness sounds. Go afield and listen for deer noises and become a better still hunter.

Bird and Small Animal Noises

One hunting season, I had carefully still hunted for several days and hadn't found the deer I wanted. With only a few minutes remaining before I had to start jogging down a canyon trail to camp, I stopped at the edge of a clearing and stood with my back against a large aspen. Several juncos and a chipmunk were rustling leaves nearby. I could see them and distinctly hear their sounds. Suddenly, the corner of my eye picked up a little spiker deer slowly mooching towards my tree. He wasn't in a hurry—no alarm. Had I not seen the deer, just heard the sound of his hoofs on the leaves, I'm positive that I would have thought his noises belonged to the chipmunk and juncos.

Sounds manufactured by ground birds and squirrels among dry leaves, however, are ordinarily a little more irregular than those of walking deer. I believe that little muley knew those small animals were there and that the chipmunk and juncos were aware that a deer was approaching. But a man, myself in this instance, could not distinguish between the sounds. When still hunting deer, a person frequently encounters magpies, jays and, rarely, coyotes and bears. Because most humans are rather awkward mammals, these wild creatures usually find us and sometimes signal a warning to other wild animals. Magpies are alert, wary birds. They may or may not be close to deer when one sees them, but they sometimes pinpoint the location of a dead one. I don't believe that muleys pay much attention to what these black and white scavengers are doing unless they squawk alarmingly a couple of times and quickly fly away. Jays (camp robbers or one of the related species) are generally friendly birds—sometimes too friendly. They often utter godawful squawks as a hunter sneaks through the trees. Guess they're trying to say hello, but it could be a signal for a deer to get-the-hell-outa-there. A chickaree squirrel is the worst pest of all. His eyesight is good, and he'll usually chatter and fuss as long as you're in or near his home territory. Perhaps, you've observed the effects of chickaree-chattering on deer. Muleys often stop feeding, check the area and sometimes scram when these bushy-tailed, reddish-brown, hell-raisers bust loose.

Winds

A mule deer's nose is very acute and readily picks up man-odor. So, if you wish to become an excellent still hunter, you must learn to read the wind: be able to detect its general direction and make a wise interpretation. Train yourself to be aware of its direction at all times, even though it isn't always possible to point your nose into the breeze.

How can a hunter determine wind direction? Almost always, autumn winds in muley country are rather strong. Their pressures can be felt on the face; grass, limbs of trees and brush are bent; rain and snow slant

downward. Therefore, direction is rather obvious, for the moment anyway. When winds are mild, some of my friends drop a handful of
crushed leaves or dust. Others, who smoke, hold a cigarette in the tips
of their fingers, away from the body. Many years ago a veteran bow
hunter showed me what I think is a good technique. He used a lightweight piece of thread which he held as high as possible above his head.
A very slight breeze causes such a thread to indicate wind direction.
Winds which fail to move the string are of little significance to a hunter
and can be ignored.

Don't believe all of the information concerning wind that over the
years has been printed. A person would become a gibbering mass of
frustrations if he were to take the advice of some of the "wind experts."
For example, one author continually writes: "Always hunt into the
wind." No qualifications; no limiting statements. A person can't—it's just
impossible—always to hunt with the wind in his face. In the West, this
would mean zigzagging over the terrain rather like a loco cayuse, for in
the hills and mountains autumn winds are sometimes as fickle as Cleo-
patra's kisses.

After a sportsman has hunted a section of muley habitat for several
years, he learns, generally, how winds (direction at a specific time of
day) move through the terrain. Thus, he may be able to travel the country much the same year after year. In one of my favorite districts I hike
two miles into the mountains before dawn and then at daybreak walk
slowly up the side of a long ravine. Almost always I will be hunting with
the wind in my face at that time of day. Wind direction may mean
almost nothing in areas where multitudes of resident and nonresident
red-shirts invade the hills opening day. Beginning with the first rifle shot,
deer start to run—a stampede which may take them in any direction.
Obviously, still hunting under such conditions is extremely difficult,
perhaps impossible.

A friend and I once sat on the side of a canyon to rest, to chat a
little, but chiefly to see if four other hunters on the opposite slope would
spook some deer in our direction. They were driving, spaced at about
75 yards, and appeared to be pussyfooting rather carefully through thick
oaks and scattered cedars. They didn't kick out any bucks, but six does
and fawns, as I recall, sneaked out ahead of those lads. Those muleys
may have heard the hunters breaking brush. However, with that steady
up-canyon breeze that morning, my friend and I were certain that those
deer were jumped chiefly because of man-odor. I don't believe those
hunters saw any of those muleys; the deer moved out too soon.

There are situations where you may want your sounds and odor to be carried into a particular patch of cover, brush and trees in which you suspect deer are hiding. Sometimes, wind carries sounds and smells long distances and, if a person skirts the edges of such cover, muleys sometimes move out and shots can be had as they clear out.

Don't let this discussion of winds, or the sage advice of the armchair experts, bug you. It's true, you'll find more deer when hunting with wind in your face than on the back of your neck. However, as we've said a number of times, wind is mighty tricky. Continue hunting anyway, but let the wind problem be a challenge. Study it and you'll walk one very important step nearer the enviable goal of being referred to by your companions as a skillful big-game hunter.

When You See a Deer

The average person, upon seeing a deer, stops abruptly. If the animal hasn't sighted the hunter, the manner in which one stops, of course, is of no significance. On the other hand, if a muley has been watching a person approach, a sudden pause often causes him to move away. If a buck runs' directly away, pass up the shot. However, watch the deer, because he often pauses for an instant before entering thick cover or crossing a ridge. When a muley is only trotting or walking, prepare to shoot, for he nearly always stops before traveling very far.

If a hunter is lucky, Mr. Buck may just stand and watch the hunter. But, there is no possible way to determine how long he will remain motionless. If a deer is inexperienced, or uncertain of identification, he may wait a few seconds before moving on, or such a deer may even walk toward the hunter. Shoot when the opportunity is good.

When a muley is unaware that a person is near, one usually has time to check the animal's sex and desirability as a trophy. A binocular is mighty handy at this time. A hunter can also estimate distance to the quarry and decide if a shot can be made from that location. If the muley is too far away for a clean, killing shot, obviously one must stalk nearer. When Mr. Antlers is partly hidden by brush and trees, a hunter must wait until the animal has moved into the open, or he must stalk to where the deer can be seen clearly. Need we say that time is important? Each elapsed second increases chances of discovery. However, to proceed in an unhurried, even casual manner, is far better than to rush, to be fumble-fingered.

A skillful still hunter tries very carefully to see Mr. Tangle Horns first, and under favorable circumstances finds that about one-third of the muleys he approaches are unaware that he is near. On the other hand, the average still hunter usually locates muleys which are alert—watching.

Yet, he finds sufficient, unalarmed deer to make the hunt interesting and profitable. Those deer which have sensed him first are usually standing or moving slowly away, so he has a fair chance of killing them.

Any deer's first instinctive concern is to remain alive. So Mr. Big Ears spends much of his time checking the environment for danger. If sighted by a muley, it's very important not to move one's rifle quickly or hurry to a spot where the deer can be seen more clearly. Nor should one drop to the ground in an attempt to hide. To move out of sight, even to walk directly away, sometimes causes deer to flee. Not everyone, upon seeing a deer he wishes to kill, can remember to continue walking nonchalantly in order to reach a better place from which to shoot. Usually, a person stops, shuffles his feet into a habitual stance and aims his rifle hurriedly.

Occasionally, a person spots a bedded deer. Because a muley usually lies in thick or semi-dense cover, the distance from your eye to his is close—averaging, in my experience, close to 26 yards. What causes a muley to play doggo, to remain hiding, I don't know. Perhaps, such a buck has instinctively found as a result of many experiences that he can thus escape his enemies. Maybe he's just lazy. Anyway, there he is lying in his bed a few yards away, and the last thing he wants you to do is stop. He doesn't seem to mind your looking in his direction, but coming to a full stop is more than he can endure. Mr. Bucko will be out of his bed and running in one motion—before you can shoulder your weapon and aim. One per cent of modern hunters—or even as high as five per cent—have a plan-of-action when they find a bedded buck. A hunter should continue walking and, when he's reached a spot where the footing is right and from which he can clearly see the deer, he should turn slowly, raise his weapon at the same time and then snap the primer.

Once I saw a friend ride a horse into plain view of a five-pointer, dismount, leisurely withdraw his .30-30 from a scabbard, assume a comfortable sitting position, jack a cartridge and shoot. The buck never wiggled a hair until the bullet plunked. Because my friend had moved very slowly, he was able to get off a shot at a deer that wasn't greatly alarmed. Had my friend, when he saw the muley, tugged wildly at the reins, shouted for his nag to stop, dismounted hurriedly, jerked his rifle from the scabbard, rushed around the horse to a shooting position, he would have had the same target and troubles as a hunter we once saw in eastern Oregon—just the fleeting glimpse of a buck's rump bobbing through the trees and a frightened horse racing for camp.

This discussion brings to mind a statement which has occasionally been repeated in outdoor literature: "Game animals know when a man is armed." Sportsmen shouldn't believe such rubbish. When an unarmed person encounters game, he has no reason to do anything that will alarm them. Generally, he merely watches the animals for a few minutes and then goes on his way. During hunting season, however, a person is trying to kill these same animals. He fusses and hurries, makes considerable noise, and the animals recognize these as hostile actions and scram. Therefore, it's important that a hunter, once he has a deer is sight, calmly—almost nonchalantly—raise his rifle. To hurry, to move with jerky motions, is pure folly, especially if the buck is alert, ready to bolt and must make only a bounce or two to reach cover.

STALKING

One of the most satisfying thrills of hunting deer—and all species of big game—comes when an animal is seen and then killed after a careful stalk, a sneak during which the quarry is unaware of the hunter's presence until struck with a bullet. The more difficult the stalk, the more gratifying the experience.

Stalking often begins where still hunting ends. A buck may be spotted through a binocular or scope a mile away. Then follows the pleasure of planning and executing the stalk. In fact, such a sneak toward game is far more enjoyable than making the kill. Stalking is even more gratifying than still hunting in several ways. Often a still hunter experiences only a few seconds of real excitement when Mr. Antlers is seen a short distance away or when he bursts from hiding. While stalking a big game animal, the thrill may endure for hours.

Among the one-half million or so hunters that go into the mountains each autumn seeking mule deer, very few can be classified as excellent stalkers. A majority of us are considerably less skilled than our grandfathers. They lived in the country—near the hills and mountains—and they hunted often, frequently depending on game for a portion of their red meat supply. Stalking is almost a forgotten technique except among archers. True, wilderness areas where this type of hunting can be practiced are becoming fewer every year. But, a majority of sportsmen today don't appear to be very interested in learning the finer points of a most exciting method of hunting deer. They're in too much of a hurry. They rush into the mountains, race around the peaks, and speed home again. An acquaintance once boasted that he had driven before dawn into a canyon near Ogden, Utah, killed a deer at daybreak and was seated at his office desk by nine A.M. This man labels this type of experience— deer hunting!

Planning the Stalk

When you have sighted deer, observe their general behavior. If eating, or bedded and chewing their cuds, they haven't been disturbed. When standing and alert, perhaps gazing in one definite direction, they're alarmed. If slowly moving, note the general direction of travel and estimate where they will be when you arrive at the location from which you intend to shoot.

Now comes the important—and pleasant—task of planning the approach. First, select a prominent landmark near the animal to serve as a guide throughout the sneak. A large rock or tree of unusual shape, size or color will make an excellent beacon. A landmark is necessary because, when the stalk is of long duration, through dense cover, or over rugged terrain, the quarry may be lost. Nothing is more disconcerting than to discover that one is uncertain of the deer's location. Moving only a hundred yards sometimes changes the entire appearance of terrain so much that one easily mistakes one ravine, ridge or clearing for another.

Before beginning the stalk, study the ground and cover en route to the deer. Trees, brush and ravines may be present, through which you can approach unseen, making the sneak a cinch. Cover may be so sparse that you must detour or crawl a considerable distance. Condition of the earth is also important: frozen, muddy, dusty or covered with leaves or snow. Wind may be wrong, or, if right when you start, change suddenly. There are a hundred factors to evaluate, and to omit one may bring disappointment. Is there sufficient time to complete the stalk, kill the deer and return to camp before dark? To remain overnight in the mountains isn't inherently dangerous, but most hunters consider such an experience very discomforting—even frightening.

Executing the Stalk

It's extremely important that a person remain alert while stalking, aware of what he is attempting to do in order that his plans will be executed properly. A hunter may have spent months, even years, dreaming of this opportunity—the chance of killing a record buck. Moreover, he may have invested a small fortune. He would be foolish to make an error and lose a trophy.

Wind is probably the most important factor to keep in mind. As we have seen, muleys really dislike man odor. Check the direction of the breeze constantly during the stalk; if it shifts, alter your sneak.

Mule deer can be approached most easily when feeding and breeding. As they gather food, their attention to danger is necessarily relaxed. A solo deer, particularly, can't keep his eyes peeled all of the time. Make your move when his head is down or screened by his body or brush. Freeze when it comes up.

Although some experts report that white-tails flick their tails just before raising or lowering the head, such is not always true of mule deer. A muley's tail is only a rope of bone and a hank of hair and can't be seen very far away. However, mule deer frequently lick their noses and move their heads when about to move to a new location.

Muley bucks are easily approached during the rut because their usual alertness is at half-mast. Consequently, most sportsmen believe they shouldn't be hunted at this time of year. A breeding buck is quite often a sorry sight. He's gaunt, sometimes with open wounds on his face and neck. His head is often carried low and occasionally he's broken off portions of his antlers. If you've been in the mountains regularly during the rutting season, you have, no doubt, had bucks walk to within spitting distance. I recall a rather comic spectacle. While sitting beside a large rock a few yards from a game trail, I looked up from a notebook to see a doe approaching quite rapidly, followed by two beat-up bucks. The doe, very startled, bounced away. But the bucks didn't know whether they wanted to run or not. After a little detour through the oaks, they slowly trotted after their Sheba, now nearly out of sight.

I nearly always wear a cap or a narrow-brimmed hat while deer hunting. Such headgear doesn't shed sunshine and rain as well as larger chapeaus, but there are other advantages. A cap can be worn at all times during a stalk but it might be necessary to leave behind a large, cowboy hat to prevent alerting the game. A back-pack should not be carried during the final stages of the sneak, either, if a person must crawl along the ground. Carrying a rifle is no problem during a sneak providing a person can remain on his feet. However, if he must travel hands-and-knees or slither across the ground, it's troublesome to keep a prized weapon from being damaged. While so traveling, I pass one arm, shoulder and head through the carrying strap and let the rifle rest on my back. Two disadvantages to this carry are: (1) the weapon wobbles and extends above the hunter's body; and (2) the rifle is in an extremely awkward position for immediate use. If you own a beat-up rifle, the appearance of which is of little concern, alternately lift and place it before you while moving along. Your weapon will then be available for almost instantaneous firing if the deer is flushed unexpectedly. However, check the muzzle for an obstruction before blasting.

A quiet, silent sneak is obviously necessary. If possible, keep the sun at your back, too, for there is less reflected light from your body and equipment for deer to see if you accidentally expose yourself. You might check on the quarry's position once or twice during the stalk, but only from locations of good concealment.

What to do when you run out of cover? Once more analyze the situation. In spite of distance, it may be best to shoot from where you are. Certainly a long shot at standing, quiet game is far better than a short or middle-distance chance at a running animal. Still, you may be able to retreat and approach from another direction. Sometimes a slow, cautious sneak, while holding a piece of leafy brush in front of one's body, works fine. I've experimented with this technique and have had reasonable success. But, once when I tried this trick on a mammoth buck which I wanted badly, the stalk went sour. He eventually saw the movement and scrammed. Muleys detect motion rather easily, and such an approach to experienced, trophy deer is sometimes impossible.

"Crawl or slide along on your gut to get a shot at a deer?" some people ask—disgusted, surprised. Yes, I've crawled miles on hands and knees to obtain shots at good trophies. And I've enjoyed every minute of the experiences. Sure, there are blunderers who kill deer almost every year without much effort—some of them top trophies. Yet, if you want to take excellent heads season after season, you may get a little dirty. Don't be afraid to crawl. It's all part of the training to become a skillful hunter.

During the stalk you may tire. Stop and rest. If the deer leaves, there'll be another day, other deer. Enjoy the experience; don't exhaust yourself. When you pause, stop behind an obstruction, where you can stand, stretch or sit.

I have never been convinced that mule deer post sentinels while resting and feeding, as some writers would have us believe. If you've observed muleys carefully, you've found, generally, that members of the herd or family group are facing in various directions where they can see, smell or hear the approach of enemies—but they have not purposely assumed such positions.

You also need to remember to avoid frightening any other deer. One alarmed animal quickly alerts the remainder of the herd, and they often bolt even though they haven't seen, smelled or heard the hunter. Glass the area carefully and keep in mind that when you find one deer, others usually are nearby. Mule deer are family and herd animals. However, old males may be living alone for one factor or another, such as eviction from the herd during the breeding season by a stronger buck.

Most deer flee when in danger, but there can be exceptions. Sometimes this exception is the herd buck, the trophy for which you've been searching a lifetime. He may delay his exit a few seconds or sneak away in a different direction.

Other species of animals sometimes foul up a person's stalk. Once, high in the Uinta Mountains of northeastern Utah, I was approaching a handsome buck but had my sneak interrupted and finally spoiled by a nervous chickaree—a reddish squirrel common to the area. I had spent considerable time trying to approach the deer, but wind and terrain just wouldn't cooperate. Finally, when everything else was apparently going all right, a chickaree began rasping from the high branches of a fir: "chit-chit-chit." I flopped on my stomach and cautiously stole a look at the buck. He was alert, but soon returned to feeding. I lay on that perfumed, forest carpet for about five minutes. Surely, I kept thinking, that little character in the tree would go away—at least decide that I meant him no harm. No, siree! The moment I moved, he chattered again. Then one of his neighbors made it a duet. I lay down again. However, the next time I peeked, the buck was gone. I was more than a little disgusted with those squirrels.

A stalking hunter occasionally spooks a coyote or a bear, animals which have senses far superior to man's and possibly mule deer's. There isn't much a hunter can do, usually, to avoid flushing them in thick cover, and if they bolt through a group of deer which a hunter is stalking, there's trouble. Deer in such circumstances never seem to stop running. Beware of grouse, too. Ruffed and varieties of Spruce and Blue don't use their wings often, but when they roar unexpectedly from underfoot, they generally frighten the hunter and warn all other game in the area that something is wrong. Ruffed grouse are ordinarily found near springs and streams; Spruce and Blues may be stumbled upon anywhere in coniferous forests. An alert hunter sometimes discovers these birds picking their way over the ground or sees them in trees. Carefully avoid alarming them.

After reaching the landmark from which you intend to shoot, check the deer. Do so with hat off, from behind brush or trees or around the corner of a rock. Move slowly. Take your time, providing the animals are quiet. If several deer are in sight and range, carefully select the animal you wish to kill. Study its antlers with a binoc.

If the animals are nervous, milling around, they're waiting only for a leader to break and move them out. It goes without saying that running deer have been disturbed. If the muleys are lying in a semi-concealed position, where a shot is questionable or impossible, it's necessary to wait until they move—perhaps until they rise to feed again. However, after a reasonable period of waiting—darkness might be approaching—you may decide to alert and cause them to stand, by tossing a rock down the slope, breaking a twig or uttering a sharp whistle. Generally, these sounds cause deer to rise quickly. But, usually, they pause a few seconds before fleeing.

You may have stalked and located deer in a location where it's necessary to plan another approach, from a different direction. A number of unforeseen circumstances may confront you. However, in typical kinds of Rocky Mountain cover, one can often get very close to deer—somewhere between 50 to 100 yards. The rule—get as close as possible—is generally true; on rare occasions you may stalk near enough to see Mr. Bucko blink his eyes!

In shooting muleys, much depends on your skill with the rifle. Remember this: only exceptional off-hand shooting keeps bullets in a 12-inch circle at 200 yards, approximately the diameter of the heart-lungs zone in a mule deer of average size. If the animal runs before you can shoot, or if you miss with the first bullet and the buck lams outta there, jump to your feet or assume a kneeling position. It's tough trying to bust running game from a rest position.

If you arrive at the location selected for shooting and fail to see the trophy, don't become discouraged. The animal may have fled. But, if the sneak has been well planned and executed, the deer should be nearby. He may have fled a short distance, entered cover and lain down. Usually, muleys don't travel far into cover before selecting a bed where they remain an indefinite period of time, the duration of rest depending upon such factors as weather, abundance of food, etc. Now you must either search for the deer or await his reappearance in the feeding area. Anyway, before exposing yourself, look over every foot of the hillsides or basin, watching carefully for movement.

Once, after a long and very difficult stalk, I became unhappy because the buck apparently had disappeared. After searching the little canyon very carefully, peering, I thought, into every shadow, I stood up, thoroughly disgusted. Then I cursed my impatience; there, less than 50 yards away, lying in the deep shade of a cedar was my trophy—motionless, watching, ready to bolt. During the stalk that muley had fed nearer than expected, and I had overlooked him while searching the middle and distant ground.

If the deer sights you during your sneak, quickly analyze the situation. Shoot if the opportunity is good. Once an experienced muley has sighted a man, rarely does the animal continue feeding—or even remain long in the immediate area. Occasionally, as we have seen, a person can trick a muley by moving carelessly, appearing not to have seen the deer, until a spot has been reached from which a shot can be made.

A stalking stratagem which a number of writers annually describe is that of "making like a four-legged animal"—in imitation of a horse, cow, deer or elk. These people even describe in some detail how two people can fool Old Dunderhead, the mule deer, by placing their arms and legs just so as they meander around the countryside. Reptile feathers! It's an insult to the instinctive alertness of deer and to the common sense of hunters to advocate that muleys can be so deceived. Friends and I have tried this four-legged, dumb-animal, stalking technique a number of times, and in every instance the deer looked aghast in our direction as though we were something that had been dropped from the bottom of the moon. Most of the deer quickly vamoosed. A deer's survival depends upon his eyesight which is approximately as sharp as that of the average man.

Let's assume that the stalk has progressed as planned. You've located a trophy and he's within range. Prepare to shoot, but only after your lungs and heart have stopped banging against your ribs. No buck fever; no fast, jerky movements. Rifle up slowly. Take a steady position. Make the initial shot a strike if at all possible, for the first bullet is worth more than all those remaining in the magazine.

A hunter, after stalking a few deer, learns that each approach varies somewhat. Therefore, a serious stalker prepares to encounter all eventualities—the usual, the unexpected. A person soon discovers, also, that he he is most successful when he stalks alone, because he creates less noise, remains out of sight more easily, and can plan and complete the sneak as he chooses.

6

Shooting Mule Deer

Before determining the right position for zipping a bullet between Mr. Bucko's ribs, bear in mind a number of basic factors having to do with rifle safety while afield. The way you handle that smoke-stick of yours means a lot, not only to the muleys, but also to your fellow sportsmen and yourself.

When still hunting or driving in dense woods, keep the rifle as much as possible in front, fairly close to the body. A deer may be encountered at any moment and a hunter must be ready to fire instantly. Here is a situation for a man with good reflex actions.

When you tire, which you will, from carrying the weapon in an up-muzzle position, drop the muzzle and let it point at the ground or to the side. You'll likely be traveling alone and need not be concerned about passing the barrel across a companion's body.

Never carry a rifle on a sling over your shoulder or across the shoulders when momentarily expecting deer. There are also occasions when you will tote a smoke-stick by choice or necessity in one hand or even place it on the ground while negotiating difficult cover. Whatever the situation, however, be watchful—be prepared to fire.

A hunter must likewise be alert while waiting at the head of a ravine or watching from his rock nest overlooking a canyon or basin. Sometimes only a few seconds are available to control a weapon and fire. Keep the rifle cradled across your legs or arm and, whatever the situation, never place it out of easy reach.

Carrying a rifle in one's hands or on a sling while riding a horse is quite awkward. Therefore, even when expecting game, I almost always leave a rifle in the scabbard. Reason? A person can badly frighten a horse by waving a rifle through the air, especially during the excitement of dismounting to shoot at game.

A good example of what not to do occurred while two friends and I were hunting in Idaho. The trip had been rather unsuccessful, and we were driving slowly out of a canyon toward home, meanwhile looking for game on adjacent mountain-sides when suddenly the driver jammed the brakes and yelled for his rifle. All firearms had been cased and stowed in the rear of the car when we broke camp. So, there followed quite a demonstration—shouting, door slamming, cussing. The herd of 10 to 12 muleys vanished long before anyone was prepared to shoot.

SHOOTING POSITIONS

When a person leaves camp to hunt for deer, he never knows where or under what conditions he will find them—standing, moving, near or far. A hunter may be in a favorable situation from which to shoot; in all likelihood, he will not. The quarry and field conditions determine the shooting position.

As I recall the many muleys that friends and I have bagged over years of hunting, most were downed while shooting from orthodox or near-standard positions. But a few were taken from awkward, unstable stances. A number of years ago while still hunting a thick grown of conifers and aspens, I turned to glance at my back-trail and saw a three-pointer melting into cover. In two seconds he would have been lost. Without shifting my feet, I turned hurriedly at the hips and blasted. Recoil nearly tipped me over, but I had my buck. On another occasion a pal downed a handsome five-pointed while perched in a tree, one leg twisted around a branch and the other dangling in thin air.

A sportsman need not be so versatile, but he should know the various orthodox firing positions and make a quick decision concerning the best one, or best variation, to use under the circumstances. Whether a person kills deer cleanly, misses or wounds often depends upon his stance. No one has a body so steady that he doesn't shimmy because of numerous movable joints, pulsating arteries and quivering muscles. No one can support a rifle as firm as a rock, even on a rock. When you see a person assume the best position available under the circumstances, you are watching a knowledgeable hunter.

After finding a deer, quickly assess the situation. If the animal hasn't seen the hunter, there is generally time to look the terrain over and select a good shooting position. Sometimes a muley remains motionless for seconds, perhaps a minute or so—even though he has discovered the hunter. Try to find an object over which to place your rifle: rock, log, tree branch, etc. Naturally, trees and logs are available in a forest, and much of western muley country abounds with ready-made rock rests. Don't forget to cushion the rifle with hand, binoc case, hat, back-pack, jacket, etc., because a rifle "shoots away" when placed directly upon or against a solid object. It's a wise hunter who realizes that one shot from a rest is worth more than the remainder of the cartridges in the magazine when fired from an unstable position.

One disadvantage of rest shooting, however, is the difficulty in hitting moving deer, particularly from prone position or from solid support. Still, if a person, when standing, can place his rifle against a tree (cushioned, of course, with a hand), he can hit moving deer. Such a rest is also quite effective when shooting uphill at moving game.

In Oregon, two friends and I met an elderly muley hunter who carried a stick about six feet long. It must have aided his marksmanship, for he was dressing out a four-pointer. He obligingly gave us a demonstration of the helpfulness of what he called his "shooting stick." Standing, he grasped the stick about five feet above the ground and dropped the forearm of the rifle across his left wrist. His legs formed two parts of a triangle; the stick the third. While sitting, he said, the stick was also of great help. He dropped into the usual sitting posture and then, with left hand on the stick at comfortable height, he placed the rifle across the top of his thumb. This kindly gentleman also demonstrated still another position, in fact, the very one from which he had killed the deer. He trust one end of the stick against his stomach just above the belt, slightly to left of buckle. Then he grasped the stick about three feet out and placed the rifle atop his thumb. Seemed very steady. I've never used such a device, but, perhaps, I shall when I reach 75, age of this veteran Oregonian.

Some individuals jokingly suggest that using any kind of a rest is a sign of infirmity. Others grumble that such a practice is unfair to game animals. On the contrary, I firmly believe that to employ a rest whenever possible is the sporting thing to do.

Practice, before going afield, is the sensible way to learn good position-shooting. If you have a friend who can demonstrate the fundamentals—excellent. Or join a shooting club. Inexpensive manuals, with photographs, are available and one can easily teach himself. It's important, under the excitement of seeing deer, to be able to automatically take a good position, without wasting time.

Prone

Of all positions, prone is least useful to muley hunters, for only rarely does a person find a situation when he can lie on his stomach. Grass, rocks and brush usually block the hunter's line of sight. Nor can this position be used on a hillside. Moreover, running shots on deer are difficult if not impossible. Shooting from an awkward, improper prone position is also an excellent way to slice an eyebrow with a scope. However, prone is very steady and occasionally an opportunity arises for a hunter to use this position.

I practice from prone regularly because I know that occasionally I shall have an opportunity to shoot at big game from this position, perhaps at long distance where a closer stalk is impossible—a chance for a buster that may top the record book. When firing from prone, one also utilizes the capabilities of his rifle, practices good trigger squeeze and relaxed shooting.

Prone shooting is easy to master. During World War II we were taught to break our fall to the ground with the rifle butt. However, I hesitate to do this with a beautiful piece of finely polished walnut, maple or myrtle. So, I stoop low, lean forward and break my fall with a left hand, meanwhile holding the rifle aloft in the right. I lie about 25 to 30 degrees from line of fire, but this varies with individuals. In a comfortable postion my feet are approximately 15 inches apart. Some persons prefer to turn their feet until the inside of the ankles are on the ground. Others rest their feet on the toes. For what it's worth, I prefer to draw my right leg (I'm right-handed) up comfortably with the inside of the right foot on the ground, the left supported by the toes. This lifts most of my chest off the ground—permits easier breathing and reduces pulse vibrations. I also hold my head high, with right eye about 3-5 inches from the scope. With the weapon in firing position, the left elbow should be directly under the weapon, with the lower arm slanting outward to the hand. Rifle forearm rests on the palm, with fingers applying only enough pressure to keep the weapon from canting. Right elbow automatically contacts the ground where comfortable. Rest the face against the stock, but don't apply noticeable pressure. The triangle made by the two elbows and the torso is very steady.

If you find that you must change position because of muscle tension or to see the quarry more clearly, keep the left elbow on the ground and shift the remainder of the body. Shift right to move sights left; shift the lower body forward to lower the aiming point.

A sling gives additional aid in steady sighting from prone. But some hunters think a sling is time-consuming to use, if not useless. Actually, a person trained to use a sling requires only two to three seconds to slip his arm through the loop and make adjustments. However, the loop should not be too tight, just enough to feel tension and to support the weapon.

Before firing (if there is time), I've made it a practice to close my eyes for a couple of seconds (following the advice of a hard-nosed but helpful Air Force sergeant), meanwhile taking a deep breath and consciously relaxing. I do not lower the rifle nor move the butt from my shoulder to chamber a second cartridge.

This somewhat brief discussion may give the impression that firing from prone is time-consuming and cluttered with details. Prone is slower than kneeling, sitting and standing, but, with a reasonable amount of practice, it's amazing how quickly the average hunter can fire. In addition, it's very reassuring to watch the sights settle, quickly and easily, on Mr. Buck's ribs and realize that one's chances of killing him are excellent, even at fairly long distance.

Kneeling

A friend and I had beat our way rather noisily out of a brushy ravine to the top of a ridge just in time to see a muley making tracks on the opposite hillside, about 100 yards away. I had killed a deer the previous day, so it was my pal's move. Later, he said that he first contemplated an offhand shot, but changed his mind in favor of sitting. However, after dropping quickly to the ground, he discovered that chaparral hid the muley. So, he shifted hurriedly into a kneeling position. Result: even after some delay and maneuvering he dropped the fat three-pronger.

Kneeling is not my favorite position, but I practice it occasionally, for, like prone, I sometimes use it. Although not as steady as sitting or prone, it is better than offhand. Kneeling is also fast and convenient for uphill firing.

When you choose to shoot from this position, keep your eyes on

Sometimes mule deer go deep into conifer forests—not to seek food, for these places are biological deserts—but to rest and hide. Such locations are excellent areas for a still hunter to look for muleys.

Left: Perhaps the most remarkable characteristic of mule deer is the tremendous size of his ears. Hemionus, his name, means mule.

Opposite: Mule deer often feed in open terrain, but almost always retire into dense cover to rest and ruminate. U.S. FOREST SERVICE PHOTO

Below: New antlers grow quickly, sometimes reaching a length of 6-7 inches in just 2-3 weeks. During summer months antlers are bulbous and covered with 'velvet'. FISH & WILDLIFE SERVICE PHOTO

Below: Large, trophy
bucks are often found high
in the mountains—particularly
during early autumn.
Although not easily found
in the above photograph,
there were approximately 20
muleys here, several of
them trophy heads.

I have never been convinced that mule deer post sentinels while resting and feeding. However, members of the herd or family group usually face in various directions where they can see, smell or hear the approach of enemies. U.S. FOREST SERVICE PHOTO

In the Kaibab Forest of northern Arizona and in southern Utah large numbers of mule deer bucks congregate. I have often seen 20-30 in one group. ZION PICTURE SHOP

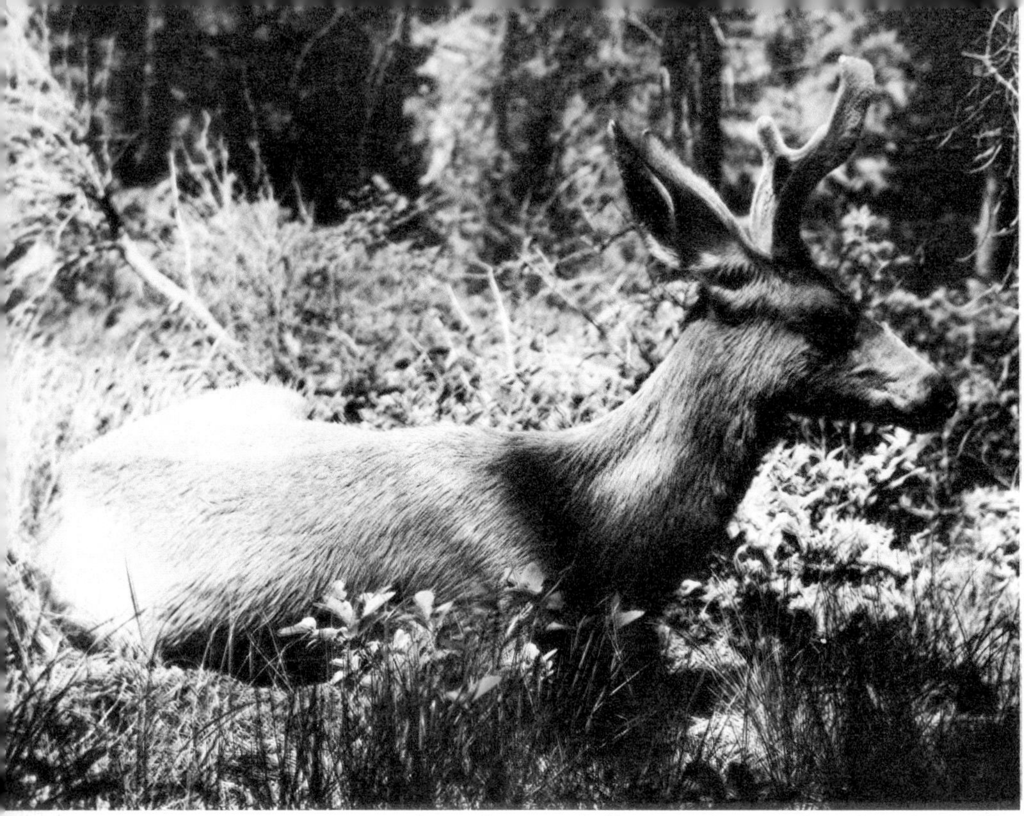

During summer months antlers are bulbous and covered with 'velvet'. This moss-like covering becomes dry during late August-early September and is scraped away on 'rubbing trees' and shrubs. U.S. Forest Service Photo

Friends and I have found that to sit or stand on a hillside, atop a ridge or cliff, where an extensive area can be watched is a very effective method to kill mule deer.

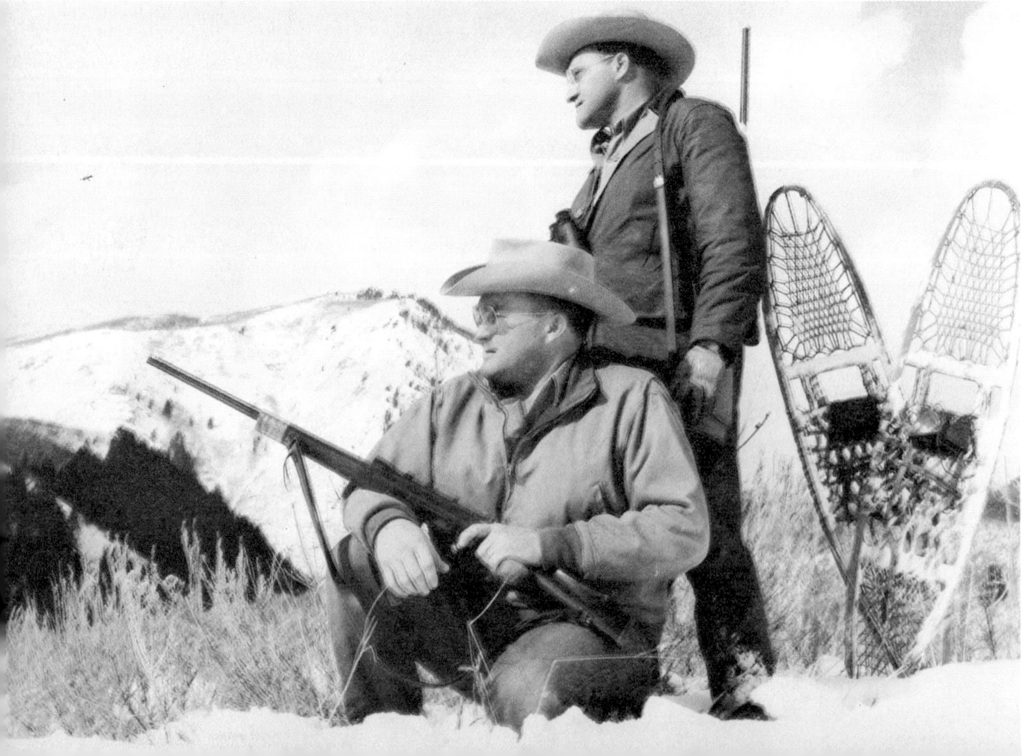

Occasionally a deer moves cautiously and slowly into a basin or along a canyon slope, stopping at the edge of a clearing, a road or slash cut through timber, to check for danger.

A *few muleys are certain to use the particular pass you are watching.*

Despite the arbitrary opinions of some of the experts, friends and I can't separate the tracks of does and bucks.

In snow the hoof-prints of deer can be followed easily even through dense thickets.

A mounted hunter can cover an unbelievable amount of terrain from dawn to dark. Elevated several feet above the ground, a horse-hunter can also more easily scan the countryside.

Above: You should, if possible, check the position of the quarry once or twice during the stalk, but only from locations of good concealment. A large, cowboy-type hat should be left behind during the final stages of the stalk.

Left: When momentarily expecting to see deer, be alert, be prepared to shoot.

Opposite, top: Take a sitting position, cushion the forearm with your hand and find the muley in the scope. Just as he sneaks out of the trees into the open, ease off the safety and squeeze the trigger!

Opposite, bottom: You're a little sad when you lift his regal head from the ground.

A top mule deer head is truly a wonderful trophy —an extreme rarity, perhaps one in 100,000 animals. WYOMING GAME & FISH COMMISSION PHOTO

Blood drains more completely from a carcass hung forequarters down. Never, if avoidable, leave a carcass on the ground overnight.

This is a tough way to bring in a carcass—but Carl Watkins, who weighed 200 pounds and was 22 years old, slung this one over his shoulders and carried it one-half mile into camp without resting.

Dragging a deer out of the mountains is irksome. In addition, dragging generally ruins some of the meat, the cape and the skin.

(Above) One of the best methods of transporting mule deer out of the hills is with horses. (Below) Some blocky quarter horses are so strong that they can carry both deer and hunter. A friend, John Knight, once owned two such horses.

(Above) Grasp a handful of the skin (from the inside) and pull downward, using a knife only when necessary to keep the separation continuing smoothly. Try to keep the hair from contacting the flesh. (Below) It's difficult to describe the exact point of separation of the legs. It's far better to show the location to a beginner and sever a leg as an illustration.

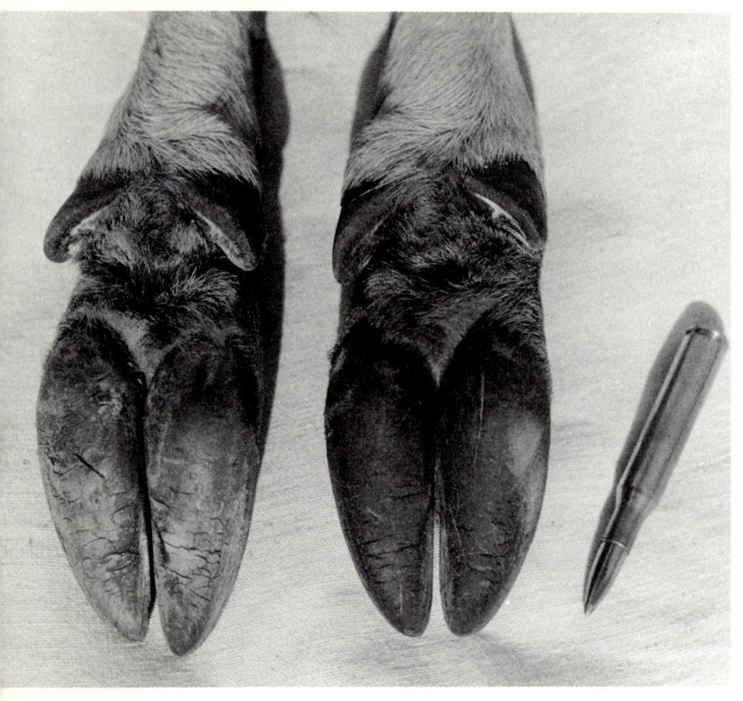

(Left) The front hoofs of large, mature mule deer are approximately four inches in length (over the curvature of the hoof) and about two inches wide.
(Left, below) The front hoofs of mule deer are somewhat larger than the rear feet and are generally heart-shaped.

Opposite: At first glance this buck appears to be an outstanding 'book' trophy; but a second look shows that several tines are missing.
MONTANA FISH & GAME DEPARTMENT PHOTO

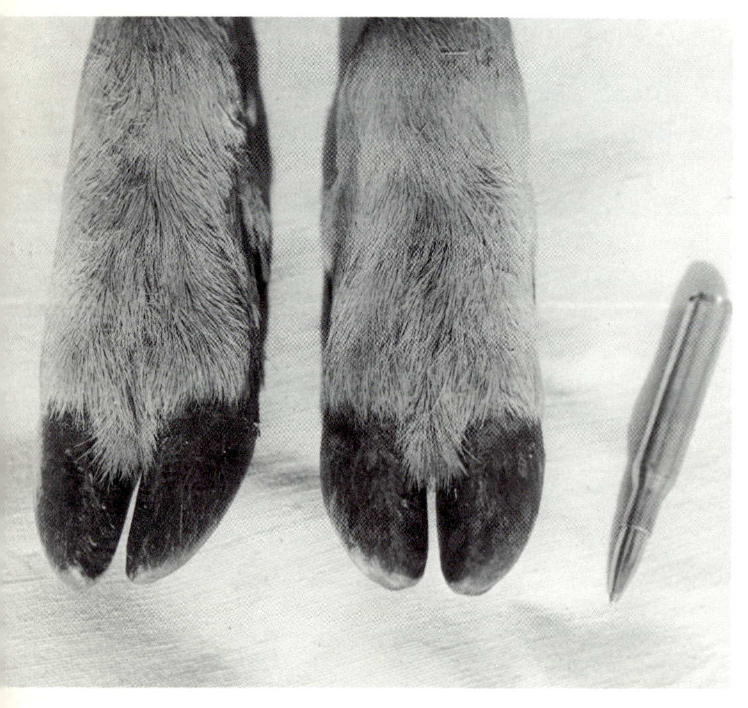

Opposite: This buck will not 'make the record book'. The tines are short, the spread too narrow and the antlers spindly.
U.S. FOREST SERVICE PHOTO

Mule deer, dead from starvation, are of no value—except to scavengers. U.S. FOREST SERVICE PHOTO

Mule deer are generally very alert creatures, but a skilled stalker can occasionally sneak near enough to see his eyes blink. Assume a steady shooting position, for often a buck will pause briefly before entering thick cover.

Mule deer don't regularly bed and feed day after day in the same area. They wander around aimlessly over their home territory, feeding wherever browse is available and bedding in edges of nearby covers. Springs, livestock watertroughs, impoundments and beaver ponds often show considerable use by deer.

Winter is a very critical period for mule deer. Deep snow forces deer to migrate onto lands often less than five percent of their summer range. An extremely harsh winter may kill one-half of them. CALIFORNIA DEPT. OF FISH & GAME PHOTO

Winter brings stark, often tragic conditions for mule deer. Much of the browse and grasses are covered with snow. IDAHO FISH & GAME DEPT. PHOTO

This young buck may not survive until spring. The snow is deep, the browse rather poor; and most of the body fat he accumulated the previous summer and autumn are gone. IDAHO FISH & GAME DEPT. PHOTO

Many sportsmen are shocked to learn that mule deer cannot be fed artificially, as livestock, for any length of time.   U.S. FOREST SERVICE PHOTO

This buck is so hungry that it allowed a man to approach within a few yards of where it was nuzzling a pile of hay.   U.S. FOREST SERVICE PHOTO

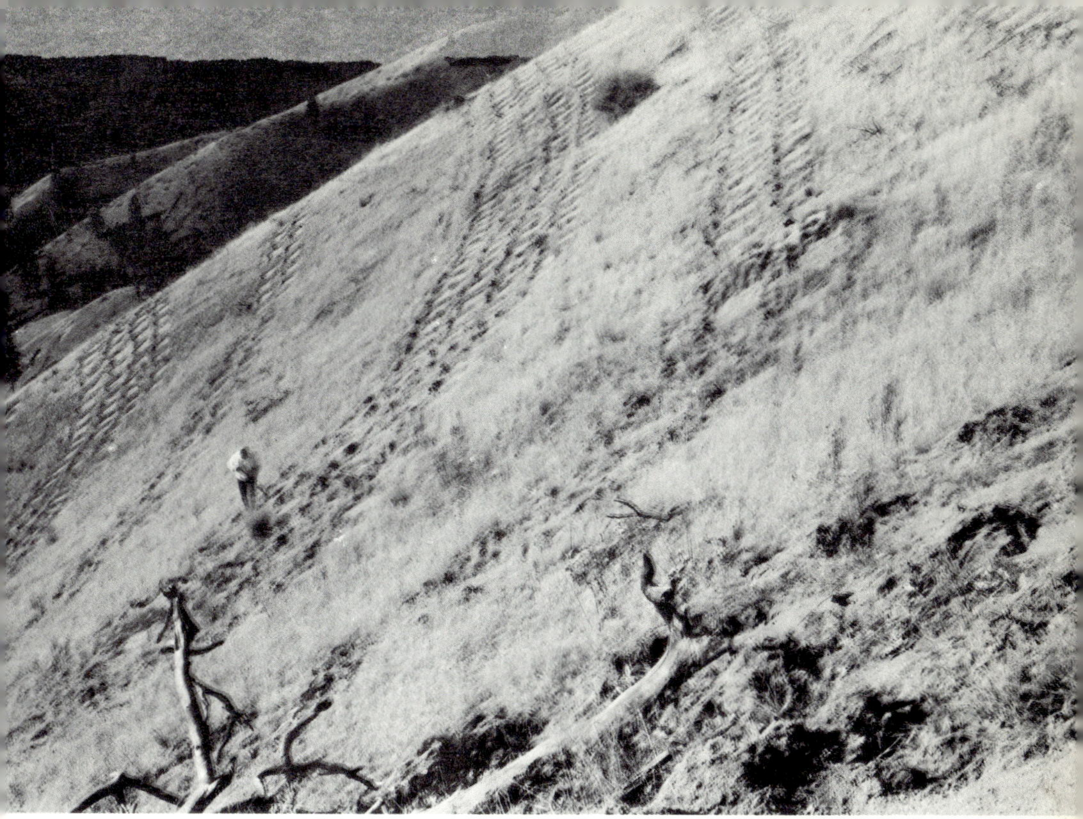

Bob Ferguson, Forest Service, plants the seeds of deer forage plants on the South Fork of the Payette River, Idaho. U.S. Forest Service Photo

Chief problem with artificial feeding is congregation of muleys, resulting in overuse—often elimination—of native browse.

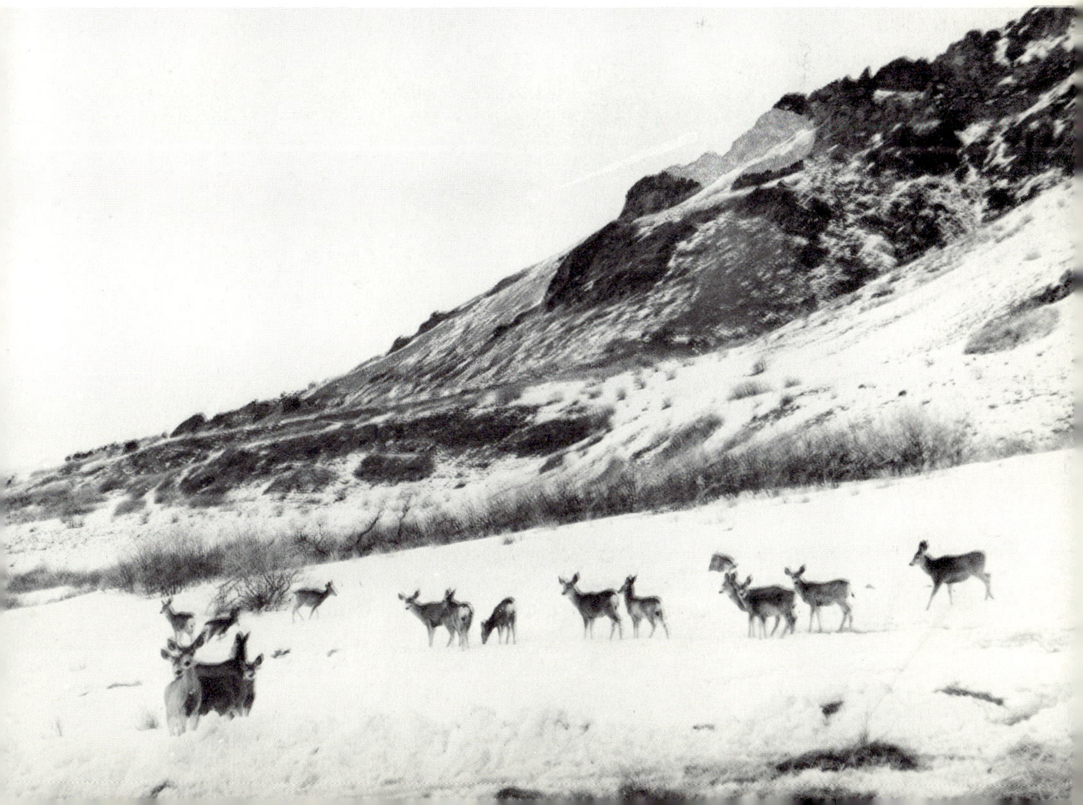

Deer seem to sense when a storm has abated and move out of cover almost immediately to browse. Periodically check a barometer during a long, bitter storm; when the mercury rises abruptly, go hunting.

the quarry, meanwhile advancing your left foot approximately 15 to 20 inches. (The procedure described is for right-handed shooters. If you are left-handed, reverse the procedure.) Then, kneel with the right leg about 60 to 90 degrees from line of fire. How the right foot is adjusted is optional, but should be an automatic response as a result of practice. Some hunters rest the right buttock on the right heel with toes curled under the foot. Others think it more steady to turn the right foot flat against the ground. For what it's worth, I prefer the first position, but point my toes into the ground. Now place your left elbow and lower portions of upper arm just inside the left knee. This puts the left elbow almost directly under the rifle, thus supporting the weapon with bone rather than wiggly muscles. Never place the left elbow on the kneecap. Too wobbly. Let the right arm drift into a relaxed position. Cheek is against the stock but without noticeable pressure. Rifle forearm rests on heel of left hand with fingers loosely gripping the wood. Keep the left foot either ahead or behind the left knee—never directly underneath. The trigger finger should touch only the trigger, so that movement isn't imparted to the stock. Body weight is well forward on the left leg.

Sitting

Many muley hunters have found that they shoot quite accurately when their bottoms are on solid Mother Earth. While sitting, good marksmen keep most of their strikes inside a 6-inch bull at 100 yards and kill standing deer at 200 yards rather easily. True, a rifle wobbles more than in prone. Nor is sitting as fast as offhand or kneeling. Yet, with practice the average person learns to fire quickly and accurately from this position. Sitting is a poor choice for close shots at rapidly moving animals. However, for walking or trotting deer—or those running beyond 100 yards—it's very much all right. This position is extremely useful for cross-canyon blasting and can generally be employed more frequently than prone because one is raised above high grass, low brush and rocks.

This position is comfortable and easily mastered. But a person should practice before the season opens, so that he can sit and fire quickly, automatically. Then, when Mr. Antlers is found, one can keep his eyes on the quarry without watching the positioning of weapon, arms and feet.

With the weapon in the left hand, break your backward fall with the right hand and, as you move the weapon into firing position, wipe dirt from the right hand on the trouser leg. Keep knees up. Now align the body about 45 degrees from line of fire. Some sportsmen, particularly those trained by the military, may face away as much as 90 degrees. This much angle is not for me. I can feel the muscles of arms, legs and torso pulling. I always shoot better when I'm comfortable. Now glance at your feet; they should be about the same distance apart as the knees. Don't sit too upright. In fact, the steadiest position is when one leans forward to the point where he can place the outside of the upper left arm and elbow against the shin bone of the lower left leg and the elbow and outside of the right upper arm inside the right knee. This moves the body weight forward and places the left forearm almost directly under the rifle, which is very desirable. On paper my bullet strikes spread noticeably when I lazily place my elbows on the kneecaps. Rest the face against the stock, but not with obvious pressure. The rifle forearm should snuggle between the pointer finger and the thumb or on palm of hand. Do not remove the rifle from firing position to chamber additional rounds.

When firing from a steep hillside, I hurriedly dig little pits for my heels to prevent sliding downhill. However, when blasting from horizontal, this is a mistake since it tends to elevate the toes and creates tension in muscles of the lower legs. Tension, remember, is a prime cause of muscle tremors. Another definite aid to accuracy while sitting is to place one's lower back against a large boulder or tree—and to use a sling.

If the above sitting position doesn't appeal to you, try one of several variations. A friend, instead of extending the feet, crosses his legs at the ankles and draws them inward near the buttocks. Then he encircles the knees with his arms, rests the rifle across his left arm at the elbow and grasps the recoil pad with his left hand for support and aiming. He admits that this variation is of little value for hitting moving game. It's amusing, also, to see him rocking back and forth as he fires a magnum rapidly.

Squatting

This is a variation of sitting and is very useful in patches of cacti, or when the ground is cold, wet or covered with snow. Squatting is steadier than offhand, but not as effective as sitting.

A number of years ago, while stalking a beautiful buck, I arrived at the lip of the little knoll from which I planned to fire, and found that the point of clay was a garden of cacti. To have stood upright would probably have alarmed the buck and offhand was questionable because of distance. Squatting saved the day. With a minimum exposure above the low sage, I was able to get away an unhurried, relaxed shot.

To assume this position, place the feet about six inches apart and then rest the buttocks against the heels. The shooter's arms can be positioned in two ways. First, force the knees together with your arms and support the weapon with a left hand immediately in front of the trigger guard. As an alternative, slide your upper arms just inside the knees and move a left hand into a normal hold on the forearm. A word of caution: consciously lean into the shot. Otherwise, you may find that the recoil tips you over.

Offhand

Best typical muley head I've shot (a respectable 186 6/8 points in the 1964 edition of the *Records of North American Big Game*) was discovered as we hiked up a rocky ridge. The buck stood hidden in dense oaks until we had nearly walked past. But, as we stopped to rest and glass the ravines on each side of our ridge, we saw him sneaking out at about 100 yards. Several trotting steps would hustle him out of sight. So, a quick, offhand shot was necessary. As he dived, head low, through a small clearing, I fired when the cross hairs had moved a few inches forward from the point of his shoulder. Reviewing the shot with a friend, we decided that dropping the muley hadn't been as difficult as it had first appeared. The buck was nearly broadside and moving at about half-speed and, although from offhand, it was a shot I had made successfully hundreds of times on jack rabbits and big game.

Although I prefer to shoot a deer from sitting—better still, from a rest—most of the muleys I've bagged were taken from offhand. This is because I love to still hunt these long-eared critters, and in fairly thick cover an offhand shot is usually the only opportunity offered. Offhand firing also affords a distinct challenge which intrigues me. However, this position is not the best. Offhand is the common, traditional method of firing a weapon. Almost all middle-agers and oldsters learned to shoot this way. We should have been taught from a bench or prone. Then many of us wouldn't be hampered with such discouraging habits as flinching. Watch big game hunters. Almost always they blast while standing, even when they could assume a more steady, accurate position.

Offhand is the least steady shooting position of all, particularly when handicapped by throbbing arteries and unsupported, tense muscles. This is especially true when game flushes nearby—the hunter is startled, and he's desperately trying to locate the quarry in the scope. Often, I'm told, many persons point their rifles in the general direction of deer—may even close their eyes—and jerk the triggers. Certainly, offhand is a poor choice for long shots, and probably more muleys are crippled and lost by huntsmen firing from this position than from all others combined. Nevertheless, a person who takes deer hunting seriously should learn to shoot reasonably well while standing, for he sometimes jumps deer at close quarters in high brush and thick trees. When game will be in view for only a short time, one must shoot quickly or not at all. Certainly, the ability to down big game from offhand separates the men from the boys.

Efficient offhand firing must be learned by most sportsmen. Only rarely does an untrained individual assume the correct stance. To become a good offhand rifleman, you must begin from prone or bench. After acquiring the basics of rifle marksmanship, you can then graduate to sitting, next kneeling and finally to offhand. Seek help from an expert if you have problems. Analyze your errors, and remember that continual practice pays good dividends. I dry-fire frequently and always expend a number of rounds while standing whenever I go to a range. Offhand firing requires more muscles; the position is inherently unsteady. A person soon learns that no one can hold a weapon absolutely steady in offhand, but regular practice helps. The best training friends and I have had is many years of blasting at long-legged, black-tailed jack rabbits. My pals are good offhand marksmen and kill 8 to 9 out of 10 standing muleys at 200 yards. My notes show that average muley hunters make only four killing strikes out of 10 at 100 yards with their first bullet.

It's very important, upon sighting a deer which requires an offhand shot, to be able to take a good stance automatically. However, field conditions often force a person to vary the standard position. While keeping your eyes on the quarry, spread your feet about 10 to 15 inches (depending on one's physical conformations), lean slightly forward, with a little more weight on the left foot (for right-handers). If the deer moves, or one is not comfortably on target, shift the feet—don't twist the body, except in an emergency.

Now move the weapon into shooting position. When possible, support the rifle with bones and ligaments, not muscles. Therefore, the arm from wrist to elbow should be perpendicular under the rifle. Rest the rifle forearm on the palm of the left hand, not on the fingers. Don't clutch the weapon in a death grip; it causes tremors. Be sure to place the right thumb around the grip. You can then control the rifle better, keep the butt against the shoulder and effect a smooth trigger release. Lift the right elbow shoulder-high, for this raises a cushion of muscle and establishes a hollow in the shoulder for the rifle stock. Occasionally, one sees a person, trained in the military, with his right elbow sky-high. Such is uncomfortable for me, for it creates tension. Head must be down on the stock but without excessive pressure.

Some marksmen shoot more accurately with the elbow resting on their hip or against the ribs. I have found this variation a little more accurate for long, standing shots. If you choose this stance, pull your left hand back near the floor plate and support the weapon in a way which seems most steady and comfortable. A friend places his thumb on the trigger guard and the remainder of his fingers on the floor plate. In this position, your torso is bent to the side.

When you are shooting at a running deer from the offhand position, be sure to extend your left hand well out on the rifle forearm for better control. This enables a shooter to keep the muzzle moving, as one does while trap shooting or blasting at crossing ducks. To stop the rifle is to wound the animal or miss it altogether.

It's important that you shoot the first time your sights look right. To dilly dally is to increase muscle tension and chances for a miss. If you don't get the shot away within four to five seconds, and the deer is still standing, quietly snipping snowberry leaves—take the rifle down, consciously relax and breathe several times.

Trigger Release and Flinchitis

During the short interval between the instant the brain telegraphs the finger muscles to pull the trigger and when the bullet leaves the barrel, most hunters flinch and vigorously jerk the trigger. Result: many deer missed or wounded. Without question, trigger release is the single most important part of the rifle firing sequence. There are no so-called "born" riflemen. Yes, there are individuals who have exceptional eyesight, muscle coordination and desire. With minimum training these persons develop into excellent shooters. However, most of us will become proficient marksmen only through long, patient practice.

Nearly all information dealing with trigger control which has appeared in magazines and books is concerned with target shooting. This data has limited value for a big-game hunter. Briefly, this system teaches a rifleman to increase pressure on the trigger only when his sight is on target. When the sight wanders, as it frequently does, the shooter maintains pressure on the trigger while trying to realign his sights. Pressure is thus increased until the weapon fires—unexpectedly. Theoretically, because the marksman doesn't know when the rifle will fire, he doesn't flinch. This "increasing pressure" method is probably all right for paper punchers and huntsmen who have the opportunity to blast at game from a rest over a rock, log or from prone. However, it has little worth for an offhand shooter and is of no value for shots at running game. In fact, it's highly possible that one's rifle might fire at the wrong time.

May I explain my method of trigger release? I practice with a particular rifle until I know the amount of finger pressure needed to activate the firing mechanism. Then I apply all of the pressure except a few ounces and, when the sight is on the animal, I pull quickly, but feather gently, the last few ounces. Thus, I *know* when the weapon will fire. I believe that I share this method with most big-game hunters—and with many target shooters—although a majority of these individuals would rather confess that they beat their wives or smoke opium than admit that they gently jerk triggers.

May I go one step further? Tests have shown that 20/100 of a second is required for the "fire message" to travel from a hunter's brain to finger muscles. During this interval a deer moves a short distance, as does the rifle sight. Should one anticipate or compensate for this slight delay? I believe so. With the rifle sight moving toward alignment, what is wrong with ordering the finger to pull the trigger a scant instant before alignment occurs? Although this method may not work for some hunters, or paper marksmen, it has proved very satisfactory for me, especially in sitting and offhand positions. However, this system requires practice.

How anyone can zap running deer, or flying birds, while using the "increasing pressure" method, I don't understand. This system takes time —too much time. Certainly it works on standing game. However, to hit a muley which is scrambling for a patch of nearby timber demands that a hunter determines the precise instant when he pulls the trigger. But, he doesn't slap or vigorously jerk the trigger. He quickly and softly presses the last few ounces of pressure when the sight picture is correct.

The trigger itself has much to do with a good release. Shape is important, preferably curved to fit the outline of one's finger. A trigger should also release each time with the same clear snap. How many pounds of pull should the trigger of a hunting rifle have? Two and one-half pounds or less is too little—probably dangerous. Five or more pounds is too much for the average man. I keep trigger pulls on my deer weapons between three to four pounds.

Thousands and thousands of old military rifles are in use for hunting and most of them have a "take-up" release trigger—an abomination. Set-triggers are no good for muley hunting, either, although GI's, while in Europe during World War II, saw a number of hunting rifles so equipped. The so-called "single-stage" trigger is best. A few hunters use trigger shoes. I don't. But I do prefer a trigger which has been scored or checkered so that my finger has firm contact even when wet from rain or perspiration. Check the trigger carefully on a rifle you contemplate buying. Cock and release the mechanism a few times. If you wish to compare the release with factory firearms having excellent triggers, check it alternately with a Winchester Model 70 or a Remington 721 or 722.

A person should also call his shots: remember the sight picture at times of trigger release on both paper targets and game. If the bullet strikes in a different location than where aimed, the shooter probably flinched.

A sportsman interested in improving his trigger release, particularly if he flinches, should practice once a week at a range. However, the expense of range practice may be a factor. Or, you may have the same problem in your city as we face in my home town, Ogden, Utah. No rifle range. In the absence of a range, dry-fire. Place a target across the room, on the barn or garage door. Practice 10 minutes each day. Eventually this practice develops a good trigger pull. One advantage of dry-firing over blasting on the range is that it's possible to detect slight movements of the sight when releasing the trigger.

Everyone knows that breathing has an important effect upon accuracy, but we hunters often fail to remember this little detail: under stress of trying to cut a muley's rib hairs with a bullet, we sometimes forget to expel enough air from our lungs so that chest and diaphragm muscles relax. Obviously, if one hurries while hunting and finds that his breathing is deep and fast, he can't release a trigger smoothly.

A rifle grip which comfortably fits a shooter's hand aids materially in accomplishing a smooth release. Another factor is which part of the finger touches a trigger. One outdoorsman has written that the second section should make contact. However, if you watch a hundred good marksmen on the range and in the field, you will find that most of them use the rounded ball of the first joint to press the trigger.

Which method is best? That which enables the shooter to pull the trigger straight back. I have small hands and cannot comfortably reach the trigger with the second section of my trigger finger. I believe that most marksmen control the trigger better when they use the ball of the first joint, for a large number of nerve ends are concentrated there. Check yourself while dry-firing and on the range and then decide which is best for you.

It's also important that a shooter move only his trigger finger. Some recruits during World War II were taught to squeeze the entire hand when pulling a trigger. This technique moves the rifle, destroys top accuracy. A shooter may even jiggle his rifle slightly if he rests part of a trigger finger against the rifle stock.

Don't blame poor marksmanship on a rifle, ammo or accessories.

Almost always the fault lies with the shooter—usually a poor trigger release. Remember this: nearly all rifles shoot much, much better than a rifleman can hold. Relaxation is probably the key to good trigger release. However, to remain loose while firing at a trophy deer bouncing around the side of yonder hill is difficult.

It's my guess that nearly all middle-agers and oldsters flinch frequently. Most of us were self-taught. We were given a .22, cartridges and told to work over the rat and sparrow populations at the barn and livestock sheds. We knew little about correct shooting positions; had had no instruction in trigger release. When sights looked right, we yanked the trigger. Consequently, over the years we've had to unravel some bad habits and learn good ones. By comparison, youngsters today are offered good marksmanship training through various organizations in school and community: scouting, hunter safety, ROTC, etc. A young fellow may start with a pellet gun, change to a .22 and finally graduate to rifles of light, medium and heavy recoil. Through such a program his chances of developing poor shooting habits are reduced. His initial training under experienced instructors stresses good trigger control, dry-firing, shooting for groups and a dozen other important details.

Have you watched a group of recruits being checked for flinching? Some close their eyes as they anticipate firing. A few raise their faces off the comb. Others thrust forward with a shoulder to counter recoil and, after a sore shoulder has developed, may push the rifle butt away from the shoulder. But the worst fault of all is when a shooter anticipates muzzle blast, recoil and noise by strenuously jerking the trigger. Result: frequent misses on game animals and paper targets.

The first step in correcting a flinching habit is the realization that one does jerk the trigger. Experts writing in books and magazines glibly outline a program to identify flinchers. The suspect is checked with an empty weapon or dummy rounds mixed with live ammo. Always results are identical: Mr. Flincher exhibits one of the above reactions and invariably in these stories ends by "nipping" or stumbling forward when he draws an empty chamber or a dummy round. Actually, it's quite difficult to check a lone individual for flinching, for he generally makes a conscious effort to avoid being trapped.

The second step is the desire to do something about flinching. One should make a list of the possible causes and eliminate them one by one. Don't overgun yourself. Buy a smaller caliber if your rifle has too much recoil. Certainly a well-placed .244 bullet is far better than a poor strike with a .338. Perhaps a recoil pad or a mechanical device to reduce recoil, muzzle blast and noise is the answer. Remember that an ultra light weapon means more recoil, and a mini-short barrel a vicious muzzle blast.

A rifle should fit the shooter. A factory stock may be too long or short. An incorrectly mounted scope or a short stock may result in a slashed eyebrow. Drop at the heel may be wrong.

A person may flinch as a result of keeping a weapon at his shoulder an unusually long time. Delays in sighting cause tremors. Result: a shooter usually jerks the trigger when sight and target approach each other. Oftentimes, a sportsman can solve his own flinching problems. If unsuccessful, seek the help of a good instructor. Occasionally a person must postpone shooting for several months—perhaps a year—then start from the beginning, preferably under the guidance of an experienced instructor.

Everyone vigorously slaps a trigger now and then. I flinch occasionally and have had several bouts with flinchitis that were so disheartening that I stopped shooting all types of weapons for a time. But, like everyone, there are also happy periods when I can do nothing wrong: when weapon swing and trigger release are as smooth as warm, flowing honey.

GUESSTIMATING THE RANGE

The average sportsman has much difficulty estimating distances to big game. As a consequence, his bullets frequently miss animals or, worse, wound game, which escapes to suffer and, perhaps, become food for scavengers.

Listen to the plight of a dude who hunted out of our camp in central Utah a number of years ago. We had guided this jasper to where a deer —heavily antlered, a trophy for which one searches a lifetime—was quietly feeding at the edge of a flat mountain park. We had watched the buck for perhaps five minutes, trying to decide what to do. Then the dude, who had boasted several times of his skill as a rifleman, decided—against advice—to shoot from where we were. The bullet smacked the buck low in the stomach. No time for additional blasts; after a couple of jumps, the muley vanished into dense aspens. When asked to guesstimate distance to where the deer had stood, the dude looked studiously across the park and said: "200 yards." We paced the distance to where the moist, black earth showed the deep tracks of the startled buck: 400 long steps. A few harsh words were exchanged with the dude when we found the bloated muley the following day. But, he had an excuse. This was his first safari after big game, and the smoggy environment of his native

California city had offered poor training for one suddenly transplanted to the clear, open spaces of mountain country.

Deer hunters, however, can do much to train themselves for guesstimating distances even though they go afield infrequently. A few minutes of practice each day for a couple of weeks before a big-game hunt pays tremendous dividends and greatly increases chances of making a clean kill. Big-game safaris are expensive and mule deer populations are declining. During a lifetime of hunting one can expect to secure only a few shots at trophy animals.

Several weeks before leaving for a hunt, measure off these distances: 25, 50, 100, 200 and 300 yards. Mark them plainly with large stakes. Next, construct a life-size deer silhouette. A cardboard cutout is satisfactory. Study the relative size of the silhouette from 25 to 300 yards. Then ask a pal to walk the paper deer out to unknown distances. To check one's accuracy, measure with a tape or count the number of paces to the silhouette. Length of step varies with individuals, but a little practice over a measured course soon teaches a person to stride at approximately one yard. A city friend who hunts infrequently found that he could guesstimate distances up to 200 yards within 15 per cent error after practicing for only one hour with a silhouette. After a few practice sessions, almost everyone finds his margin of error no worse than 10 per cent for distances up to 300 yards. Now take the cardboard muley to a place where there are large rocks, shrubs and trees. Play the game again. Some hunters take mounted heads, even whole mounted deer, and place them at various distances to sharpen their estimates.

Even after long years of hunting, many sportsmen consistently underestimate yardage to animals standing in bright light. Our California dude had such trouble with the trophy buck. A crystal-clear day with a bright sun at our backs caused that muley to project against the background like a fly on a cream cake. Deer silhouetted against a bright sky or contrasting backgrounds, such as light-colored rocks, also appear much nearer than they really are. Yardage which puzzles many hunters is that stretching across level terrain, over patches of open snow, water, etc., where there is little or no vegetation to assist a person in guesstimating. When the day is hazy, foggy, or rainy, or if one is hunting in the dim light of dawn or dusk, old Big Ears is probably nearer than one dares believe. Likewise, yardage to game located up- or downhill is nearly always overestimated. If a hunter is kneeling or lying down when he spots a deer, invariably he overestimates the distance. Same is true when background and the animal blend together; when game is seen over broken ground or in shade; when heat waves are rising from the earth; and when only part of the animal can be seen. Distances most difficult of all to estimate are those across canyons and ravines, where animals always appear much farther than one thinks.

Guesstimates sometimes indicate that deer are too far away for probable, clean kills. If conditions (terrain and behavior of the quarry) are favorable, a hunter should stalk to a point from which a killing shot can be made. However, one shouldn't approach so near that the animal becomes frightened and offers only a running opportunity. Certainly one medium-distance poke at a standing muley is better than several blasts at a spooked, bouncing animal. The best rule: shoot at the shoulder-heart-lungs area no farther than one can hit a paper target of the same size. But to follow this advice one must know the approximate distance to the animal. The type of rifle one carries must be considered also. If a person is armed with a .30-30—class weapon and suspects distance to a deer is 400 yards or beyond, he certainly should sneak nearer before blasting. As a person's skill at guesstimating yardage increases, he can "stretch" his range—as much as 100 yards—after building confidence in his ability to hit game at known distances. A hunter learns what his rifle, ammo and sights can do under various situations.

Occasionally, one's companions can assist in guesstimating. If there is sufficient time, several guesses of yardage to game can be averaged. Also, ask a hunting pal to call your shots. He can see where they're hitting better than you. Remember, however, that a puff of dust from dry earth or rocks often rises or drifts laterally with the wind.

A serious big game hunter always paces, if possible, the distance from point of shooting to where a deer is hit. This is the "test of the pudding." When it's impossible to verify yardage—as across a canyon—one can, if he remembers the sight picture at time of firing, check the amount of bullet drop and arrive at an approximate figure.

A few hunters have asked why, when there is so much emphasis on flat-shooting magnums, it's necessary to estimate range. Certainly, a weapon whose trajectory is relatively "flat" out to 200 or 300 yards is of great assistance to deer hunters. Surveys, however, show that less than 10 per cent of muley hunters own super-pooper weapons, although the percentage is increasing. Most muley hunters estimate distances beyond 100 yards so poorly that dependence upon super magnums only causes more extreme long-range blasting—consequently more missing and wounding. It's a matter of education, I suppose. Convince a man that the probability of making a kill beyond 200 yards with his weapon is not good and a deer may have been saved which he might harvest another day—when within range of his rifle.

To assist hunters in guesstimating, inventors for many years have been trying to devise range-finding sights. When binoculars and rifle scopes were invented, technicians decided that the long awaited opportunity had arrived. The Germans etched distance scales on binocs and scopes. Then Americans placed two or more wires across the sight picture of a rifle scope. One popular glass shows 6 inches between wires at 100 yards. Scopes are also made with posts projecting a known distance above the cross hairs. Or, as most everyone knows, one can buy rifle scopes equipped with small dots which cover a definite number of inches at various distances. Redfield Gun Sight Company developed several years ago a telescopic sight which eliminiates much of the uncertainty of estimating distances. Many sportsmen consider this device of inestimable value, particularly beginners and individuals who hunt infrequently. Surely more deer will be killed cleanly (fewer wounded) when sportsmen use such a device than if the same hunters were equipped with rifles bearing iron or conventional telescopic sights. Two reference wires are located near the top of the field of view (sight picture). After finding a deer, turn the power selector ring until the animal's body is bracketed between the two wires. The projecting scale at the bottom of the sight picture then shows distance to Mr. Bucko. Finally, turn the power ring to magnification you wish to use, compensate for bullet trajectory to the deer and squeeze the trigger. Sounds complicated? Not at all, but don't be disappointed when you find that this scope isn't 100 per cent accurate in determining distance.

Over the years I've debated with fellow sportsmen many times about the innovations which have affected this delightful sport of deer hunting: binoculars, magnum rifle, rifle scopes, devices to attract deer by scent or sound, range finders, etc. How far can we go while using these aids and retain a semblance of the sport? Surely, there is a limit. On the other hand, should we follow the advice of a growing segment of hunters and retreat to using bows and arrows and muzzle-loading rifles? Should we ban by statute or common consent the use of devices which make killing a deer almost a mechanical act?

The answers lie in one's heritage, one's experiences, one's aspirations. No one admires accurate, beautiful firearms more than I. And I also own and use several rifle scopes and binoculars. However, I find that to spook through quiet, autumn woods with bow and arrows is almost intoxicating. I must be part Indian. Surely, we hunters must concede the game certain advantages if we are to prevent the sport from deteriorating into mere slaughter. Perhaps, the use of binoculars and rifle scopes is permissible. On the other hand, artificial devices to attract deer to a hidden rifleman, or a range-estimator from which a person could read data for an easy kill, even at extended ranges, is not sporting, in my opinion. I may be old-fashioned, but I hope that no one ever markets a precise range finder which would sell for a few dollars and could be carried in one's shirt pocket.

How can a man who insists on hunting with iron sights use them to guesstimate distance? Subtending is the answer—placing an object of known size against the deer's body. First, check your sights on a measured piece of paper at 100 yards. Assuming that your front blade covers 6 inches at this distance, it likewise blacks-out—subtends—12 inches at 200 yards, 18 inches at 300 yards. The average mule deer's body is about four feet long. Let's assume that you've located Mr. Bucko standing on yonder hillside peacefully eating tender aspen leaves. You plunk your posterior on the earth for steady sighting and find that the blade covers about one-fourth of the muley's body. Two hundred yards away. Not a difficult shot for an experienced person who is carefully sighted in, assumes a steady position and remembers a few details such as correct trigger release. Let's assume, however, that while glassing the vast expanse of the basin at the head of Utah's Mill Canyon, you locate a deer just below the game trail that leads into some conifers. When the sight blade is placed against the deer's hide, you discover that, except for his head, he nearly disappears. The distance is the better part of 700 to 800 yards. Better sneak a mite closer!

Many hunters specify cross wires when purchasing a rifle scope. An improvement, in my humble opinion, is a suspended dot, one that subtends about 3 to 4 inches at 100 yards. Although cross wires can also be used to estimate range, a dot is much more functional.

Guesstimating pays well in still another way. If you've chosen to sit in a rocky nest opening morning, estimate distances to those locations where deer are most likely to appear. Then, when Mr. Antlers sneaks over yonder ridge, placing the scope dot on the correct spot on his rib cage is fairly simple. Guesstimating distance to big game isn't difficult. A few hours of practice may fill the freezer with meat and hang a trophy head on the wall of the den!

HITTING 'EM AT LONG RANGE

For a number of years I've been recording some interesting data about super riflemen in a little brown notebook. Page two has a quotation from a national sporting magazine: "Range was a good 700 yards . . . I fired . . . buck went down on second shot." On the same page is an excerpt from another article: "Buck was about 550 yards away . . . held for his neck and killed him with my first shot." An entry on another page of my notebook tells of an outdoor writer who killed a doe "with a head shot at 600-700 paces." Still another hunter dropped his buck at 625 yards with an 86 gr. .25-20 bullet. How many corral lengths did this ruben hold above that deer to make such a distant kill? He didn't say. A gun editor once wrote that his wife killed a running deer at 600 yards. This same writer also reports that while in the company of an hombre in Canada or Alaska he saw the man hit a caribou at 700 yards with a .270. The critter was finally finished off at about 1,200 yards.

Few of us are as skilled as the above group of experts. In fact, by comparison most of us are rather poor shooters. After observing service personnel during 27 years of active and reserve military duty and after watching civilians at rifle ranges and big game hunters in the mountains for about 40 years, I'm convinced that a majority of U.S. citizens are bum marksmen. We mule deer hunters have trouble hitting game in spite of the stories we relate with gusto around campfires. Perhaps, only one in 25 is a fair shot. We do well to hit a running deer at 50 yards—anywhere on its hairy side. And at 100 yards—not a long shot—many of us frequently miss standing deer, offhand.

What is a long shot? I could be wrong but, in my opinion, a long shot is that distance beyond the point-blank range of a specific rifle. Beyond point-blank range, most everyone knows, a bullet starts to drop considerably, and a hunter must compensate if he intends to hit a deer. For instance, the .30-06, which is probably used as much by mule deer hunters as any caliber, when zeroed at 200 yards, throws a Western SP, 150 gr. bullet nearly 5 feet low at 500 yards and 30 odd feet low at 1,000 yards. A .270, 150 gr. bullet of the same type drops a little farther. And a .30-30, .300 Savage, a .303 and similar calibers often seen on deer safaris do even more poorly.

Why are long shots so difficult? Chiefly because we are unable to estimate distances to game animals with much accuracy. Even after considerable practice, as we have seen, most sportsmen can't guesstimate point-bank range (100 to perhaps 300 yards) more accurately than 90 per cent. And at long-range—let's assume a deer has been located at 500 yards—a majority of us can't determine whether the animal is standing at 400 yards or 600. Obviously, then, we're apt to miss the deer or hit it on the fringes.

For example, a buck of average size runs about 15-22 inches from backbone to brisket. Assume that a hunter has located such a deer. Is the animal 300, 400 or 500 yards away? Our hunter finally decides that Mr.

Bucko is 500 yards away. Like most of us, he overestimates. Actually, the deer is standing at 400 yards, and to hit him in the middle of the ribs at this distance requires a holdover of only one foot. But, the dude, believing the yardage is 500, holds about 4 feet over the buck, shoots above his back and misses by 2 feet. Clearly, long-range shooting is not for beginners and once-a-year muley hunters who fire only a few rounds each season.

What are the skills, then, of a man who is qualified to make long shots? First, he's developed the ability to guesstimate range with not more than a 10 per cent error or is using a scope with a built-in estimating device. He has also acquired an accurate, flat-shooting weapon, tuned it with appropriate ammo and has practiced (he doesn't depend upon a manufacturer's trajectory table) until he can throw strikes from a bench at 300 yards into a 12-inch bull, the approximate size of the heart-lungs area of a deer. (Obviously, if he can't do this trick on paper, he can't lay those slugs into an animal's boiler room, either. Don't believe the lunkheads who alibi that they may not be able to print good groups on paper but just show them something wrapped in hair!) He's also chosen a good bullet: a pointed slug that rides the wind. He knows, too, that at long-range, bullet energy is greatly reduced and bullet expansion sometimes negligible. (For example, a western SP, 150 gr. bullet in the .30-06 has 2,930 foot pounds of energy at the muzzle, but this is reduced to 1,510 at only 300 yards.) And, he's also learned to use a good riflescope. Iron sights are of little value for long-range shooting. How can one hit a deer when the front blade covers the target?

Now we've found a muley hunter who is prepared to make those strikes out yonder—when he can't stalk nearer. And there will be occasions when a person can't approach as near as he might wish. Muley country is open country, and deer have excellent eyes. Mr. Sportsman may not be able to stalk nearer because of an impassable canyon, approaching darkness, onset of a storm, presence of other deer in the neighborhood, etc. Mule deer are becoming "wilder," too, as the years roll onward. They spook more easily—are more difficult to approach. So, a medium to long shot may be necessary—certainly preferable to a short, running try. In localities which feature crowds of hunters, a skillful marksman may elect to try for a bucko at long-range, for chances of his remaining undisturbed, permitting a stalk, are rather remote.

A few individuals I know have spent as much as $500 on a deer safari and never located a desirable trophy until it was a now-or-never proposition. In such situations I've seen hunters blast at muleys as long as they were in sight, although the possibility of hitting them anywhere was extremely slight. Likewise, shots at muleys wearing trophy headgear are difficult to refuse even under nearly impossible circumstances. A few veteran hunters also spurn the easy, close shot for they derive satisfaction only in the long or difficult attempt. But are these reasonable excuses for shooting at extreme ranges—that one-in-a-thousand chance?

One advantage of long distance shooting is that a marksman generally has time to guesstimate range, recall the bullet's trajectory, assume a good position and effect a smooth trigger release. Under these ideal conditions a good rifleman has a reasonable chance of hitting a muley at long-range.

As we have seen, mule deer vary in size from about 15-22 inches from back to brisket. Inside this area the boiler room is located: heart and lungs. Such a target, the experts say, shouldn't be too difficult to hit at long range. True, the finest American marksmen with the best available equipment can lay all their bullets in a 36-inch target at 1,000 yards, and should be able to smack a large deer in the heart-lungs area with regularity at 500 yards. But these are exceptional men. Other marksmen cannot score quite this well, although there are a number of them who are capable of keeping most of their bullets within a 12-inch bull at 200 yards, offhand with a sporting weapon. These shooters have also proved that they score as accurately out to 400 or 500 yards from a rest position. Therefore, given excellent equipment these individuals are qualified to shoot at deer up to 500 yards. But the animal must be motionless and the hunter sitting, prone or with his rifle resting over a padded log, rock, etc.

Often mule deer are jumped accidentally or through carelessness and, although they bounce away quite rapidly, almost always they pause and look back at the source of their fright before trotting over a ridge or into timber. Fall into a steady position because, in all likelihood, you'll have a quartering or broadside try for a trophy. If inclined to become flustered when you spot Mr. Antlers on yonder hillside, prepare a "trajectory schedule," listing bullet rise and drop from muzzle out to the long-range capability of your weapon, and attach it to the stock with clear, waterproof tape. Another item: ask a friend to call your strikes on deer or misses on nearby rocks or earth. Generally, it's difficult for a shooter to spot his strikes at long-range. But, even from out yonder, when the wind is right, one can often hear the plunk of a bullet on flesh.

One of the real joys of deer hunting is listening to a parade of campfire stories. However, when stomachs are bulging, most muley hunters exaggerate a little about distances at which they kill deer. A number of hunters are also inclined to remember the good shots and forget the misses. Unfortunately, many youngsters and beginners hear these tall-tales and believe them. Then they go into the hills and smoke up deer at long-range. If the results were only wasted ammunition, few would complain. National sporting magazines are guilty, too. Their editors and corps of writers often regale their readers with long-shot tales and type-writer "bullistics." Without question, a few hunters occasionally do kill game at tremendous distances, but these are accidents where a smidgen of skill is combined with a huge quantity of luck. Unfortunately, this leads to indiscriminate blasting by the general public and the wounding, western game managers report, of large numbers of animals.

Many hunters fail to realize the consequences of wounding deer. As a 7-year-old I was horrified by the sight of a young buck, shot through the back, bawling in agony as it dragged itself laboriously toward cover. Too many hunters shoot too fast and too far. If a bullet can't be put into a deer's locker room with a hold on top of his back, distance is usually too great. Such a hold at 300 yards with my deer rifles results in a strike in the heart-lungs. Most of my deer have been killed at distances ranging from 50 to 200 yards.

Before making that long shot, ask yourself: (1) Can I stalk nearer? (2) Can I guesstimate the range? (3) Do I have the ability and equip-ment to hit at the estimated range? If there is no reasonable chance of cleanly killing the deer, pass up the shot. Yes, it's true; there will be another day, another deer.

RUNNING SHOTS

When Mr. Average Hunter locates mule deer, he usually finds them moving, traveling at varying speeds from a walk to a frightened, rapid run. Because this person wishes to kill a deer, and hesitates about wait-ing for the fairly easy, standing opportunity, he generally blasts at Mr. Buck despite the fact that chances for a kill are poor. It may be all right for exceptional marksmen to blast at some running muleys, because they usually make clean, quick kills. However, the amateur generally finds himself missing moving animals, or, if he hits, gut- or ham-shooting them. Until he has had some experience on other moving targets that will im-prove his marksmanship, the beginner should not attempt running shots. An experienced hunter can often approach mule deer and kill them before they become alarmed and bounce away. But, there are occasions when he chooses to cut them down running. However, his skills are good and he need not go home with clean hands even though he hasn't had a standing, broadside opportunity.

It's apparent after talking with a number of beginners that most of them, because of insufficient training and practice, usually hold smack on a running deer when they jerk the trigger. Obviously, this is wrong, for, to hit a deer which is moving in any direction except toward or away from the hunter, a person must place the bullet, not where the animal is presently located, but where it will be in a short time.

Banging at jack rabbits is probably the best substitute for shooting at deer that western hunters can find. Jacks sit, hop lazily along or zip cross-country, zigging and zagging, about as fast as any muley ever ran. After many years of blasting at these long-eared varmints, a hunter can, when concentrating, kill about one out of five with his first bullet. If one takes the best opportunities—those bunnies 50 to 75 yards away and running over fairly level and unobstructed terrain—his average sometimes rises to 30 to 40 per cent. And under nearly all circumstances a person rarely misses a rabbit (actually jack rabbits are hares) by so great a margin that he would have failed to connect with a deer, generally in the high spine-shoulder-heart-lungs region.

Most deer hunters, unfortunately, do not live in or near areas where jack rabbits are abundant. However, other animals and objects can be used for practice. Firing at waterfowl, upland and nonprotected birds and regularly visiting trap and skeet clubs improve one's shooting; so does blasting at cardboard targets inserted into automobile tires and rolled downhill. Developing skill to kill running deer begins with knowing precisely what to do and then practicing—but not on deer. The ideal way involves teaching and demonstration by skilled marksmen, followed with practice on jack rabbits, running deer targets, etc.

A beginner must learn to call his shots, to remember clearly the sight-picture—the place on the target where his sights were aligned when he pulled the trigger. He also must learn to shoot quickly, to squeeze the trigger immediately when the relation of sight and target looks right because, similar to running-deer targets, game animals move rapidly and disappear rather quickly, especially in thick brush and trees.

One occasionally encounters individuals who believe, because they can daylight targets from a shooting bench, that they are likewise exceptional shots on running deer. At the bench is the proper place to learn a number of important details, such as trigger squeeze; but having these skills is no assurance that a person will kill moving deer consistently. In fact, the worst marksman on running game in my circle of acquaintances is a man who could probably pick up more than his share of awards while shooting from traditional positions at paper targets. Almost anyone can learn, after a little practice, to hit stationary targets, but to place strikes on running deer is much more difficult.

Because a hunter under present conditions can't possibly hope to kill enough deer during his lifetime to materially improve his marksmanship, he must depend on training at skeet-traps, the rifle range, rolling tire-targets and at varmints such as jack rabbits. A basketball player or golfer who participates in only one game each season won't break any records. Neither will a hunter who rarely practices kill many running deer.

Spot Shooting

Learning a method of shooting that consistently drops deer is a problem with many hunters. Most beginners start by spot shooting. They push the barrel out in front of a moving deer or clay pigeon the distance they believe to be about right, stop the weapon and press the trigger. Frequently, the result is a miss—and a disappointed hunter.

Sustained Lead

Probably the best technique is to swing in front of a target, establish a definite lead, and, while maintaining this distance, squeeze the trigger and follow through with the weapon. This method is consistently reliable, and almost anyone with a reasonable amount of practice on running-deer targets, jack rabbits and clay birds can kill moving deer. If a lead in front of the target places a bullet in the deer's paper-paunch, increase the distance. By varying the lead a person can discover approximately where he must align his sight to strike a running deer at any speed and distance in the lungs-heart area.

Fast Swing

Several excellent shots on running deer have told me that they use what is called a fast swing. They bring the rifle quickly from behind and, when the sights have passed about the right distance in front of the animal, they press the trigger and keep swinging. The swing is rapid—so rapid, in fact, that one pal maintains that he presses the trigger while the scope dot is still on the animal's ribs.

Certainly the fast swing is very effective for a person with good muscular coordination and eyes. This method, however, calls for considerable practice on jack rabbits and at the clay-bird and running-deer ranges.

After hunting mule deer for more than 40 years, I generally fast swing animals which are running rapidly and within 50 to 75 yards, especially if they are about to disappear into cover. Beyond this range, I use a sustained lead because even when aiming at medium distances, it's very difficult to control a fast swing of the barrel and snap the primer at precisely the right moment. However, every person has a different reaction time, and only by practicing regularly can he discover which technique is best for him.

How Far to Lead Running Game

Successful, experienced hunters are occasionally asked to indicate the distance they lead running deer for a strike in the lungs-heart. It's nearly impossible to answer this question because almost every shooting situation is different. Sportsmen use a large variety of rifles with varying velocities. Distance from hunter to deer likewise varies considerably, as does the angle at which the deer is moving. There are also other factors such as size of the deer and rapidity with which a person swings a rifle.

However, a number of hunters, particularly those who have had little or no success in killing running deer, insist on receiving an answer. For these sportsmen, let's solve this simple problem: a muley buck at 100 yards is bouncing broadside across a mountain park at 15 m.p.h. The hunter has a rifle which fires a bullet across 100 yards at an average velocity of 3,000 feet per second. How far must a sportsman lead this buck to place a bullet into his lungs? We find by simple arithmetic that our bullet requires one-tenth of a second to reach the deer. However, the muley has also moved 2.2 feet while the bullet is in flight. Assuming that the lungs lie about one foot behind the front of the shoulders, a person must aim approximately 1.2 feet in front of the brisket to hit the target, the lungs. At 200 yards the lead would be approximately 3.4 feet in front of the brisket and so on out to the theoretical limits of the range of the rifle. However, very few hunters stand much chance of cleanly dropping running deer beyond 100 yards.

Obviously, the solution of this example problem is of limited value except to indicate, in general, the lead a person could use in a picture-book situation. Under actual field conditions the average hunter rarely has such a shot. Usually, the animal is quartering, moving up- or down-slope, and is varying his speed, all of which complicate the situation.

Some of my friends believe that strikes on quartering deer are not as difficult as the 90 degree angle, broadside blast for the simple reason that less lead is required. Assuming that a buck is approaching or running from a hunter at a 45 degree angle, a person must only hold about 6 inches in front of the shoulders to hit the lungs, providing, of course, that the deer is 100 yards away, running at 15 m.p.h., doesn't zigzag, and the shooter swings his rifle and follows through! To kill cleanly, (which usually means a strike through the lungs-heart-shoulder area) when animals are traveling up- or downhill, is sometimes difficult. Almost every good shot can hit a buck moving upslope; the animal is generally traveling rather slowly and only a small amount of lead is required. However, placement of a bullet to reach the boiler room—not a strike in the guts or hams—is a problem. And through or over most iron sights, much of the animal is hidden from view when the shooter pulls ahead to establish a lead. While going downslope, a deer moves more rapidly. Yet, this shot—when a deer is moving toward the hunter—is easier than when an animal is climbing uphill, simply because the aiming point, the shoulders, are in view. A person can quickly calculate the approximate lead, pull ahead and squeeze.

Sights For Running Deer

The increasing number of hunters afield each year with scoped rifles clearly indicates the value of optics in helping sportsmen kill mule deer. Everyone in my circle of deer hunting friends has from one to a dozen scoped rifles. And, except for casual plinking, no one in the group uses iron sights.

Use the best scopes for making running shots—clear, sharp types such as Redfield, Lyman and Leupold equipped with medium cross hairs or dots. Cross hairs, because of horizontal and vertical positions of the wires, assist a hunter materially in keeping his sight on a moving animal. However, a floating dot is better, for the black dot remains more definite and obvious in the field of view and can be moved more quickly and accurately in front of deer and maintained in position. No one runs fast enough to give me a scope with a post reticle. Obviously, a scope should be mounted low on a rifle, have a wide field of view and good eye relief. A scope of 2½X-4X is best for most hunters for running shots. Personally, I prefer four-power, with a three-minute dot.

Iron sights? A buckhorn is an abomination, of little value. One handicaps himself with such a sight because the ears protrude so high that a deer is partly hidden and can only be followed during a running shot with difficulty. A very open sight, the blade of which is curved slightly over a white line or arrowhead isn't too bad. But, a peep is best of all. I used such a sight for years before I could afford a good scope and found it quite satisfactory, particularly on close, running game. A peep is fast, accurate and easily mastered.

Rifles For Running Deer

It's very important that a rifle accommodate a person's stance, face, arm and neck length. Perhaps one hunter in ten can walk into a sports store and buy a rifle off the rack that is 100 per cent right. The stock may be inches too long or short; the comb too high or low. One of several other factors may result in a poor fit and cause inaccurate shooting.

I generally manufacture my own stocks. Among my special favorites is a .270 built up from a Mauser action with a Kenneth Hooper barrel. The stock I made from a plank of well-seasoned Utah black walnut, with a one-half inch castoff to the right and a comb which just fits my face. When I locate a deer and raise this rifle, Mr. Buck is there in the scope. No need to juggle the weapon to find him.

This particular rifle weighs 8½ pounds when equipped with carrying sling and a four-power scope. So much weight may sound a little excessive to many hunters, but I prefer a slightly heavier weapon than do most sportsmen because such a firearm swings smoothly and accurately, much better than a featherweight. However, such a rifle seems quite heavy after a day of hard hunting. I learned a number of years ago that an extra pound or so in a rifle remarkably improves a person's chances on running game. For example, I can kill more running jack rabbits with a 9 pound .220 Swift than with a .22-250 that weighs 7½ pounds. A smooth, fluid swing and follow-through are the important factors in hitting running game. Therefore, a weapon which is sufficiently heavy to stabilize motion is highly desirable.

BUCK FEVER

Buck fever can be a tiger on one's back—punishing, painful, disastrous to accurate shooting. Or it can add a pleasurable zest to the hunt.

I often recall an October morning when a friend failed to dislodge the demon tiger from his back and lost a magnificent, trophy mule deer. Low clouds were spitting tiny, round snow pellets when Frank and I left camp at daybreak. We hiked for an hour along an abandoned logging road, then turned off into a rocky ravine that after a quarter-mile sliced into a mountain basin which nearly every season has produced two or three good muley bucks.

Suddenly, Frank, who was in the lead, turned abruptly and without speaking, pointed to tracks in the snow. Mule deer tracks, extremely large and fresh—so fresh, in fact, that very few snow pellets had fallen into the prints. We both checked the wind: square into our faces. Like hounds we followed the tracks as they led northward through the rocky gorge. Then Frank stopped a second time, knelt and pressed his hand to a pile of droppings that were still warm. His lips parted into a tantalizing smile. We sneaked slowly and carefully across the lip of the basin, paused and, as I started to position a binocular, Frank expelled his breath like maybe he'd been kicked in the stomach by a cayuse. There stood the grey-faced veteran, broadside at about 125 yards. In a very characteristic muley pose: head high, motionless, watching us.

Frank had found the tracks and had seen the buck first. Obviously, the shot was his. Should be easy. Over the years my companion had killed a number of good bucks, but never a real first-rate, trophy book buster. Thinking that Frank would fire immediately, I held the deer in the binoc. But, after waiting several seconds for the muzzle blast, I glanced at my pal. His stance was awkward and the muzzle of his rifle was pointing a series of figure eights against the sky. Watching Mr. Bucko again, I saw him mince a couple of steps. He was ready to move out. Then, almost simultaneously a puff of dark earth erupted in the snow above his withers and I heard the bellow of Frank's '06. A miss.

Instead of keeping his rifle in shooting position while jacking another cartridge, Frank lowered his weapon and stared darkly and open-mouthed at the running muley. The expression on his face was a tragic one. "Why don't you shoot!" he yelled. For a reason which my friend wouldn't have understood, I didn't fire but continued to watch the big muley bounce around the hillside. Just as the deer reached the edge of some conifers, Frank blasted a second and final time. We discovered later that the buck had escaped untouched.

We squatted on our heels, and Frank puffed rapidly on a cigarette. "All my life I've searched for a trophy like that, and then I flub my chance," he complained in a husky, hesitant voice. "Why the hell did I have to miss!"

I looked at my pal. In addition to a very painful expression, beads of perspiration spotted his upper lip although the day was bitterly cold. No need to tell Frank why he had missed that muley. He knew that buster probably would have made the record book—and that a friendly sports editor would have printed his photo with the trophy in the local newspaper.

Frank's reactions were quite typical of hunters suffering from buck fever. And there are additional reactions we can discuss. They run the gamut from slight excitement to uncontrolled fright. Everyone has seen, or heard stories of, sportsmen shucking cartridges out of their rifles, thinking all the while that they were firing at game. Some hunters, upon seeing a buck they want very much, have fired bullets into the air or ground. Others, reportedly, have thrown their rifles at retreating deer. Apparently the fever causes a hunter to forget a step or two in the mechanics of aiming and firing. Oftentimes, there is no memory of the sight picture at time of shooting and occasionally the person's mind is a blank.

Several decades have passed since I killed that first mule deer, but the memories are still vividly clear: sitting on a high rock overlooking a shallow canyon, eating a dry sandwich, luxuriating in a warming sun and a panoramic vista of thousands of acres of red-brown oaks, dark green conifers and yellow-leafed aspens.

The muley wasn't large, just a fat forky-horn. Hunters over the ridge had spooked him out and their shooting alerted me. True, I was only a kid, but I had seen my father and other relatives kill a few muleys, so I shouldn't have developed the fever. But I did, and how I laid that first bullet from the old Krag into the buck's ribs I'll never know for I really had the shakes. He ran until about 200 yards separated his pelt from my rifle and stopped with head up, watching.

I've never told all of the details of what happened but now is a good time to confess. Fumbling, hurriedly, I fired 18 times; and the only additional damage suffered by that patient muley—and he never moved appreciably from where he first stopped—was a skin burn. That buck just didn't know that he was supposed to die! When I searched my pockets for additional ammo, it seemed impossible that I was down to the twentieth and last cartridge, but that very fact was sobering and caused some semblance of reason to filter into my excited brain. Climbing off the rock, I sluggered down the slope to within 50 steps of the buck, placed the barrel across the dead branch of a convenient tree and took him through the ribs. As the muley fell, the fever hit me again. My father and a friend, approximately a mile away, were packing out a buck on a horse, and they heard the barrage followed by my Comanche war whoops. When questioned later, I lied. I told Dad that the very crude buckhorn sight on the Krag had been the cause of the poor shooting. However, he knew the truth, possibly because he had once found himself in an identical predicament. Sure, I had had a fabulous case of the fever.

Buck fever isn't restricted to individuals who hunt big game. Some persons suffer from the fever while participating in athletic events or engaging the enemy in combat. I've been told that a prominent, national entertainer often vomits before a performance, and that many public speakers are miserable when they face an audience.

The symptoms? We've already discussed several physical reactions. When a trophy buck breaks from cover and your mouth becomes dust-dry, hands shake and your voice is jerky and tremulous, perspiration pops from your skin, your heartbeat and breathing are twice the normal rate, muscles tense and legs rubbery—you've become a victim of old buck fever itself!

The cause of buck fever isn't hard to explain: merely the excitement generated while endeavoring to accomplish something which one wants desperately to do. Actually, the person afflicted is afraid of not doing well. A powerful substance, adrenalin, is released into the bloodstream and causes the symptoms listed previously. This may be quite all right if an individual is running from a charging lion, but is disastrous when one must smoothly control nerves, muscles and bones responsible for accurate shooting. When companions are present, fear of criticism or ridicule if one misses game usually causes an intensification of the reaction. There is damage to a person's ego, to one's pride. Fear of failure and ridicule are very realistic, basic fears. Sportsmen so affected should hunt alone. The individual who has already established himself as an excellent game shot wishes to keep that reputation, and it's a saddening experience to see hunters begin to miss—and develop buck fever—when poor eyesight and other physical disabilities appear with advancing age. Hunting a new species of game animal may cause buck fever. A hunting pal missed a bull elk at about 150 yards—from a rest position—after waiting 19 years for a wapiti permit. It struck me a series of low blows the first time I hunted white-tails, goats, antelope and elk. A good friend experiences a massive case of buck fever if a muley flushes suddenly and is close by. However, he is calm when he spots a deer in the distance and must make a sneak.

To avoid buck fever, at least its most troublesome symptoms, a person must try to understand the causes. This is half the battle. Certainly a sportsman should hunt as often as possible. To get to know one's weapon through frequent, regular practice helps build confidence so that a person automatically completes the firing steps. To rush through the aiming and firing sequence is often ruinous for a hunter suffering from buck fever. Such an individual should make a determined effort to proceed slowly. An individual who is a chronic sufferer from buck fever has told me that to counter his fumbling, hurried aiming and firing he counts to 10—after seeing the deer and before blasting. A hunting companion carries an unloaded weapon. Therefore, he must place a round into the magazine after the deer appears; and this series of mechanical steps prevents him from suffering from tremors. Breathing deeply several times after a deer has been found has helped some individuals. If it's possible to take a rest position, do so since steady, aligned sights aids materially in counteracting buck fever.

Beginning deer hunters are often troubled. They try too hard, as I did that October day many years ago. Eagerly, intently these youngsters want to drop that first deer. This is understandable, for in many hunting circles in the West to have killed a deer, particularly a record buck muley, is somewhat of a status symbol. Fortunately, the miserable effects of buck fever tend to diminish after a person has bagged a few head of big game. However, today with reduced bag limits the average hunter is indeed skillful or lucky, perhaps both, if he kills a deer each fall. Therefore, because of limited experience he may suffer the devastating effects of the fever every hunting season.

Some persons resort to alcohol and drugs to subdue the demon tiger, but this is a poor, regrettable approach. So what, if we miss killing a particular deer? A person has done nothing concretely for which he should feel ashamed. Certainly, there will be another day, another animal. Probably, too much emphasis—pressure—is placed upon an individual to bag some venison, anyway. One should hunt only because he gains a pleasurable experience and the basis for happy, unforgettable memories. If a person's days afield become successively less enjoyable—perhaps even painful—because of severe reactions, he should sell his weapons and choose another sport. The right amount of buck fever can insure a scintillating, tingling hunting adventure. Too much is often distressing—even disastrous. Too little, and the hunt leaves one with a feeling of useless slaughter and disappointment.

7

Making Shots Count

PLACEMENT OF BULLETS

The few seconds for which you've been waiting months, possibly even years, has arrived—when you will try to kill a deer. However, it's your responsibility to endeavor to drop that deer quickly, cleanly, and, of course, with a minimum destruction of meat. You have no right to shoot unless a good shot is possible.

Among the many topics of deer hunting lore there are few about which so much bull has been written as the placement of shots. Unfortunately, far too much of the "expert" material concerning this subject printed in sporting magazines and books over the past 30 years is the result of inexperience, poor observation and fuzzy thinking. We've been reading year after year the same old story, following nearly the same wording with identical, trite cliches and drawings.

Brain-Head Shots

Several experts have written that an excellent way to dispatch big game, including deer, is to hit them in the brain. Perhaps elephant or

African buffalo should be killed by this type of shot. I don't know; I've never killed either of these species. However, with rare exception, I do know that it's a poor shot for the average man to make on mule deer.

Some outdoor writers have inferred that because large, domestic animals can be dropped very easily by a brain shot with a pip-squeak .22 rifle, that this type of shot is likewise effective for deer. While a lad on a farm, I killed, or saw killed, perhaps a hundred pigs, sheep and beef critters with a .22 rifle. However, these animals were tied, or were quietly standing in a corral within only a few feet or yards from the rifle muzzle. I don't recall one animal that didn't drop immediately after the bullet had smashed into its brain. One of these small bullets will likewise kill a large mule deer under similar circumstances. I know, for I've seen it happen. Mule deer, however, aren't usually killed within a few feet or yards from a rifle.

In offhand, competitive shooting it has been proved that only excellent riflemen, using very accurate weapons equipped with the finest of scopes, can keep most of their bullet strikes on a 6-inch target at 100 yards. These are the sharpshooters—one in several hundred riflemen. However, the average rifleman has difficulty placing bullets in an area roughly 15 by 15 inches, the approximate size of the shoulder-heart-lungs region of a deer. His chance of hitting the brain are minimal. Brain cavities of adult deer measure three to four inches long and two to three inches wide—quite a small target. The head of a mule deer isn't much larger than the entire body of a western black-tailed jackrabbit. Most riflemen can't consistently kill these big-eared hares while shooting offhand, at 100 yards, when the animals are motionless. And when the bunnies are running, very good riflemen, men who shoot from 500 to 1000 rounds each year at running jacks, bust only about one fifth of them with their first bullet. Experienced hunters sometimes have an opportunity to blast at stationary deer because they have the skills necessary to approach close to the quarry. Amateurs soon discover that they, generally, do not have stationary targets. Therefore, if the beginner—or the semi-experienced hunter—can't hit the relatively small brain of a standing deer at 100 yards, how can he possibly hope to strike this same target while it is bouncing away?

Some hunters argue that a bullet needn't hit the brain, that a near miss kills. That may be true. Modern, high-velocity rifles frequently impart a great amount of shock. Too often, however, the bullet rips a chunk out of the deer's head and knocks him flat, after which he recovers and races away.

While hunting Brown's Park in northeastern Utah a number of years ago, I embarrassingly demonstrated my marksmanship to three companions. A small, spiker buck had walked out of a ravine and was standing broadside, facing us at about 50 yards. I decided to make a grand exhibition. I'd blast that little critter through the brain, offhand. The buck dropped at the shot, but was up and running within seconds. The bullet had torn away part of both jaws. When the muley stopped at about 100 yards, I killed him with a bullet through the lungs. Had this head-shot deer escaped, he might have bled to death within a short time. A deer with its jaw torn away will eventually starve to death, probably under painful circumstances.

I cannot agree with hunters, and with some of the experts, who advocate that a shot at the head usually results in either a very dead deer or a clean miss. Anyway, why should we want to chance a miss—when we shoot at game to kill? There are far better locations on a deer to place bullets—locations that are much easier to hit than the head and result in a clean, relatively quick death. Some individuals also say that if the head is missed, particularly on running deer, that the bullet may strike the neck or body. Occasionally, that might happen! Sportsmen who are primarily trophy hunters avoid head and neck strikes because it's rather difficult for a taxidermist to patch holes in the skins of short-haired animals such as deer.

Neck Shots

Here again some of the experts have written some wild-eyed, unreliable advice. One man reports that he makes a practice of shooting for the neck up to 200 yards, advising fellow hunters that such is an excellent way to kill deer. Another guide cautioned his dude: "Let him come as close as he will, then shoot for the neck. That way you won't spoil any meat." Neck vertebrae, excluding the longish spines, are only about three inches in diameter, rather a small target beyond 50 yards.

True, a near miss of these neck bones can drop a deer, as when the bullet strikes the arteries or windpipe, or when it imparts a large amount of shock to nervous tissue. Another writer has said that deer struck in the neck either drop dead in their tracks or are missed clean. Rabbit feathers! Similar to the head shot, plenty of deer hit in the thick neck muscles escape, perhaps to die later. Remember, too, high neck wounds bleed very little, making a follow-up difficult.

Spine Shots

A survey made by the National Rifle Association from compiled data of both white-tail and mule deer hunters disclosed that 85 per cent of deer struck in the spine dropped in their tracks. Perhaps that is the reason behind a statement by one writer that a bullet strike anywhere along the neck or backbone is an instant killer.

Almost all hits in the neck or chest vertebrae kill mule deer instantly. Deer struck in abdominal and pelvic vertebrae also collapse, but they frequently pull themselves toward cover by means of their front legs. All of these animals eventually die and almost all of them are recovered by hunters, but such shots should be avoided if possible. A rear spine strike destroys some of the best meat on the animal and apparently causes much suffering—a broken-down deer, laboriously dragging itself along, frequently bawling in agony, is a pitiful sight.

Rear End Shots

For years I've been speculating why so many hunters take tail end shots at big game. Such shooting shows poor judgment. When a deer is smacked in the hams, it suffers a painful injury, is often difficult to recover, and much of the best meat is ruined. The bouncing rump of a deer is a very difficult target, and, fortunately, many misses occur. Sportsmen pass up this shot. If a hunter postpones shooting for a few moments, a muley, unless badly frightened, may characteristically pause during its flight, offering a quartering or broadside shot.

Stop for an hour at any checking station and look at the sorry lot of deer being carried out of the hills—many of them ham-shot, unfit to eat, carcasses which eventually are fed to pets or thrown into garbage cans. Experts who advocate rear end shots are wrong. I become extremely disgusted when I read their instructions about how to hold low between the rear legs in order to send a bullet through the guts to reach the heart-lungs region. Especially sickening are detailed instructions about hitting the end of the tail vertebrae, exactly between the hams, to "break down a deer," or aiming just over the withers of animals to strike the neck or head.

Paunch Shots

Placing a bullet in the stomach-intestines should be avoided whenever possible. Although a National Rifle Association survey showed that 44 per cent of deer hit in this region dropped in their tracks, with a still higher percentage followed up and killed, too many paunch-shot muleys escape.

It would be ridiculous, however, to write that skilled marksmen never smack deer in the stomach-intestines. Such happens occasionally to everyone who hunts muleys year after year. Quartering and running shots are notoriously bad in this respect: even though one aims at the heart-lungs, the bullet or fragments sometimes slash through the paunch and burst this smelly mass of partly digested food. Recently I read several paragraphs which attempted to soothe the feelings of those hunters whose ability to hit game in a vital area is so poor that they frequently strike the paunch. The gist of the advice was: it's perfectly all right to shoot at the middle portion of deer, providing one does so with a super-duper magnum rifle. Deer, thus hit, this writer said, nearly always go down and, although they may not be dead, can easily be given a finishing shot. Nothing was said about the stinking, sickening, meat-spoiling mess of stomach contents that must be cleaned out of the carcass. It's almost impossible to tidy up the meat of a gut-shot deer in the field. Result: venison which is objectionable to both sight and taste.

Shoulder Shots

A large number of deer are smacked in the shoulders. Generally, a good bullet, fired from a rifle of reasonable caliber, striking this area knocks an animal down, although death may not be instantaneous. The bullet, however, ruins a considerable quantity of meat, although it can't be classified as the best meat on the animal.

Under hunting conditions, when a person is handicapped by poor light, when an animal is moving or the distance considerable, etc., a sportsman usually doesn't have the picture book, broadside deer at which to shoot. To place a bullet into the vital heart-lungs area, it's frequently necessary to aim at a point on the shoulders. If the animal drops and remains down, only flesh near the bullet strike is ruined. If, however, the deer runs some distance before falling, expect a considerable quantity of meat to be spoiled, for bloody fluids scatter in muscle tissues.

Generally, a shoulder strike damages bone and muscle to such an extent that the animal is anchored, a very desirable situation. Today, when the woods are swarming with hunters, a portion of which don't hesitate to swipe a nice buck, it's important to place bullets that stop deer within a short distance.

Heart Shots

It's been interesting over the years to see where some experts place the hearts of mule deer in their cutaway drawings. They have located this organ in the strangest positions: mid-body, up with the lungs; rearward, nearly in line with the diaphragm. Yet, a person wouldn't be too wrong if he aimed for the spots in which these experts indicate the heart is situated, for the deer would likely be killed. The heart, nevertheless, would remain untouched.

Actually, the heart lies much lower and more forward than the average hunter suspects. To strike this organ one should aim about four to five inches above the bottom of the brisket and approximately seven to eight inches behind the point of the brisket. Obviously, this presents a couple of problems. First, a hunter while thus aiming low and forward could miss the animal, although a strike in the front legs or higher on the body are possibilities. Second, portions of the front legs "shield" the heart of a broadside deer, but a good bullet should penetrate sufficiently. However, I've seen high-speed, rapidly expanding bullets blowup on bones and shoulder muscles and never reach the heart. Let's assume that the hunter does hit the deer's heart. Almost always such a strike is fatal within a short time, although some heart-shot deer continue running for 100 yards or so.

Lung Shots

The lungs are by far the best place of all to hit a deer. Most of the muleys that I've bagged, I'm proud to say, were killed with bullets through one or both lungs. All deer either fell where hit or ran only a short distance. Only two were not recovered. These animals ran about 100 yards and were pounced on by thieves.

One distinct advantage of the lung shot is that a rifleman has a fairly large target area. Even though he misses these two large organs, chances are good for a strike in the heart below, the spine above or forward in the shoulders, all of which, as pointed out previously, anchor a deer or make recovery possible within a reasonable distance. Most lung-hit animals not dropped on the spot can be followed easily. Usually, a bullet rips a fairly large hole, and the blood-trail is very apparent even on multicolored autumn leaves. Lungs of deer are easily reached by a bullet, too, especially on a broadside shot, for an excellent bullet slices soft rib bones with little difficulty. If, however, a hunter takes a frontal-lungs shot, his bulet must push through considerable shoulder muscles and bone.

The best pose for a deer to be in for a strike in the lungs, of course, is broadside—a shot which the average hunter rarely has. However, a good huntsman, the man who has studied the problems and spent a number of years in the mountains, has the know-how to find and approach deer and often has broadside—at least quartering—shots at the lungs area. This man also has the patience to wait, if necessary, until he has a reasonably clear blast at the lungs—which is quite important. The beginner? His is the responsibility of developing skills until his shots result in reasonably clean kills—rather than an exploding mess of bloody meat, a disgraceful waste of valuable protein.

SCOPES AND OPEN SIGHTS

The controversy over the merits of scopes and open sights is almost dead. Very few individuals today argue the advantages of iron sights; for most western hunters have found that they can place their bullets much better with scoped rifles even on fairly close, running deer. Bullet strikes in the heart-lungs area which previously were rather difficult beyond 100 yards with open sights are now commonplace with the aid of a scope. A variable scope is best: use 2X-3X power while still hunting in timber; 4X-5X while nest and pass hunting; and 7X-9X for longish shots across canyons and basins.

REACTION TO BULLET STRIKES

Everyone who hunts mule deer knows that each muley reacts somewhat individually to bullet strikes because of temperament, degree of alarm, etc. But over the years sportsmen have observed definite generalities, and the following are some you'll hear around evening campfires.

If a deer falls instantly, as though poleaxed, he's been hit in the brain, forward portion of the spine or base of the antlers. When shot through the brain or spine in front of the diaphragm, he's yours. However, as previously indicated, grazing strikes in these areas may only stun momentarily and the animal may rise and race away. A mule deer blasted through the brain doesn't behave like a forest grouse whose head has been snipped off by a hot slug. A grouse is a fright: jumping and thrashing about on the forest floor. A muley may only quiver a bit before dying.

Friends and I have never seen a deer killed by a strike on its antlers. Usually, they flip their noses upward and shake their heads. But a solid smack near the base of an antler sometimes knocks a buck askiddle. And he may appear to be dead. In several deer camps I've heard stories of bucks so grounded. The scenario is almost monotonous: lucky nimrod rushes up, thrusts his knife into the sticking point, but, while skinning the carcass, fails to locate a bullet wound—anywhere. Then a hunter-pal arrives and points to a trace of metal on one of the antlers.

When a deer buckles in the middle, he's taken a bullet in the mid-spine. If he humps up, but remains standing and extends his neck, he's been hit in the stomach or intestines. Struck in the face, a muley often elevates his head and staggers backward. Sometimes he vigorously shakes his head.

Once, while hunting with a friend, I shot a buck that rose on his hind legs and tumbled backward down a hillside. The '06 bullet had smashed his heart. Other hunters tell of identical experiences. Another very characteristic reaction of a heart-shot muley is to start running quickly, go rapidly from 10 to 100 yards and then collapse in mid-stride. Muleys sometimes jerk their front legs upward when struck in the heart.

If a deer limps or drags a leg, the cause is clear. If a walking animal appears to fall forward, but quickly catches himself, he's been struck on a front leg. If his posterior lurches to the side, a rear leg has been damaged.

Several years ago I overheard two friends comparing notes: both had placed bullets into the upper diaphragm region of two large bucks. Both deer had jumped quickly to the side and "swapped ends." Years ago in the Delores River district of eastern Utah I saw a buck stop when hit in the lungs, extend his neck and then drop dead. And what experienced hunter hasn't seen a deer jump into the air when a slug exploded beneath him, spraying him with bits of gravel or lead?

Have you ever banged a muley amidships when his stomach was filled with mushy, chewed browse? Beginners often smack animals in the guts—and everyone who hunts deer year after year will occasionally be so unlucky. The "wunk" sound of a stomach strike isn't easily forgotten. Nor is the "ponk" echoing from a strike on the hams, heavy shoulder or neck muscles.

However, the most unusual sound is made when a slug smacks a deer's antlers. Two of us were sitting back-to-back on a large log in an Oregon forest when my companion sighted a buck sneaking toward us down a logging road. Without comment, he quickly fired. We both heard a "ka-rack," a sound not unlike that made when a person snaps an inch-thick piece of dry aspen over his knee. The buck escaped, but I believe my friend still has part of an antler which he keeps as a conversation piece.

At close range a rifle report may cover the sound of a bullet strike, but at mid-range (100 yards) one ordinarily hears them both. Long distance hits may be audible, depending upon a favorable wind. Be alert, also, for cries of wounded deer. Only rarely do they utter sounds, though suffering from terrible wounds. But friends and I have heard muleys wounded in the rear spine and kidney-loin area sometimes bleat much like domestic sheep.

Unalarmed mule deer usually drop in their tracks from heart-lungs shots—but not always, even when smacked with super magnums. Sometimes they stagger for a few seconds before toppling over. Though knocked to earth, some rise and run a hundred steps or so, even with heart or lungs in shreds. Frightened, hard-running muleys occasionally show no indication of being hit—never even breaking stride though struck in the heart, lungs or stomach. It's amazing the amount of punishment fired-up animals can absorb when their nervous systems have already been shocked with one or more bullets.

Although sure-footed, deer occasionally stumble because of rodent burrows, rocks, logs, etc. But usually, when deer break stride, they've been hit. Standing, quiet muleys may merely "hitch" a shoulder when hit. A pal shot at a five-pointer and saw the buck double-step, shuffle his feet. He found the rascal dead just under the far lip of a ridge. A momentary break from standing or walking into a brisk trot or run generally indicates a bullet has gone home. A bounding mule deer has approximately the grace of a flying whistler swan and a change in his high, crisp bound may indicate he's absorbed a bullet. The bounce suddenly becomes less high—and more awkward.

Other hunters have told me that muleys often revolve their tails when hit. This may be true, but I haven't observed such behavior. Some writers claim that "both muleys and white-tails clamp their tails down" upon being struck with a bullet. They may do; I don't know. It's very difficult to see what a muley's small, scrumpy tail is doing. After shooting at a deer I usually watch for more interesting reactions.

Have you occasionally seen a small cloud of dust, hair, snow or water fly from a muley's pelt after a bullet strike? Muleys sometimes urinate upon being hit and such evidence can be found along their escape trails. However, don't place too much emphasis on this fact alone. It may be a coincidence—the deer reacting just like we human animals upon being frightened and just having to visit the bathroom. When a deer, particularly a doe, leaves the herd, chances are the animal has been hit. However, nearly everyone knows that old, experienced bucks sometimes split away from the herd even though not wounded.

If a pal is near, ask him to call your shots. But remember that a bullet may glance from a bone or pass through the animal and ricochet from a branch or rock and appear to have missed. An Idaho friend had such an experience: bullet zipped through a deer, struck a rock beyond, ricocheted and stirred dust about 10 feet away. May I add my humble opinion to the pleas of many big game managers that most wounded deer could be recovered if hunters would observe a deer's reaction when hit? True, the animal may only be creased, but it could be a mortal wound. Regardless of observation, particularly if the sight picture and trigger release were good, a hunter should go for a look-see to the spot where the deer was at time of firing.

WHEN YOU HIT YOUR DEER

When Mr. Muley Buck goes down, don't make the mistake, as I did when a youngster, of dashing toward a deer, whooping like a Comanche. While down in a ravine, where I couldn't see the deer, the four-pointer recovered and escaped. You might remember a bit of granddad's advice which has paid well for me on several later occasions: "When an animal is grounded, quickly chamber another cartridge and remain in a good position—where you can watch. Only when reasonably sure that the creature is anchored, should you walk toward him." A possible exception to the above statement: in heavily hunted localities, go immediately to the grounded animal—for an obvious reason.

A few muleys—approximately 15 per cent—rise and endeavor to run away. From an advantageous position, with rifle ready, it's possible to prevent most escapes. Usually, a deer moves slowly upon rising, and another bullet can easily be placed into the heart-lungs-shoulders. But keep shooting as long as the opportunity is good, even though the slugs may smack the hams or other undesirable locations. To prevent a suffering animal from escaping is now of utmost importance. If unable to score another strike, or if the animal continues running even though hit again, carefully note its direction of escape.

When a muley shows no indication of rising—a minute is long enough to wait—carefully note his location. Find a strikingly different object near the animal such as a prominent rock, tree, etc.

Now, remove that piece of brightly colored toilet paper (Have you ever tried to locate white john-tissue against a background of snow?) which you've brought along for this specific function, and attach it to a bush or tree near where the shooting occurred. Don't leave a handkerchief, coat or hat. In all likelihood, you won't want to retrace your footsteps—and you could become disoriented and lose these items.

As you hike toward the deer, glance back at the john-paper occasionally, for with every footstep scenery changes. It's especially troublesome during periods of fog, rain or snow. A man I casually know follows a compass heading to his deer. When a person must detour from a straight course because of a canyon or impassable brush or trees, a little horse sense is mighty handy, and it's here that a friend can be very helpful. He'll likely volunteer to remain on the spot and direct you with hand signals. Neither should yell if another method of communication is impossible. To shout in the hills, except in an emergency, is to identify yourself as a very amateur woodsman, a block-head. If the deer can't be found, you've either chosen a poor landmark or you are confused. Retrace your footsteps to the toilet paper and relocate the deer. A friend once backtracked three times before finding his buck. The only possible "mark," a red sandstone boulder, became hidden by 10-foot high scrub oaks as he approached his muley.

After finding your deer, don't lay your rifle aside, unsheathe your knife and walk near the animal—no matter how dead he may appear. Shoot him again if he is still alive. This is a merciful thing to do, and it could save you much trouble, perhaps your life. Carry a round or two with completely jacketed bullets. A small hole through the neck vertebrae where they join the head is immediately fatal and doesn't materially damage a cape for mounting. A hole between the eyes is much more difficult to repair.

How does one determine whether a deer is dead—or merely in shock? An old-timer whom I met long decades ago in the woods near Ashton, Idaho, appears to have a good answer: "It's a matter of experience, son. Sure, it's all right to kick a deer in the rump from a spot where he can't get you with his hind hoofs or his antlers. But look at his head. Most always his mouth is open, his tongue hanging loose. Eyes are also open and vacant—dull. Beware of a muley whose eyes are squinty closed and whose nostrils are oozing bubbly blood. The legs of a dead muley will be extended—not pulled up under his body. He's relaxed; and, when you push him with your boot—remember, from his topside—he'll roll like a bag of jelly. All this—coupled with the fact that he's taken a bullet through a vital part of his body—generally makes him a very dead muley —but not always."

A hunter's presence, his voice—especially his touch—sometimes gives a deer the impetus to rise and run—occasionally toward a hunter. Don't immediately straddle a deer for picture-taking or sticking. Throat cutting is unnecessary and a bloody practice, anyway.

Many stories of bucks which have risen and battled humans are related with flourish around campfires. Now it's my turn.

While a youngster—but I should have known better—I experienced some embarrassment with a three-pointer! As the buck ran quartering away up the side of the ravine, my bullet struck him in the left shoulder, breaking the bone. He thumped hard to the ground but rose and ran swiftly, in spite of his handicap. A blood-trail led us about one-quarter mile to where he lay, head up, beneath a large piñon tree.

An older friend nudged the buck with the muzzle of his rifle and then with his toe. "Go in and stick 'im," he urged. I hesitated, but the eyes of several experienced companions ringing the buck gave me courage. After placing my '06 against the trunk of a tree, I walked slowly toward the muley, knife in hand. Upon feeling my fingers on his right antler, he rose to his feet more quickly than 16 cats. My circulation froze; the knife flew. Somehow I managed to latch onto the muley's antlers. There we stood: eyeball to eyeball. I wished that I was 49 miles away. As the deer pushed me around in a small cloud of dust, someone shouted: "Stand clear! When he's broadside, I'll blast 'im!" "Gawd, no!" from another friend. "You'll hit Roby!"

Even with a broken leg and after losing a large quantity of blood, the buck, I'm sure, would have injured me but for the action of a courageous friend. A big bruiser, well over 200 pounds, he spread his arms and engulfed that deer in a magnificent, all-pro football tackle. Down we three went into the dirt and the pine needles. Several more bodies quickly joined the melee of twisting bodies and, happily, someone remembered to cut the deer's throat.

LOOK BEFORE YOU LEAVE

Two friends and I were sitting in our jeep straddling a low ridge near Cottonwood Creek, on the north slope of Utah's Uinta Mountains, when someone spotted four muleys. They were moving toward us, up a shallow ravine. The deer, all females, apparently sensed that humans were near; they were very alert, trotting a few steps, pausing, rotating their big ears. Another hunter was standing beside his truck, approximately 100 steps farther up the ridge, placing him about 200 yards away from the buckskins. Although each of our permits entitled us to a buck and one antlerless animal, we were trophy hunting and not interested in does. However, the stranger was.

He opened up and, after several ka-oomphs from his rifle, we saw one of the deer flip around and then run-limp up the ravine. The shooter climbed into his truck, and we thought that he was going to follow the cripple up the draw, for it was passable some distance for four-wheel drive vehicles. Instead, he reversed over to the road and was soon out of sight in the cedars. We cussed a little and vowed that we would have words with a certain jasper owning a red truck when we encountered him again.

Temperatures were low that morning, and I was shivering cold. However, a little exercise would take care of that problem. Two or three inches of new snow and a good blood-trail made following the doe easy. After about a mile of tracking, I shot the suffering critter and hung the carcass in a tree. The stranger's bullet had clipped the bone in the doe's left front leg near the "knee."

Forest Lake Basin, over the hill from Alta ski resort near Salt Lake City, Utah, is very difficult to hunt. Still, through the years this tangle of conifers, aspens and maples has produced a number of beautiful trophies. The second weekend of the season found me sitting on a limestone rock at the head of the basin. Another hunter was likewise perched on a rock to the south, about 300 yards away.

I was dreaming of a high-antlered buck that I had seen in the same area the previous week, when shots erupted to the west. I turned my alert button full up and began glassing a little park near where the shooting had occurred. Suddenly the man across the basin began blasting at a buck racing across another clearing midway between us. I heard the telltale wunk of a bullet meeting flesh, but the muley continued running until hidden by trees. After about five minutes, the hunter was still sitting on his rock. So, cupping my hands, I called. "Missed him!" came the reply. Only after some encouragement did the stranger agree to hike down into the bottom of the basin to have a look.

I was there first and had already found the deer but decided to stand aside to see what this jasper would do. There was no snow, but a thin carpet of wet leaves covered the ground. Using a fair blood-trail and disturbed leaves, a high school sophomore could have found that muley. However, after a few minutes of flubbing around, this joker was ready to give up and hike back to his perch in the rocks. Here was one of the few times in my life that I've wanted to kick a fellow human in the gut. Instead, I led him to the fallen monarch which I'm sure was the buck I had seen the previous weekend.

These are a couple of instances where hunters could easily have recovered deer which they had hit. Over many years of hunting, companions and I have found a number of wounded and dead deer, some of them magnificent trophies that were wasted, in most instances, because hunters failed to go where the deer were when fired upon. Why do hunters fail to "look before they leave"? First, too many persons don't watch for small telltale strike-reactions when they shoot at deer. If a muley doesn't drop or struggle violently, many nimrods conclude that they've missed. After all, they've read in a dozen widely distributed shooting and hunting magazines about the devastating effects of magnum rifles on big game! Second, many hunters are too lazy.

When there is no obvious evidence of a bullet strike, many hunters go on their way looking for other deer. A few walk to where the critter was standing if the animal showed slight wounding, but fail to pursue further when there is little evidence on the earth of a strike. Nearly all hunters take a look if the muley indicated it was in major trouble before slipping away into cover. And, when a large quantity of blood is found, most hunters follow until a deer has been located, darkness or weather prevents further search, or until the animal stops bleeding.

Not many muleys rise and run away when a good bullet is properly placed—perhaps 15 per cent. But occasionally animals struck in the heart-lungs run as far as 100 yards. The chief problem is that large numbers of muleys are struck in poor locations—around the fringes. Nearly all creased animals try to escape. Even though there is no evidence that a bullet has been placed into a deer, a sportsman always goes and has a look-see. As we have previously noted, a bullet can pass through a game animal, ricochet from a branch or stone and stir dust some distance away, giving the impression of a miss. When you arrive at the spot where Mr. Antlers was fired upon and find obvious evidence of wounding—and there are other hunters in the area—saddle up shank's pony and follow the animal's trail immediately.

However, in primitive areas or localities where it is unlikely that a thief will clamp his tag on your trophy, proceed more slowly. First, survey the scene from a short distance away. Don't destroy the spoor with your big feet. Blood is the easy, obvious clue, and even a small amount quickly draws attention. But don't let an absence of the red stuff discourage or befuddle you. A wound may not bleed for several yards— perhaps only a drop here and there out to 50 or 60 paces—when a bullet enters the heart-lungs cavity and disintegrates.

If a deer is hit when standing, entrance and exit holes may shift to another location when the deer moves, and the wound may bleed little —perhaps not at all. Sometimes pieces of dislodged fat also plug wound channels. If you regularly read outdoor magazines, you know that some writers explain in minute detail how to interpret blood sign: a little means this, a great pool, that; light colored blood one thing, dark another. I've always been very skeptical of placing too much importance on the color of deer blood. As a biologist I know that blood exiting by way of a large artery from one side of the heart is bright red, having recently been oxygenated by the lungs; while blood being collected by veins and channeled back toward the other side of the heart is dark red. But once arterial and venous bloods have been mixed by a bullet wound and then spilled on earth, grass, leaves, rocks and snow, it's nearly impossible for the average sportsman—and the experts—to know whether it is arterial or venous blood, or the location from where it originated.

An uncle with whom I've hunted on umpteen occasions, once summed up the "blood situation" quite well: "A little blood at the site where a deer has been hit, or along it's escape trail, usually means a superficial wound. However, the animal could be filling up inside. Entrance wounds don't bleed much. Exit wounds inflicted at close and medium range are larger and pass considerable blood. But a bullet at long range may zip unexpanded through a deer and leave insignificant holes. At long distance a bullet slows considerably, loses energy, and an animal can absorb the damage and run away. Death may result only from internal bleeding and when organs such as the heart, lungs and kidneys no longer function. A large amount of blood at the site of bullet strike and along the escape route indicates a major wound. But remember that a little blood on snow looks like gallons. When blood and stomach contents are mixed, the facts are obvious. About the only really significant conclusion I reach upon finding blood on the spot where I've hit a deer, is that the animal is wounded—and I have a job to do: to track that muley down."

No blood? Then look for other evidence. Deer hair is brittle and a bullet cuts or loosens a surprising amount that is easily found on snow, less easily on bare earth and rocks. However, among leaves, scattered rocks and in grass, finding cut hair is very difficult. You will probably find hair before blood, when you hit a running animal. Wounds in the face and lower legs, where hair is short, leave little or no hair-evidence.

Stomach and intestinal contents are almost as obvious on snow as blood, but are often overlooked if a deer is hit when standing or running through vegetation or rocks.

You may find a piece of fat that has been blown out of the animal. A companion and I once came upon a discouraged hunter who was certain that he had hit a buck. "Sights looked good; even heard the bullet plop," he insisted. But there was no evidence on the ground: blood, stomach contents, hair—nothing. Then my pal retrieved a 2-3-inch piece of fat hanging in sage several feet away. The stranger immediately became interested again. And the following day when we passed his camp, he showed us a mature buck that he had found less than an hour's distance from that piece of fat. Muleys during the fall almost always carry considerable fat in the visceral cavity, along the back near the loins and over the hams.

Usually one can also find tracks, especially in snow and moist earth. Yet, on hardpan earth and rocks, hoof prints may be impossible to locate. Under these conditions a deer appears to have flown out of the area. One may have trouble reading tracks when other deer have moved over the ground. However, if the muley was alone when hit, some interpretation can be made, particularly if the animal staggered about. A bit of proof, coupled with observations at time of shooting, amounts to considerable evidence of a wounded deer. However, remember this: normal tracks leading out of the area certainly do not indicate that the animal is unharmed. But most hunters don't know the usual tracking patterns of walking, trotting and running deer.

Perhaps as many as 75 per cent of the deer which rise and race away could be recovered. Several years ago I read that if the number of game animals left to rot each autumn were known, it would be considered a national disgrace. Assume each deer you shoot at has been hit. *Always*— I repeat—*always* go and have a look before leaving, particularly when the sights looked good at trigger release. On-the-spot evidence may determine whether a person should follow a deer's trail for 300 yards or 3 miles. Unravel the story of what happened; it's often more exciting than the actual shooting.

TO WAIT OR TO PUSH YOUR DEER

Spokesmen for the school of thought who advocate: "Sit down, smoke a cigarette and wait for your buck to stiffen up or bleed to death," have been writing outdoor books and magazine articles for a long time. And in recent years the following quotes have appeared, indicating that the school is still very much alive:

"When the animal has been shot through the shoulder or legs, wait fifteen minutes before following the trail."

"If the game lies down for a short time the wound will stiffen and the animal will not rise as quickly when approached."

"A stomach-shot deer should be waited out for a slightly longer time, twenty minutes or so."

I strongly suspect that the authors of these and similar statements are merely rewriting questionable advice which has been monotonously repeated through the decades—not to inform hungry outdoor readers but to sell copy. The original group of "wait and stiffen" writers-sportsmen black powder weapons which shot lead bullets which expanded very little. Consequently, a slug zipped through an animal, death resulting chiefly from hemorrhage, not shock. In the meantime, Mr. Antlers ran on his way until a vital organ no longer functioned or his blood bank was drained.

Weapons and bullets have changed since then. So have people; a number of citizens don't hesitate to steal venison. If you operate in an area where large numbers of hunters are thrashing about, take this advice: follow a wounded deer as quickly as possible. Shooting attracts other men. Often, possession is ten-tenths of the law.

Act quickly then—follow the deer for 300 to 400 yards. As we've previously seen, nearly all animals hit in the heart-lungs are found before you've hiked 100 steps—also some of those struck in the paunch, shoulder, hams and neck. If a muley is still going strong at 400 yards, stop and analyze the situation. You probably need to suck in several gallons of air, anyway. Meanwhile, decide whether it is best to wait or to follow. When a deer is still bleeding copiously, continue in hot pursuit. In primitive areas, however, waiting causes no harm. The animal is bleeding to death, is likely some distance ahead and will continue in flight until it dies on its feet or lies down, never to rise again.

A muley struck in the visceral cavity can sometimes travel for hours and miles if pressed, perhaps equally as far if not pressed. In spite of what the experts write, no one knows what a stomach-wounded animal will, or can, do. Such a deer may lie down within a hundred yards; or it may lead you a merry chase covering 15 miles. Friends and I have also found that some deer, when struck in the legs—even those with broken limbs—may travel long distances once the initial shock subsides. However, sometimes they find a nearby thicket of brush or trees and hole up. We've discovered also that very sick deer lie down immediately, while those that have recovered from initial shock may remain standing in thick cover and watch, very alertly, not only their back-trail, but in all directions.

"Stiffen up" is a term that has been overworked by outdoor writers. What does it mean? I wrote to an author who frequently uses the words for his definition. However, he must have suspected entrapment, for he never replied. A wounded creature, man or lower animal, doesn't stiffen. His ability to move after wounding depends chiefly upon shock and amount of tissue destruction. "Stiffen" is a poor term, and a writer who uses the word in his little essays usually errs in several other ways, too.

Waiting 20 to 30 minutes after wounding a game animal often enables the creature to recover from shock, to outdistance the hunter or find a place to hide where it may be impossible to dig him out. Deer, especially those struck on the fringes, often travel almost normally after the effects of shock have subsided.

Another important item to remember is that blood and other trail signs are most distinct immediately after a deer has passed. Rain and snow can quickly obliterate spoor. Other animals may also erase or obscure tracks and blood. When a deer is shot late in the afternoon, it's imperative that one follow immediately because a muley recovered the following day, although alive, is of questionable value, except as a trophy. Another very important consideration is that a quick follow-up ends the suffering of a sensitive creature. The above advice doesn't stand up 100 per cent in the face of field experience. But it will, perhaps, as often as 90 per cent of the time.

FIND THOSE CRIPPLES

Every sportsman endeavors to kill his deer quickly and cleanly at the location where the animal is fired upon. But, even excellent marksmen occasionally strike a deer on the fringes because of unseen branches deflecting a bullet, movement of the animal, tricky wind—or for one of the other 19 possibilities. However, every autumn thousands of mule deer are wounded and run away because some damn fool was stretching the trajectory of his weapon. Yet, at least 75 per cent of these cripples could be recovered were the hunter to exercise common sense and diligence.

Deer not found within 100 to 200 yards of where struck almost always have been smacked in the stomach-intestines, legs, neck—somewhere on the edges. And, as we've seen, there is no possible way to determine how far these animals will travel before dying, if they die at all. Yet, one point should be clear: the hunter has a job to do—to follow the animal until there is reason to believe the wound is insignificant, impossible conditions arise preventing further search or, happily, the critter is found.

Where do wounded deer go? Once again we must deal with generalities based upon years of observation. Most severely wounded muleys run as though blind. These animals are recovered within a few yards. Muleys less seriously wounded—those whose senses are still operative— were probably nearly 100 per cent correct. For they were armed with run in a direction offering the best escape route. This is their home ground; they know the terrain. Their course may be the same they would follow if not wounded, at least until out of the hunter's sight. When a person knows the country well, he can sometimes determine where a deer will go in its attempt to escape. Several experts have written that wounded deer go toward water. I haven't found this to be true of mule deer.

Gravity often answers our question. Deer with broken limbs find uphill travel more difficult. A muley winged in a front leg can still move very well, although not as fast as a normal buckskin. A broken rear leg, however, really hampers a deer. Over open terrain a horseman can easily run down a muley with a broken leg. An animal whose strength is ebbing rapidly usually lies down or, when pushed, goes downhill. But don't rely on these observations 100 per cent. Lightly wounded deer may travel through fairly open country, even along game trails and forest roads, endeavoring to manufacture space. But, on the other hand, they may head for cover. Friends and I have found that nearly all badly wounded deer endeavor to find a patch of dense brush or trees. Here they are difficult to locate and shoot, because they are fighting for their lives. It may be a merry game for a hunter but not for a deer.

Once a deer is out of sight, a hunter, obviously, must depend upon blood, tracks and other trail spoor to follow the animal. Only rarely does a trail appear as though the buck were carrying a can of red paint with a hole in the bottom. But as long as bleeding is regular, the spatterings are easy to follow, particularly on snow—a little more difficult on grass, rocks and earth. When a blood trail is obvious, a woodsman can watch some distance ahead. With his eyes up, he may see Mr. Big Ears if he flushes. But, when blood sign is sporadic or absent for some distance, trailing becomes more difficult. When this happens, mark the spot where blood was last seen with a bit of toilet paper or handkerchief. Then find the next splotch.

When blood disappears on large rock outcroppings or on dry, hard earth, search in the general direction the animal has been traveling to locate the next bit of blood. When this fails, use the "circle method." If a deer is following a forest road or game trail, the task is fairly simple. During a rain- or snowstorm casual blood sign is easily obliterated, and then a person must rely upon tracks. However, during a heavy rain- or snowfall, tracks may even disappear. Blood spoor isn't always found on the earth—sometimes on bushes, rocks and trees beside the trail.

Trying to deduce where an animal has been hit from blood and other evidence found along a trail is often difficult. Once a companion was certain that we were following a leg-crippled muley. Later, we discovered that the deer was bleeding from the mouth. However, when blood is found right in the tracks, in all likelihood there is a wound somewhere on the leg. Evidence that a foot is being dragged is easily detected in snow, dust and soft mud—almost impossible otherwise.

Signs along a trail may indicate that you are following a sick animal: continued heavy bleeding, staggering, stomach contents, falling, etc. Then your buck may turn sharply aside, seeking seclusion—to lie down, a bed from which he may never rise. A muley often turns abruptly aside after spotting his pursuer.

A little blood along a trail, particularly after a woodsman has followed a deer for a long distance, often adds up to a considerable amount, especially on snow. A muley can travel for 10 miles or more while regularly dripping blood. Compared with man, they have tremendous stamina.

When blood disappears or becomes sporadic, a woodsman must then follow tracks. In snow, except where the animal is traveling with other deer, hoofprints can be followed, even through dense thickets, by a child with a 50-pound anchor around his neck. In mud or soft earth, the task is only slightly more difficult. Following tracks over dusty earth is also fairly simple. But tracking in leaves is something else. Among freshly fallen leaves little evidence remains that can be found except by a deerhound. However, leaves which have been on the ground for several weeks, especially those which have been covered with snow or moistened with rain, are disturbed by a passing deer to the extent that an observant person can follow the animal's course. Especially when the muley is running. Obviously, relatively dry leaves found on top of wet ones must have been churned upward by the deer's hoofs. Conifer needles and deciduous leaves lying on top of a forest floor are bleached a different shade of green, brown, yellow or grey than those underneath. Viewed from a distance of 25 yards or so, one can often detect these slight variations in shade and follow a wounded animal.

Probably the most difficult tracking is over large, flat rocks and hardpan, areas where once-moist earth has been baked iron-hard. To follow deer across such places is nearly impossible. Skilled trackers then note the general direction the muley has been traveling and, failing to pick up tracks when rocks and hardpan give way to soil again, circle or course back and forth until they relocate the trail. Traveling deer generally head in a definite direction, drifting aside only when obstructions appear.

Your muley's trail may also cross those of other deer—many times in good deer habitat. If you stray to other tracks, you'll botch the entire operation. Occasionally, too, you will drive other deer before you and their spoor may obscure, even obliterate, those you are following.

When one must move from one drop of blood to another, constantly watching the ground, a pal can be very helpful. One hunter walks some distance to the side—perhaps along the elevated side of a ravine, while the other trails. Frequently, a wounded animal can be found and killed more easily using this technique. Or, when a muley is obviously headed up or down a canyon and traveling slowly, a single hunter can hike some distance up the hillside, glass for a minute or so—even walk some distance—then descend again into the bottom to cut the tracks.

Deer fooprints, separated by 10 or so feet, indicate that something— probably you—has spooked the buck and he is racing away. Wobbling tracks indicate a staggering deer—one in trouble—particularly if the tracks suddenly flounder downhill. However, it's very difficult for the casual muley hunter to realize that a deer is wobbling, for a little experience is necessary before a person can detect and interpret the nonsynchron- ized hoofprints of a wounded muley.

Crippled deer occasionally lie down, and the trailer should study these locations for a few minutes. Did the deer lose considerable blood? The very fact that the animal made a bed indicates that he is in trouble. However, a deer usually lies down several times—and at more frequent intervals—before making his final bed. When a deer falls while ascending or descending a hill, he's in deep difficulty. An animal may also tumble as he runs. These locations are easily found, for the skid marks are ob- vious, being marked by blood and hair on stones and branches.

To be able to follow a deer up- or cross-wind is a choice measure of luck. Almost never have I recovered a muley that was wounded on the fringes when I had to sneak along his trail with my nose to the ground and trail down-wind. But, whether you are following down-, cross- or up-wind, be constantly aware of its direction.

Stop occasionally and look ahead. A muley, suddenly aware that he is being followed, often jumps and runs like a scalded monkey. There- after, he'll watch his back-trail and be immeasurably more alert and difficult to find. When a traveling muley enters a jungle of brush or trees, plan a surprise. Check the wind and circle to the other side of the jungle. If, after a reasonable period, the rascal doesn't appear, still hunt back through the cover. Look to the rear occasionally. The animal is battling for his life and instinctively may do something that is more than a match for your ingenuity.

When trailing conditions are difficult, your task is sometimes enor- mous. The animal could be hiding scant feet away in a dense tangle and be overlooked. Deer are masters, particularly when wounded, at remaining immobile for a long time—then, after a hunter has passed, slipping away into another part of the cover. Older, experienced deer sometimes make trailing very difficult—but extremely interesting. If you fail to locate Mr. Antlers by still hunting, he may have stolen out of the tangle. Skirt the edge of the cover and pick up his trail again. When a companion is available, use this bit of stratagem: one hunter circles to the far side of the cover while the second man follows the trail. Two friends have successfully used this little scheme several times. Another acquaintance abandons the spoor and still hunts when a muley enters a thicket, watching the wind carefully and moving very slowly.

When you locate a wounded muley, about 20 per cent of the time he will be partly concealed by a rock, bush or tree—watching, ostrichlike. He may instinctively believe that he is concealed. Then it's a head, neck or spine shot. Seventy per cent of the time you'll find a flushed, moving animal. Shooting under these circumstances is difficult and conditions determine what should be done. However, try as best you can to anchor him—for several reasons, one of which is that if you miss, or wound slightly, he will never again seem to stop. He knows he's being followed, and additional fright or a wound adds impetus to his escape. Don't worry too much about spoiling meat or a trophy head. Primary concern is to end the suffering of a wounded animal. Five per cent of the time your muley will be lying or standing in the open. He's not long for this world, and you can approach near enough to be certain of a killing strike. The remaining 5 per cent? The animal is dead. You're a little sad when you lift his regal head from the ground, but you're also happy that you've come to the end of the trail.

I'm occasionally asked if birds and other small animals locate and markdown wounded deer. Hunters have told me that they have had magpies and jays locate, even follow, their wounded muleys. This has not happened to me. Magpies, however, soon discover a dead muley. I've found a number of carcasses while prowling the mountains after the deer season had closed by watching these black and white scavengers. With a glass, sit in good deer habitat where you can see for miles. Invariably, you'll discover a group of quarreling magpies flipping through the air near a carcass.

Severely crippled and starving deer attract coyotes, particularly during late winter-early spring when rodents are still in the deepfreeze. On two occasions I've killed coyotes that were harassing muleys with broken legs. Generally, coyotes don't bother a dead muley for several days. But not always. A number of years ago I had the misfortune to wound a blocky five-pointer just at dusk, and darkness fell before we could find him. We were on his trail at day-break and located his remains an hour later. Coyotes had found him during the night and had left little except antlers, skin and bones.

Sportsmen often inquire how far a deer should be trailed. Much depends upon evidence found at the shooting site and along the trail. I always follow tracks for 200 to 300 yards even though there is no indication of a bullet strike. Is it asking too much that a hunter trail for at least a quarter-mile or so when there is a drop of blood here and there? The following may sound like a waste of energy—and foolish—but I once pursued a gut-shot muley for an entire day before ending the animal's misery. Would you also follow a deer dragging a broken leg for seven hours? All men who cherish the honor of being called sportsmen would do as much. Briefly, one should follow until he is certain that the wound is of little consequence to the deer; until darkness makes further pursuit impossible—and then he should return the following day; or until the trail is unquestionably lost.

For many years I've been recording in a little yellow notebook some extremely interesting information outdoor authors have written about tracking wounded big game.

One sage has written: "Tracks of deer and other hoofed big game animals are as individual as fingerprints." That should interest the FBI! This writer continues; he endeavors to prove that it is not too difficult a chore to follow an animal's specific tracks because of little irregularities, such as a hoof's slightly wavy edge. Admittedly, animal tracks do vary somewhat but not to the extent that this man indicates. As a matter of fact, good, clearly defined deer footprints are difficult to find; and to follow one animal's tracks using small deformations when his prints are intermingled with those of other deer—impossible!

Another matter which is occasionally debated around evening camp-fires—whether a mule deer will jump far to the side, to confuse a trailing hunter—has been answered by a widely read hunter-editor. He writes: "Many times when trailing old wise mule bucks . . . I have found where they have doubled back their trail, then jumped high and wide over some big wind fall in an effort to confuse anyone tracking them." This writer is confused—I mean he's confusing the muley with another four-legged critter which does engage in the acrobatics he's described above.

Many years ago there developed a group of trackers-authors whom a friend refers to as the "raindrop and sprig of grass school." Occasionally, a book or magazine essay still appears by a professor belonging to this college. Such was a chapter from a recent book of hunting lore in which the author found it fairly simple to trail a deer by means of rain-drops knocked from disturbed leaves and a bent sprig of grass here and there. Pardner, doff your hat, for there is a real expert!

Another author wrote that he didn't start on a deer's trail until dark. Using a flashlight and on his hands and knees, he carefully parted grass stems here and there with his fingers. "Suddenly . . . he held it up to the light . . . three strands of coarse, greyish-white deer hair." The man continued for a considerable distance and discovered not one, but two dead deer. Wow!

My little notebook also contains an item concerning an expert tracker who trailed a deer by means of drops of blood here and there—during a rainstorm. One of his ancestors must have been crossed with a wet blood-hound. Another writer points out in a very professional manner that "a deer will try to throw trackers off his trail by following footprints made by other deer." Jaspers have been hanged for less!

Over the years a hodge-podge of unreliable information has been concocted and repeated about tracking big game. It started, I believe, with stories extolling the supposed skills of American Indians, Africans and frontiersmen. These individuals were attributed skills which they didn't possess. Stories of how these super-woodsmen could follow an animal by an infinitesimal bit of blood here and there, a turned leaf, a disturbed bit of sand, a blade of grass slowly moving back into position were read by millions of gullibles. I doubt that these "tracking masters" could read trail sign any better than some modern big-game hunters. We've likewise proved false the fabled marksmanship feats of the law-men, the badmen and hunters of the American frontier.

There is nothing hanky-panky, nothing mystical, about trailing wounded game. Observation is the key. True, some of the best trackers I know have spent a considerable part of their lives in the hills. But, essentially, following a wounded critter is merely the application of horse sense and determination. To develop an appreciable amount of skill in tracking requires several years of experience—learning what to do and what to look for. Unfortunately, few modern hunters have the time or inclination. To maintain a high degree of alertness is important while following game. Interest often drops to half-mast within an hour or a mile or so, especially when spoor is difficult to follow. Inclement weather also discourages many hunters.

Would you believe that only about 10 per cent of the deer hunting public is capable of successfully following a wounded deer by tracking a drop of blood here and there? An acquaintance maintains this figure is too high. In the face of reports from Western game managers that the crippling loss of deer runs from 10 to 40 per cent, every hunter should develop an appreciable amount of trailing skill so that he can subscribe to the sportsman's code which encourages hunters to recover wounded game. True, we can't locate all cripples, but almost everyone can acquire sufficient skill to reduce the crippling loss considerably. Of course, if a person has the price of admission, he can rely upon a guide to trail his wounded animals.

There is much satisfaction in recovering a deer that might otherwise rot or be eaten by scavengers. In fact, when every detail goes just right—luck, weather, etc.—and you have located a deer which might have been lost, you've experienced one of the genuine thrills of hunting.

OWNERSHIP OF DEER

Disputes over ownership of dead or wounded big game animals date back many years. It was Gaius, an ancient Roman, who wrote a landmark statement which became law for centuries: "One does not become the proprietor of a wild beast which he has wounded, but which he has not effectively taken . . . Pursuit alone vests in the sportsman no property in the animal pursued." English and American courts followed the Roman law, and they decided in several instances that a hunter was entitled to the game only if he had "deprived the animal of its natural liberty . . . and brought it within his power." Possession, the courts ruled, was: "actual, physical, bodily seizure of the animal." An early New York case has often been referred to by courts. One Fenning wounded a deer and his dogs chased it for six miles. But a second man, Fargo, finally killed and claimed the animal. Fenning sued but the court ruled that he had no right because he had not "deprived the deer of its natural liberty."

However, such reasoning is sometimes faulty—and has resulted in the awarding of game animals to jaspers who had "put in only finishing shots." Fortunately, recent American decisions have taken a more realistic viewpoint, and courts have ruled that game belongs to the man who has sufficient control over an animal that its escape is "improbable." A Wisconsin court appears to take such a realistic, fair attitude: "Game belongs to the person who has it in circumstances that escape is improbable, if not impossible." Thus, mortal wounding and immediate pursuit has been deemed possession. So, actually, "taking a game animal with the hands" is no longer necessary to establish ownership.

However, over several decades of hunting muleys, I can't recall a single dispute over ownership which has been contested in court. The matter is usually decided on the spot—then and there. Court litigation is expensive and the case may sit on the calendar for years. What happens to the carcass in the meantime? Obviously, everyone loses except the lawyers and judge. Usually, a person gains possession of a carcass if he knows the law, argues forcefully—and has a couple of armed pals nearby. We must be realistic. In spite of court rulings, possession is probably still "nine points of the law." Therefore, try as best you can to "make the first shot count." Drop the deer "on the spot." And follow previous advice to trail quickly a wounded deer—without waiting for the animal to "stiffen up."

Ideally, each case of disputed ownership should be decided on facts. This entails a calm examination of the deer by the interested parties— entrance and exit bullet wounds, whether a particular wound was mortal, identification of spent bullets, etc. Sportsmanship should prevail. But, face the facts; a considerable number of potential thieves are in the mountains each autumn. I believe that an occasional human corpse found in the woods is the result of a dispute over a muley carcass.

8

After You Kill That Deer

DRESSING THAT MULEY

For most hunters the pleasure stops when a muley has been killed. However, before an animal can be eaten, the carcass must be dressed, hauled out of the hills, skinned and butchered. And these tasks most individuals dislike. Consequently, they do an unsatisfactory job. Result: tons of venison are thrown away each fall or fed to pets. This is unfortunate, for venison is expensive—far more than prime beef. Prepared properly, venison is delicious, too—although it can't be compared with the best cuts of beef. But how delicious would prime Hereford be if shot through the guts, chased a mile or so, dragged through mud, leaves and dust, not cooled immediately, nor aged sufficiently and then butchered poorly? It, too, would have a "gamey" flavor!

Most hunters do an unsatisfactory job because they don't know the simple steps to follow in dressing, skinning and butchering a deer carcass. Too, thousands of youngsters hunt for the first time each autumn. Of course, if a person can afford a guide, he can stand aside and let the hired help dirty his hands. But some guides don't cape, dress and skin

animals too well. So, a hunter should be capable of doing the job himself. Remember, how you handle the carcass during the first hour or two
is the deciding factor between delicious and not-so-tasty steaks and
roasts.

The task is easy to learn and accomplish. In fact, one can learn all
essential steps by reading, but the best way is to watch an experienced
outdoorsman and actually participate. It may be possible to visit a
slaughter house or a ranch where domestic animals are being processed.

Before starting to dress your deer, expose some film to assist in re-
membering a remarkable event—the killing of a wonderful game animal.
Better still, if a companion is present, ask him to operate the camera and
record the various steps beginning with your finding the lifeless trophy
until the animal is skinned. Photograph the muley, if possible, where it
fell. However, if necessary to move the deer because of unfavorable light
or other conditions, do not drag if you plan a head-mount or a tanned
hair-skin.

Only rarely does a muley die in a precipitous area where it's necessary to anchor the carcass with a rope to a rock or tree for dressing. If
the head or skin has no trophy value, the animal should be moved to a
place where dressing can be conveniently accomplished, preferably beneath a tree for shade and hanging.

To start, remove your coat, wristwatch and roll up your sleeves, for
you'll have a little blood with which to contend. Grasp one or more of
the muley's legs and turn the animal on its back. From the rear spread
his legs and place them on the outside of your two legs. Then, lift the
penis and cut through the skin beside this organ, back to the anus. Tie
the end of the penis to prevent urine spillage and separate the organ
back to where it enters the body. Females are often still "in milk" during
September and October. Grasp the udder, pull outward and cut all connective tissues around the bag. You may spill a little milk and, although
it may look a little messy, no material harm has been done.

Next, carefully make an incision two to three inches long through
the peritoneum (the tough layer of muscle between the skin and abdo-
men-intestines) in the area from which the penis or udder has been
removed. A bit of intestine may protrude through this small opening.
Stomach and intestines have very thin walls and can easily be cut with
a careless flick of a knife. So, be careful not to puncture them or the
result is a mess. Stomach and intestinal contents impart a very offensive
smell and taste to meat.

Palm up, thrust pointer and middle fingers into this opening, spread
and pull upward. This usually elevates the skin and peritoneum away

from the paunch and intestines. Insert the knife between the fingers, cutting edge up (slicing upward doesn't cut as much hair—hair which falls into the carcass and dulls a knife). Keeping the blade parallel with the incision, cut the skin and peritoneum forward to the rib cage. If you plan to transport the animal immediately, and there is the possibility of flies, dust, leaves, etc. entering the incision, you may wish to keep this opening as small as possible. Actually, a better procedure is to open the carcass from pelvis to rib cage and then close the opening by sewing with stout string.

Now roll the animal onto its side again, preferably with legs pointing downhill. Grasp the edge of the anus (in females this bit of surgery also includes the vaginal tract) and cut around the tube(s)—as deep as the knife will reach. Pull the tube(s) out and tie securely with string. Then reach inside the abdominal cavity and pull the paunch and intestines out, snipping tag ends of connective tissues here and there where these organs attach to the body wall. Be careful. Don't burst the bladder, a tough little sac but easily punctured with a knife. Obviously, front and rear ends of the intestinal tract are still attached. Now, from the inside grasp the rear end, the large intestine which leads to the anus, and pull into the abdominal cavity, using a knife to cut remaining tissues.

With the paunch and intestines out, there is enough space in which to work with a knife to remove the diaphragm, a thin yet tough sheet of muscle separating thoracic (chest) and abdominal cavities like a curtain. Pierce the diaphragm near the edge of the body and run the knife completely around the body. Slicing into the diaphragm is usually accompanied with a gush of warm blood which has collected in the forward portion of the body around the heart and lungs. Then reach inside the chest cavity and sever with a knife the windpipe and gullet as far forward as possible. The gullet (also called esophagus) is smooth to one's touch, but the windpipe looks and feels like a corrugated radiator hose. Grasp the lungs and heart and forcibly pull them out of the body.

You have now earned a short rest. But, before you stretch out in the lazy autumn sunshine, spread eagle the carcass on the ground to drain, incision down.

Don't forget to save the liver and heart, for these organs supply a tasty respite from usual camp fare when properly prepared. Cut the top off the heart, and remove the organ from the sac enclosing it. Place the heart upside down on snow or a clean rock to drain for a minute or two. Also drain the liver (a muley doesn't have a gall bladder, so you needn't worry about spilling bile). Then, if possible, immerse the two organs in a stream or cover with snow. Lacking such conveniences, slip them into a plastic bag and add a little water from your canteen. Changing the water two to three times eliminates most body heat and fluids. By all means don't expose the liver and heart to the air until a crust forms.

When a carcass is to be left in the woods overnight, split the pelvic bones (the aitchbones) at their junction, the symphysis. An ordinary sheath- or a hefty pocketknife can be forced through these bones on a young deer, but it's necessary to use a hatchet or a large, heavy knife on an older animal. This permits access of air to the thick, upper hams. Likewise, the rib cage can be split down to the neck and propped open for rapid cooling. During inclement weather the meat may become wet and, when left uncovered, open flesh is an invitation to scavenger birds and blowflies. In some western localities, jays and magpies sometimes peck at a carcass; to prevent this, or to reduce damage, bag the animal or surround with leafy branches. Opening a deer from neck to anus also permits the introduction of hair and other contaminants during dressing and transporting.

When toting a back-pack or riding a horse, I always carry three very useful items: a tiny, fist-size hoist, several No. 20 spikes, and 25 feet of rope. Once a deer has been opened from anus to neck, it can be hoisted by one man, either head or tail up, in which position internal organs practically fall out. Lacking such a hoist, one man, after removing the viscera, can hang a small deer with a short section of 3/8-inch rope. It's far from easy, but with one arm around the carcass, pull on the rope with the other. A medium to large buck is a job for two to three men. Antlers can also be wedged between branches—and a split hock thrust over a stubbed limb. The spikes are for anchoring the hoist, a rope or the animal's rear legs when there are no low branches on a tree, such as mature aspen.

Never, if at all possible, leave a carcass smack on the ground overnight. And, where there is a choice of a place to hang a deer, select a shaded area, for obvious reasons. Another item to remember: blood drains more completely from a carcass hung forequarters down, especially when the head has been removed. However, the head and neck, unless removed, generally become soiled with blood and body fluids when hung in this position. There are definite advantages when a deer is suspended head up. Besides being much easier to hang, particularly when a hunter is alone, the critter's hide sheds rain and snow better. The cape is also protected from filth and, high in the air, is less likely to be damaged by small animals. On the other hand, there is little opportunity for body fluids to escape. Consequently, much blood remains in the veins and arteries, especially in those of the hams, which can provide some of the best meat. Such fluid retention clearly defeats the purpose of hanging, which is to drain off the animal's body fluids.

The dressing procedure is modified when you kill your muley in a treeless area. Then, the dressed carcass, when left in the field overnight, should be placed, incision upward, across a pile of brush or head-size rocks. Try always to elevate the carcass, at least the hindquarters. When necessary to leave the muley directly on the ground, wedge the animal on its back and prop open the body cavity with short sections of branches.

Whether you hang the deer up or leave it on the ground, always prop the body cavity open. If rain or snow threatens, you may choose to turn the carcass onto its side. However, I've never found that a rain or snow shower particularly diminished the keeping qualities of venison, although a carcass left exposed to several days of continuous warm rain may spoil.

When I have my druthers, I dress, skin, cut away all bullet-shattered flesh, remove all blood with a moistened cloth, half or quarter and enclose the sectioned carcass in muslin sacks—right where the animal fell. Result: blood drains away and the carcass cools quickly. Then we return the following day with a packhorse. Air temperature isn't nearly as important as generally believed. Most deer spoil because of residual body heat. However, warm air, coupled with warm, moist meat, are conditions which encourage growth of bacteria that start meat spoilage.

Most muley hunters by necessity must transport a carcass out of the mountains immediately. When this is the case, keep the body opening to a minimum—eight to ten inches is sufficient. Don't cut the skin back to the arms—or forward through the brisket. Then, after removing the stomach, intestines, heart, lungs, etc., use the point of a knife and two to three feet of cord or small rope, to cross-stitch the incision. Closing this opening prevents any soiling of clothing and horse and saddle with blood and introduction of dust, leaves, etc. Immediately upon arrival at camp, complete the dressing and skinning.

During his step-by-step description of dressing our deer, you've noted that not once have we mentioned "sticking" the muley. Sticking and throat cutting serve no useful function, although occasionally we still read such advice in outdoor magazines and books. Actually, your bullet started the bleeding process and properly dressing an animal completes the job. A trophy hunter avoids all cuts on the head and neck, for the prime purpose of his hunting is the head. Cutting an animal's throat or sticking makes a taxidermist's job quite difficult.

A misconception has grown concerning the necessity of removing a deer's testicles immediately after death. There is not one shred of evidence that a buck's gonads, or their contents, contaminate the meat in any way. Another bit of erroneous trivia that has been kept alive over the years is the belief that scent glands must be removed from the rear legs. Again there is not one trifle of evidence that these glands can by themselves contaminate meat. The only possible way for these secretions to reach the meat is by transfer from hands and knife. And it's not a difficult chore for a careful individual to dress and skin a carcass without fouling the meat with fluids from these scent glands. Still, if you are a skeptic, cut them away, then cleanse hands and knife before continuing the dressing. The tarsal scent glands are on the inside of the rear legs at the hocks; the metatarsal glands, roughly four to five inches below the hock, on the rear-outside. Hair in these glands appears to grow in bunches, and on end.

The real spoiler of good venison isn't scent; it's hair, dirt, urine, intestinal and stomach contents and slowly dissipating body heat.

Another warning we've been hearing from the experts over the years is: "Don't use water to cleanse the carcass of a deer." Instead, one current writer advises us to wipe the body cavity with grass, moss or leaves. One certain way to cause a carcass to look-like-hell is to try to remove blood with leaves, moss and grass!

While hunting with two friends in Idaho, I was astounded to see one of them drag my gutted, hard-earned muley to a nearby creek and plunge the entire animal into water. The carcass was immersed before I could guess my companion's intentions and protest. But, in spite of the fact that we kept the venison for more than two weeks without mechanical refrigeration, the meat didn't spoil. It's much simpler, and more effective, to bring along a piece of absorbent cloth and, dampened from a stream or canteen, cleanse the inside of the muley's carcass. During late November and December hunts I've often used compressed balls of snow, like a sponge, to cleanse the body cavity. Followed with a cloth rubdown, the flesh dries in a few minutes, glazes in about one hour. If gut-shot, always use liberal amounts of snow or water to wash away intestinal contents.

We've also been frequently advised to "smear blood over the carcass to discourage blowflies." Actually, painting with blood attracts these critters and the carcass will frighten the wife and kids when you take it home. Appearance of wild meat has a great deal to do with one's appetite. When blowflies are numerous (usually in early fall when temperatures are still high), it's sometimes difficult to prevent these insects from depositing eggs on meat. They especially seek out moist flesh and dark, hidden recesses. Don't depend, either, on the experts' advice that smearing pepper over the meat will keep flies away. Instead, enclose your muley in a muslin bag. What about those yellow hornets buzzing around a carcass? Some hunters inform me that hornets chase blowflies away. I don't know the exact role of these bees. I do know that blowflies lay eggs on the meat in spite of the hornets. It may be necessary, if transportation isn't immediately available, to cut branches and switch the flies away until darkness or friends with the packhorse or jeep arrive. Whatever the trouble, one must try to save his venison. There is little satisfaction in taking home maggot-infested meat.

Should the hunter find it necessary to leave the deer in the woods overnight, he may be concerned that wild, four-legged critters or birds will destroy his prize. Some birds, especially magpies, often peck away at exposed flesh but, unless left for several days, little damage results. Coyotes often destroy a game animal which has not been found, but these yodelers rarely approach cleaned game for days, fearful of man's ingenuity. A wise person, nevertheless, scuffs the ground to imitate a trap-set and suspends the cloth used to cleanse the animal where it will be agitated by the wind. This crude scarecrow is very effective.

All grass-eating and browsing animals bloat quickly after death. Gas accumulates in the digestive system and it's imperative that the intestinal tract be removed immediately, especially when air temperatures are high or when the carcass is lying in the sun. If, after a buck has been located, the abdomen is obviously rounded and gas can be expelled when one stands on the side of the animal, a hunter will be lucky to save the meat. Venison may even sour within hours if left on snow. To repeat: air temperature is not the primary consideration; dissipation of body heat is the important factor. Every autumn a number of deer are carried home atop vehicles, stuffed between bumper and grille, etc. It's little wonder that many wives refuse to cook the rank stuff. I never cease to be amazed at the poor treatment given potentially good meat. Apparently some hunters care little about the economic value of their kills. But, after spending considerable money and time, it's foolish to waste venison. If a hunter isn't interested in the meat value of his kill, he should give it to a less fortunate person.

When dressing a deer, note the bullet path and damage to tissue and bone. The results may confirm your satisfaction with the bullet. On the other hand, you may wish to try another type during a subsequent hunt. Try to locate the bullet or fragments, for such verifies correct expansion and serves as an excellent conversation piece.

A word of explanation: deer blood may cause your skin to erupt into a mild infection. Unless I wash away the blood immediately after cleaning a deer, a number of small eruptions appear on my hands and remain for several days.

Cleaning and dressing a muley may sound involved, messy and time-consuming, but actually it's quite simple and can be accomplished by an amateur in 20 to 30 minutes.

TRANSPORTING THAT MULEY OUT OF THE HILLS

For most muley hunters the task of moving a carcass to camp is arduous. Consequently, thousands of individuals don't wander far from roads, hoping to drop a buckskin near their wheels. However, killing a muley beside a well-traveled thoroughfare is the exception.

Recent years have seen a vast increase in the number of two- and four-wheel drive vehicles. Hunters roam the hills in or on these machines much like horsemen, and it's amazing to see them traverse steep, rugged terrain. However, a growing avalanche of criticism is presently building against those individuals who use these vehicles unwisely in the mountains.

Perhaps the next best method of moving a muley out of the hills is with a horse. For a number of years friends and I have owned several horses and they have canceled most of the aches and pains of toting deer. The simplest, cleanest way to carry a carcass on a horse: halve or quarter the skinned animal. Then the sections, incased in cloth bags or plastics, are inserted into two large canvas pouches. We use surplus Air Force parachute cargo bags and suspend them on the sides of a riding saddle. This method is especially practicable if your horse is skittish. And some horses are diabolically rambunctious. Only a few horses stand docilely and calmly load deer the first time. Most never feel completely comfortable when they smell deer odors and see the carcass moving toward them through the air.

A simple blindfold often calms a horse, although when a friend placed his jacket over the head of a mare, she thrashed about and kicked him on the thigh. Tying up a front leg generally immobilizes a cayuse. Twisting or biting a horse's ears and smearing deer blood on his nostrils? I've often thought that these bits of torture further irritate an animal and cause him to be more difficult. An excitable nag can often be calmed if a person stands near his head, to the side, talks quietly and pats him on the neck.

Let's assume that the horse is standing calmly, cinches have been tightened comfortably. Cut a 3-4-inch hole through the deer's skin and flesh at a point where the weight of the deer is divided, usually near the diaphragm—and approximately 4-5 inches above the rear end of the brisket. When inexperienced and undecided about the "balance point," place the carcass into the saddle, balance and cut a hole through the body wall near the horn on the saddle. Next, lift the deer high enough to clear the cantle, pass the horn through the hole and gentle the carcass into the saddle. For an obvious reason, this is called the "buttonhole" method. Finally, with a small rope (quarter-inch works fine) secure the pierced upper legs (the lower portions have been removed just below the "elbows" and hocks) to the front cinchrings. Make the ties through both sides of the rings; otherwise, they may twist and gouge the horse. Then, pull the head up, toward the cantle, particularly when the animal is antlered, and tie securely with rope. This elevates the antlers, where they can't prong the horse, and over his back where they can't easily grab at trees and brush. A very large head should be removed, particularly when a mount is planned, and tied to the top of the carcass. When loading a muley on a hillside, place the horse downhill from the carcass and parallel with the slope.

As the horse is led away, someone should walk behind. From this position he can easily detect an unbalanced load. When necessary to shift the muley, loosen the ties, adjust the load to balance and retighten the ropes. One horse with which I'm acquainted merely stops and stands quietly when a saddle and carcass twists off-balance. However, most horses won't tolerate a big-game carcass dangling between their legs. Often they kick and thrash about, may even run or fall and injure themselves.

A very small deer can be tied behind the cantle, but most muleys are so large that they must be carried in the saddle itself. However, I've never seen a muley so big that a 1,000-pound horse couldn't carry it. In fact, some blocky quarter horses are so strong that they can carry both deer and hunter, the rider sitting behind or atop the deer. A small muley can also be sling-hitched to a Decker saddle, or a person can section the carcass and tie into mantas. However, I like the "buttonhole" method, for a person can then bring a deer to camp on the horse he has ridden. Better still, when two horses are available, pack one and ride the other.

Many muley hunters use deer carts to tote their animals out of the mountains. A friend and I built one a number of years ago, and we still use it for some special occasions. Constructed of 1¾-inch electrical conduit and a 22-inch bicycle wheel, the cart is six feet long and 24 inches wide. A two-man outfit, this rig will easily carry the largest muley that ever lived. Although a deer cart functions best over level, clear ground, two reasonably strong men can push, pull and lift such a loaded vehicle through unbelievably rough, rocky territory.

A sportsman, unlucky enough to be without a trail vehicle, horse or a deer cart, faces a tiresome task if distance to camp is far or over steep, rugged terrain. In such situations, friends and I sometimes use pack-boards. We divide the muley, cutting through the spine at the end of the rib cage and lash one-half to a packboard. The head is discarded when it has no value. Otherwise, we cape the animal, sever the head behind the ears and lash both to the top of the pack. I've never seen the muley that a man of medium strength couldn't pack out in two trips. We rest-stop near a log, rock or slope if possible, to assist in regaining our feet. When this is impossible, we rise from a hands-and-knees position.

When a deer has been killed a great distance from camp or in an extremely precipitous location, particularly when a hunter can complete only one trip, cut-strip the meat from the bones, wrap in canvas or plastic and lash to a pack-board or stow in a rucksack. Quartering a carcass, which enables one person to move the meat easily, is simple. With a saw or hatchet, cut or chop the animal down the middle of the spine. Next, divide each half into two nearly equal portions.

Friends and I used to carry a number of deer right on our backs; even after 40 years, I can still recall the aches, pains, the sweat. However, we were young then, bursting with strength and enthusiasm. Once I killed a smallish buck on Pahvant Mountain and a friend, who weighed 200 pounds and was 22 years old, slung the carcass over his shoulders and carried it one-half mile into camp without resting. He arranged the carcass in the most comfortable position across his shoulders, grasped an antler with one hand and a rear leg with the other.

An acquaintance knapsacks his deer, when they are small. After dressing the carcass, he passes each front leg through a slit cut between the hock and the tendon. Then he runs his knife between the skin and bone, just above the front hoofs, and thrusts a small branch through these openings, locking the legs in place. When a companion is present, lifting the carcass over his head, onto his shoulders— *a la* horsecollar—is fairly simple. Otherwise, he moves the carcass near a rock or log. Again, this is backbreaking toil and when my friend reaches camp, his shirt is invariably splotched with blood and perspiration. When a deer's weight doesn't exceed two-thirds that of the hunter, the animal can be carried a short distance. But, face it; toting a muley to camp in this way isn't an enjoyable experience. Only a fairly strong man in excellent physical condition should carry a muley on his back.

When only 16, I was hunting with an uncle near Kanosh, Utah. He killed a very large five-pointer, and somewhere in those cedar-choked hills he found a dry quaking aspen pole about 12 feet long. With short sections of rope, we bound the muley's legs and head to the pole and, with a rifle slung over one shoulder and the quaker pole over the other, we started to camp, our heels sinking six inches into the sandstone rocks. The rough terrain made keeping-in-step-walking impossible, and the swinging carcass was troublesome. Before we had gone a quarter-mile, I hated every ounce of that muley's body. A slight improvement is made by tying the deer tightly between two poles, then resting the supports on the shoulders of each man. But, soon this method likewise becomes painfully tiresome and, after a long carry, one is apt to vow never to hunt muleys again.

Dragging a deer out of the mountains is equally irksome. In addition, dragging generally ruins some of the meat, the cape and skin. However, when you must drag an animal, close the incision, and remove the cape if the animal is a trophy. Lacking a rope, you must tow the carcass by the head or legs. However, a smart muley hunter always carries a piece of rope. Most hunters merely tie one end around a female's neck, next to the ears, or to a buck's antlers—or pass the rope through a slit cut in the lower jaw. The other end is tied to a 2-3-foot section of stout branch—a tow bar. One person can make considerable progress downhill or over snow. But, uphill, or when the animal is large, the task is formidable. Two persons make the job easier, but it is never a pleasant experience. Once, while horse hunting alone, I killed a buck too heavy to lift into the saddle. However, I had the buck in camp in about 30 minutes. A simple matter of attaching a rope to the muley's antlers, followed by two turns around the saddle horn—then a tow over crusted snow.

With a minimum of time and effort, a person can build a one- or two-man skid, a travois. Place two dry (green ones are too heavy and bend), 10-foot quaking-aspen or conifer poles about 3 feet apart on the ground. To these poles lash five to six crossbars with wire or rope. The front crossbar should be approximately 4-5 feet long when two hunters will make the haul. Otherwise, the front bar can be the same length as the others—or left open like the front of a buggy. Once I saw two hunters bring a muley out of the hills lashed on such a travois—and pulled by a horse. The trail had been extremely dusty and the carcass was so dirty that it was ghostlike.

A word of warning: a certain percentage of hunters are trigger-happy and shoot at anything wearing deer hair. Therefore, dress yourself in red or blaze-orange and attach liberal yardage of the same cloth to your horse and the carcass. Just good life insurance. It's also an excellent idea to whistle or sing a merry song as you return to camp with a carcass. A hunter I know carries a muffled horse bell in a saddlebag and suspends it around his horse's neck when coming back with a deer. He also returns after dark whenever possible.

SKINNING

Circumstances, as we've seen, determine whether skinning should be done immediately or postponed. However, when convenient, remove the pelt soon after death—unless you intend to pack out the carcass whole, in which case you may want to leave the skin on to protect the meat from soiling or bruising. The skin is easily removed shortly after death. Still, this chore isn't too difficult after rigor mortis. However, once a carcass has frozen, the job is laborious.

Some muley hunters believe that if a deer remains unskinned for one or more days the hide imparts a taint to the meat. I doubt this. Opinions differ whether a deer should be suspended head or tail up for skinning. Eastern friends almost always skin their white-tails with antlers up, while most Westerners prefer the head-down approach. After skinning a considerable number of domestic and wild critters, I usually suspend a deer by its hind legs. The same method is used in commercial slaughterhouses. Friends and I have even skinned a few deer on the ground. However, these were exceptional occasions. Usually a tree wasn't available. Skinning on bare earth generally means a dirty carcass, although when done on a flat rock or snow, the job is fast and clean.

If you have a choice, start the skinning on the ground, then elevate the carcass. With the deer held or wedged on its back, tuck one of the animal's rear hoofs between your legs, about knee high, and insert the edge-up tip of a skinning knife under the skin 4-5 inches below the "knee" and split the skin down to the pelvis, or aitchbones. Next, ring the skin on the leg where you first inserted the knife. With thumb and pointer finger, pull the edge of the skin outward and cut away from the bone and flesh for several inches along the entire incision. Do likewise with the other rear leg. Next, sever the tail where it joins the body. Use a small saw or a knife other than the skinning blade, for cutting through tail vertebrae dulls the edge. Now, thrust the ends of a gambrel stick through the two obvious holes at the hocks (the "knee" joints) and elevate the rear of the carcass about chest high. During all phases of skinning, endeavor carefully to keep the hair side of the skin from contacting the flesh. Grasp a handful of the skin (from the inside) and pull downward, using a knife only when necessary to keep the separation continuing smoothly. Islands of fat and muscle tissue here and there may pull away with the pelt. Then some special care is needed to restart the skinning process. Try to keep the fat on the carcass—makes for a professional job.

Once the hindquarters are free of skin, the knife can be laid aside. Thrust your fist, or even elbow, between the hide and flesh with sufficient force to separate the two, somewhat like peeling a banana. Result: a very neat and efficient job. Continue elevating the carcass to insure a comfortable working position. Professional skinners use this method, and the task for them (and for you after a couple of tries) is surprisingly simple and rapid.

Upon reaching the forequarters, pull the skin over the legs and with cutting edge up, knife the skin from the brisket (point of the chest) down the leg to a point well below the "elbows." Snip here and there with the knife and use a clenched fist to free the skin down to the neck. Because neck skin and muscles adhere very tenaciously, much of this portion of the skinning is blade work. Push or pull forcefully downward on the skin and separate with a knife. Next, remove the head and legs. Cut through the heavy neck muscles, windpipe and esophagus just back of the ears and, while someone prevents the carcass from turning, grasp the antlers (buck) or ears (doe) and twist abruptly. This disconnects the head from the neck vertebrae.

Legs are easily removed—one minute is sufficient. However, I've found it difficult to describe the exact point of separation. It's far better to indicate the location to a beginner and actually sever a leg as an illustration, for the separation point is fairly well concealed on an unskinned leg. Anyway, about 4-5 inches below the "knee buckle," or approximately 15-17 inches from point of toe; and about 1½-2 inches below the "elbow," or 14-16 inches from point of front toes, are the correct locations to disconnect the legs. Ring these joints with a knife, cutting tendons and soft tissues, then pop the muley's legs over your folded leg just above your knee—if the carcass is on the ground or conveniently within reach. If suspended, hold the hoof in one hand and strike the front of the joint with the heel of your other hand. By all means, don't remove the rear legs at the "knees" or hocks, for this separates the large Achilles tendon, making it impossible thereafter to suspend the deer with a gambrel. Some sportsmen saw or axe the legs off. This invariably results in jagged ends which perforate muslin cooling bags and puncture hands.

Separation at the joints leaves rounded, smooth surfaces. Chopping off muley legs during cold weather may also nick an axe blade. Remember, also, when feasible, to postpone leg removal to the end of the dressing-skinning process, for knife contact with bone results in a dull blade.

You've decided to skin your muley with head up? The procedure is somewhat the same as with antlers down, particularly if the cape has previously been removed. However, if one must start with the neck skin, a minor problem arises because, as noted previously, neck skin clings tenaciously to the muscle. And the separation always involves much knife work, removal of hair, some of which invariably tumbles into the body cavity or adheres to the flesh. However, once the shoulder region has been reached, skinning progresses easily and rapidly. Upon reaching the hind legs, case them out without the usual cuts from "knee" to "aitch-bone."

Next, make a longitudinal cut through the chest and down the underside of the neck and remove the windpipe and gullet. Use a saw to cut through the brisket, although a large knife functions very well. However, this dulls the blade. Now, cut away all flesh and bone sur-rounding bullet wounds and pieces of fat which birds may have pecked. Bacteria go to work immediately in these areas. Remove all hair from the carcass. Warm water and a sponge or piece of towel work fine. Hair which remains on the flesh quickly dulls the appetite of a person who cooks and eats the flesh. It's very important that you take home a clean, appetizing carcass. About an hour after skinning and cleansing, a glaze forms on the meat. This protective surface effectively diminishes dehy-dration and is a deterrent to blowflies.

Next, enclose the entire carcass in a muslin bag, particularly when flies are a problem. It's surprising how many of the two-winged pests survive freezing nights in the mountains. Fly maggots (they hatch in about five to six days) are easily found, but it requires sharp eyes to locate the whitish eggs. A bag likewise prevents dust, etc. from soiling the muley.

Caring for a carcass in camp is quite simple. After sundown suspend the muley where road dust, human thieves and camp dogs can't reach the carcass. At sunrise retrieve the deer, wrap in canvas and stow be-tween sleeping bags or other insulating materials. Or, if you choose, hang the carcass on the shady side of a trailer, camper or trees when tempera-tures remain low during the sunny portion of the day. Handled in this manner, a carcass keeps well for several weeks.

One final word: while homeward bound, don't place the deer atop your car, or attached to the bumpers. Too much heat and dust. It's far better to enclose it in canvas and stow inside the automobile—away from fuel cans.

BUTCHERING

If you choose not to process the meat yourself, take the carcass at once to a commercial meat cutter. However, when you have the facilities and a desire to turn that muley into delicious chops, steaks, roasts and hamburger, hang the carcass (in garage, cellar, shed or basement if temperatures are sufficiently low—not above 50 degrees F.) for seven to 10 days. Aging meat permits enzymatic action, or something, to tenderize muscle cells.

Whenever possible, I process my own venison. This results in almost no cost and much, much better meat. Too many professional cutters freeze deer carcasses and then cut them up with a band saw which deposits a thin layer of bone-meat dust on the flesh—which to me is undesirable. Obviously, commercial cutters, burdened with a flood of deer during a short hunting season, don't have time to meticulously cut and package venison, as described below, for everyone. It would be very costly, too. Then came an experience which convinced me that never again would I take a deer to a professional meat cutter. As we entered the driveway of this estabilshment, we saw, hanging in an open shed, perhaps 20 to 30 muleys and 25 or so additional carcasses in piles on the concrete, some in the sun. The only occasion when I've seen more flies was at an open meat market in Africa.

I returned home and skinned and butchered the buck myself. Actual working time was about two hours. I had also saved a few dollars. Professional cutters may charge from 10 to 12 cents per pound to cut and wrap a carcass. Let's assume that your muley weighs 150 pounds. This multiplies to a figure of approximately $15. The task of butchering a muley is quite simple and can be accomplished in your basement, kitchen or garage. Want to try? Place the carcass belly-side down on a table or large wooden box. A covered floor works fine, but the necessary bending and kneeling is unpleasant on one's back and knees. Or, begin butchering with the muley hanging head down, if you wish.

First, make two shallow cuts (your hunting knife can be used) from shoulder to rump—immediately beside the backbone. Now, with your fingers strip the dry, paper-like tissue and shallow layer of fat covering the loins down over the ribs. Underneath lie two long strips of meat, some of the finest on the carcass. After making bisecting cuts near the shoulders and rump, run the knife down each side of the backbone to a depth of about 2-3 inches. Snipping here and there with the knife, peel out the loins. Cut into steaks or roasts, whatever your choice. For what it's worth, I separate each side of the loin meat into two or three family-size chunks which can either be roasted as is or cut into steaks when partly thawed. Meat has less tendency to lose moisture when left in larger pieces. If you decide to steak the meat at this time, remember that meat consists of fibers and cells. Thus, for tender meat cut across the "grain" of the muscles. Another suggestion: roughly wrap each piece of venison in wax paper, then place into an airtight plastic bag. Finally, identify individual types and cuts of meat with a Magic Marker.

Next, remove the front legs. After tipping the carcass upon its side, grasp the end of the leg, lift up and outward and sever the leg from the body with a knife. It is easily done—no bones to cut. It has always seemed remarkable that a deer's front legs were attached to the body only by muscle and tendon! Bone the meat, remove islands of fat (muley fat eventually becomes rancid—rank smell and taste), roll and tie into roasts. When there is ample time, I also carefully remove all tendons and connective tissues. This necessarily leaves a portion of the meat in rather small pieces, but just right for stew. This part of the carcass also makes excellent hamburger. There is much waste flesh on the front legs—likewise on the neck and ribs. But I kennel one or two dogs, and this waste is reserved for the canines. The meat goes into plastic bags and frozen. Venison should always be cooked before feeding to dogs; otherwise, they may become infested with worms.

Next, with a knife (a saw isn't necessary) sever the rear legs at the hip joints. Place the legs on the cutting table and with a very sharp, very thin-bladed knife trim away all fat and the thin, tough "glaze membrane." Then remove the long bones and separate the hams into their natural divisions and package.

Two pieces of meat remain to be removed: the "hanging loins," located at the top of the body cavity, beside the vertebrae, between the ribs and the rear legs. These pieces, although smallish, are perhaps the best on the animal. Peel them out as you did with the regular loins.

There is still about 10 to 15 pounds of flesh clinging to the muley's bones, but this is meat which I roughly trim and package for the dogs. Little remains, now, except the bones. Thus, we have reduced a 150-pound carcass to approximately 75 pounds of delicious meat.

Cared for properly, from killing to cooking, most venison is tender, delicious. Writers often refer to excellent venison as "sweet" meat. The word, sweet, is a poor choice. Actually, deer flesh has a taste and odor of its own—quite different from elk, sheep and antelope.

NOW LET'S EAT IT

Quality meat, whether it be beef or bison, is produced from an animal "on the gain." And a muley is no exception. The best venison I've eaten came from a long-two-year-old buck collected in September. His credentials were the very best: young, fat and slain as he stood drowsing in the shade of an aspen. Still, the meat didn't taste quite as delicious as prime beef or elk, but it was mighty close. The chief reason excellent to very prominent "gamy" flavor. Therefore, it's wise to disguise this taste which is somewhat offensive to many individuals. However, no attempt should be made to drown the meat in 39 herbs and concoctions until the stew, roast or fries resembles a Yurdish buloosh. This is what many recipes found in hunting books and periodicals tell a cook to do. One should consider the age of the deer and cut of meat before deciding on a cooking method. Venison is somewhat "drier" than beef and cooking time should be a mite shorter. Moreover, deer lead a much more vigorous life than beef animals, and muscle tissues are tougher.

Shall we begin with those portions of the deer which can be eaten soon after the kill—liver and heart? Both were removed during field dressing. Back at camp immerse the liver in cold water for at least 30 minutes. Then slice into one-half inch steaks and soak again in cold water for 5 minutes to remove undesirable blood and juices. Drain and cover again for 5 minutes with boiling water to which one-fourth cup of vinegar has been added. Drain again, pepper and roll in flour. Then fry in bacon fat. Just before done to satisfy individual taste, sprinkle with salt. I prefer all meats well done—to eliminate various parasites. All fried venison should be served piping hot, on warm plates. Hearts of all big-game animals can be eaten immediately, and we usually fry a liberal portion of both liver and heart from the first muley brought to camp. If not done at kill-site, remove the heart's top—chiefly fat, connective tissues and blood vessels. If possible, soak the heart about an hour in salt water and parboil for 15-20 minutes. Next, slice, pepper and cover with flour and fry in bacon fat. As with all fried venison, salt should be added only when the meat is nearly done; otherwise, fluids are drawn from the meat.

Venison steak is probably *the* favorite among muley hunters. A friend prefers his Swiss style. His wife cuts the meat into the "right size and thickness," removes all fat (This is very important, for venison fat is chiefly responsible for the bad flavor.) and applies a liberal amount of salt, pepper, paprika and flour. Then she fries an onion in pork fat until the rings are brown. Now the meat is seared on both sides, after which a mixture of sour cream and water is added, the pan covered and allowed to slowly simmer until done. Or try Swiss steak this way: Season with salt and pepper and dust with flour. Fry until nearly done in pork fat or olive oil. Then add a small sliced onion, a dash of caraway seeds, a squirt of lemon juice, two cups of sour cream, cover and cook slowly for about one and a half hours. Serve with cinnamon toast, red currant jelly, French fried potatoes and a good wine—Burgundy or claret.

My mother fried venison in the following way: She placed the peppered one-half inch steaks into a preheated, heavy-iron fry-pan, seared each side and then alternately turned until the "red" had disappeared. (She also knew about meat parasites.) Then she poured some diced onions over the meat, added salt and simmered for an additional three to four minutes. (Almost forgot—she also cooked venison in pork fat.) Then she served each of us a piece of sizzling meat and a spoonful of onions. We kids always added a pat of real butter to the top of the steak. Venison has a tendency toward dryness and the butter also adds a bit of flavor.

Some individuals tell me they've had wonderful luck broiling venison, but my attempts were all failures. Most of the natural juices are lost and one ends with a darkish hunk of dried leather.

A mountain dinner I shall never forget was prepared in the following way, in a Dutch oven. As nearly as I remember, this lady dusted several pounds of venison steaks with flour and seared both sides in hot pork fat. Then she placed one small onion (ringed), several sliced carrots and potatoes on the meat and sprinkled the lot with salt, pepper and celery salt. The lid on, the oven was placed into a depression in the ground and covered with a mound of hot, glowing embers. What a delicious meal when we returned from fishing three hours later!

The Robinson family's favorite venison roast begins with a four-to-five-pound piece of meat from which all fat has been trimmed. Mix in a separate container one can of tomato soup, one-quarter cup of soy sauce, two teaspoons of sugar, and one teaspoon of ginger. Place the meat into a roasting pan, and pour the above mixture over the meat. Anchor rings of one onion on the roast; cover the pan and cook at 300 degrees F. for four to five hours.

A friend prefers his roast prepared with numerous slits into which slivers of bacon or ham, previously dusted with salt and pepper, are thrust. Bay leaves are added to the roasting pan and the cooking meat moistened occasionally with orange juice. A Texas friend believes that venison roasts should be soaked in sour wine for several days in a refrigerator. Then he places bay leaves and cloves on top of the meat and cooks slowly, basting with the same sour wine. My grandfather was 100 per cent opposed to roasting venison with sage, bay leaves, onion and the other sundry herbs and concoctions. "Season only with pepper and cook in salty pork drippings. Why ruin the natural, wonderful flavor?" he insisted.

Stewing is one of my favorite methods of cooking venison. Place into a Dutch oven or deep, heavy fry-pan or kettle, a small chili pepper, a squirt of vinegar, two or three chopped onions, a dash of sage powder and one-half cup of cooking fat. Place the oven on the fire and when this mixture begins to bubble, add two to three pounds of venison cubed into one-inch pieces. When the meat is almost done, add two or three large potatoes and several carrots (both sliced or diced), a large can of tomatoes and two teaspoons of salt. Cook for approximately one additional hour. A few minutes before serving, thicken the fluid with flour.

For the poorer cuts, try meat loaf. Grind approximately one pound each of venison and ham and mix with the following: two or three eggs; one teaspoon Worchestershire sauce; salt and pepper; one-half cup of chopped onions; one cup of bread crumbs and one cup of milk. Mold into a moist, pliable loaf and cook for approximately one hour at 375 to 400 degrees in an uncovered pan.

Anyone for venison burgers? Combine equal parts of ground beef and venison, to which are added finely chopped onions, salt, pepper and a dash of horseradish. Cook quickly in a hot fry-pan with just enough pork fat to keep from burning. Serve on heated buns, complimented with raw onion rings, relish and a mixture of catsup-mustard.

It was as a youngster that I first ate a superb venison dish, prepared by my father in deer camp. I had eaten my portion before I knew the ingredients: scrambled muley brains and eggs, seasoned with salt, pepper and chili sauce. I've cooked this combination on several occasions since but have never been able to persuade hunting companions to consume their portions. And that's a pity! However, once I did succeed in tricking two friends into eating another mule deer product: Rocky Mountain oysters. We had killed two bucks and I brought their livers, hearts and, unknown to my companions, the oysters (testes) to camp. While the two friends were skinning the deer, I prepared supper—and the oysters—just as I had cooked and seen them prepared since a youngster on the sheep ranges. Liver, heart, and oysters were all steaked and fried together, with onions and mushroms. After we had all stuffed our stomachs and were lazily sipping coffee, I casually asked for their reaction to eating the oysters. The first response on their faces was disbelief, then slight anger, finally green resignation. Both later agreed that the "oysters tasted fine."

9

Heads Are What Count

Although trophy hunting had interested sportsmen here and there in the U.S. for many years, it wasn't until 1887 that a core organization was formed to collect and rank heads under direction of Theodore Roosevelt, later to become president. Then a young man, Mr. Roosevelt gathered around him a group of enthusiastic American riflemen who proposed to "promote manly sport with the rifle among the large game of the wilderness." The club was limited to 100 members, each of whom had killed in fair chase at least 3 species of North American big game. Its members sought to emphasize quality of trophies, rather than quantity, and in 1896 set standards for ranking heads. The organization was called the Boone & Crockett Club. By 1932 a fair number of trophies had been evaluated, and the Boone & Crockett Club decided to publish a book showing their rankings. Prentiss Gray was editor. Subsequently, interest in trophy hunting increased and, with new standards, it was decided to publish another record book in 1939.

During the 1920's, 30's and early 40's, mule deer trophies were generally judged by outside spread and number of points. Using extreme spread as a criterion, a head collected by Arthur Henke, in 1940, near Glenwood Springs, Colorado, is thought by a number of trophy hunters "to be the world's record head . . . everything considered." Measurements: outside curve, 29 inches; circumference of beams, 5¼ inches; number of points: right 16, left 19; outside spread, 47 7/8 inches. Antlers/skull plate weighing 11 pounds, 4 ounces. However, this head doesn't appear in the 1964 edition of the Boone & Crockett record book. Although eye-catching, the antlers lack uniformity and, detached from the skull, might serve as clubs for Neanderthal cavemen.

In 1950 a somewhat "new" system of scoring heads was developed; consequently, still another edition of the book appeared in 1952. It was thought that this would be the last record book for many years, but such an avalanche of heads was submitted that a fifth edition was released in 1964. The 1952 record book listed 848 trophies; the 1958, 2,509; and the 1964 book, 5,072. Another edition appeared late in 1971.

The characteristics of a good muley head have been debated for many years. As a boy, I remember Dad and his hunting cronies analyzing the merits of various muley heads. Much emphasis, 30-40 years ago, was given to number of tines; but most value was placed upon antler spread. Lists of deer with extremely wide spreads were regularly published by sporting magazines. Much was wrong, however, with evaluating heads on basis of extreme spread or number of tines. The main objection was that most of these heads were not handsome. In fact, it would be difficult to label many of them as anything other than an ugly monstrosity.

Mr. Gray suggested that heads be judged upon amount of bone material. He actually constructed a water tank in which antlers were immersed and the displaced water computed. But this system had problems. For example, it was found that some antlers absorbed considerable water. Someone then tried to prove that a better method was to make a plaster cast of the antlers and fill the empty spaces with buckshot. Again, insurmountable problems. Why not weigh antlers, someone suggested. At first glance, this system sounds feasible. However, it was found that fresh antlers weigh considerably more than older ones. And then a few hunters found they could add an appreciable amount when heads were kept immersed in water until weighed.

Finally, Dr. James L. Clark, American Museum of Natural History, and Grancel Fitz, Boone & Crockett, devised a system that has weathered criticism since 1950—although it does have some bugs. This system ranks heads by: (1) amount of bone material; and (2) symmetry. The Clark-Fitz system changed considerably the previous rankings of heads.

In fact, none of the top 10 muley heads listed for a number of years in hunting books and magazines appear in the 1964 record book. Briefly, under the present Boone & Crockett Club system, a mule deer head is measured with a one-quarter inch steel tape. The total inches of inside spread, main beams, length of the four additional tines, and circumference of several sections of the antlers are added. From this, total the differences between the above measurements and total length of abnormal points are subtracted. This is the way a typical head is evaluated. Nontypical antlers are measured in the same way except that the total length of all abnormal tines is included. The official measurer and a witness then sign the application; the owner completes a "fair chase" affidavit; and the application is forwarded to the Boone & Crockett Club office, currently at the Pittsburgh Museum, Pittsburgh, Pa. If the head is an extraordinary one, perhaps one of the four or five best, the Boone & Crockett judging committee will suggest that the head be sent to them for re-evaluation. These heads are then suitably displayed with other species at a white-tie awards event, to which the fortunate hunter is invited. The head then appears in its appropriate place when the next record book is published.

Correctly measuring a head is somewhat difficult, requiring careful attention and unbiased judgment. In most instances, no two individuals measure a mule deer head and arrive at an identical point total. In fact, I've seen a careful, competent, neutral individual come up with three results in three attempts. For example, deciding where to place a tape on the edge of the burr, particularly a mounted head, for measuring length of antler beam is sometimes difficult, and can result easily in a difference of a half-inch. Likewise, it's difficult to follow the turning of an antler with a steel tape. A slight miscabobble—a small difference of measuring—say four-eighths of an inch, can change considerably the placement of a trophy in the book. For instance, in the 1964 records there are 50 heads ranked between 185 and 186 points, 38 between 187 and 188. Obviously, it behooves the measurer to proceed as carefully as humanly possible. Even after measuring hundreds of heads of various species of North American big game for the Boone & Crockett competitions, I still fuss and worry that I might accidentally make a mistake. However, the heads that I've measured which have won awards, and have been called in by the Boone & Crockett Club, have checked out almost exactly with my measurements. I try always to measure when I'm relaxed, not rushed for time—when in the right frame of mind. I measure each distance three times—and more if there is a variation of one-sixteenth of an inch or more.

On November 25, 1926, Ed Broder arrived by horse-drawn sled at Chip Lake, Alberta, Canada, to hunt deer. Coming upon large muley tracks in nearby woods, he trailed and just at dark saw a buck at approximately 200 yards. Firing his .32 Winchester, Mr. Broder dropped the deer with a bullet through its spine. Where and why the head from this muley hung unrecognized for so many years is unknown to me. However, when measured in 1960, it created a mild sensation; its total score of 355 2/8 surpassed the 1958 non-typical muley record, a head in the National Collections, by 56 5/8 points. "Perhaps the most outstanding trophy ever recorded," is how this remarkable trophy was described in the *1964 Records of North American Big Game.* Yet, it is my own opinion that this head is quite ugly. With 22 tines (right antler) and 21 (left) it has the symmetry of a squawberry bush, with branches running every-which-way.

Even worse is the No. 2 non-typical head, a deer killed near Chama, New Mexico, with 17 and 16 tines. These unattractive antlers feature a club-like appendage hanging from the right antler, numerous tines erupting here and there, one even projecting several inches above the right eye. Same can be said for the No. 1 non-typical head in the 1952 and 1958 books (now fifth in the 1964 records).

Characteristics identifying an excellent trophy are a matter of personal opinion because beauty and symmetry are abstract qualities. After functioning for a number of years as trophy measurer for the Boone & Crockett Club, and after having seen a few thousand mule deer during approximately 40 years of traveling through muley country, I have a definite opinion concerning what constitutes an excellent muley head. Trophy heads should be representatives of the species. Oddball, many-tined heads are no more typical of mule deer than the circus fat man, the side-show freak with 39 toes and fingers are representative of man.

The antler types I consider most outstanding lie between the so-called typical five-pointer and the multi-tined, non-typical heads previously discussed. These are heads with seven to 10 tines on each side, and they are grown by very mature, old bucks. These heads are seldom found in record books, for they have too many tines (thus are penalized) to be included among the typical and not enough to qualify in the non-typical group.

It's unfortunate that a third division for muley heads hasn't been established. I discussed this by letter with the late Grancel Fitz of the Boone & Crockett Club. His reply was that there was little chance. Consequently, hundreds of excellent trophies are ignored, trophies which in my opinion are far better than most of the typical and non-typical heads in the book. A typical head of 10 points (all tines counted) is a little bare, a little austere for my taste. Moreover, such a head is often developed by a mature but comparatively young animal. Only when a deer reaches full maturity, perhaps during declining years, does he develop the additional tines which make his head such a remarkably handsome trophy.

ONE FOR THE RECORD BOOK

If a person has difficulty evaluating a trophy mule deer with a tape on the floor of his den, he'll have a somewhat greater problem with an animal as it stands alive, perhaps several hundred yards from his rifle. Light will probably be poor, and the buck likely will be standing against a background of blending vegetation. Under such conditions, a good binocular is absolutely necessary. However, an experienced trophy hunter can roughly estimate the trophy-value of a head in four or five seconds, for he has probably looked over hundreds of muley heads—including a number of good mounted trophies in his gun room. He knows that a head should have a beam length of approximately 2 feet since, of the 420 typical muley heads in the 1964 record book, only 39 fail to have at least one main beam of 24 inches. Likewise, he knows that the average width of a large muley's head is about 7 inches and length of ear about 8. Through a binoc he multiplies the head width or ear length three times to the top of the longest tine (usually the rear point). An additional measurement he keeps in mind is 21 inches: distance from ear tip to ear tip when a large buck is carrying his ears horizontally. This distance he uses to guesstimate inside spread, which, hopefully, will be about the same as length of main beams.

Does the animal have both brow tines, and do the three rearmost tines extend upward 12 or so inches? Have any of the prongs been broken? Check also for "froggy" points, those extra tines which project from regularly placed beams or tines. Three or 4 of these generally kill chances of a typical head making the book. After all, only 22 points separate the minimum score, 195, from the top head, presently 217. Another important consideration is thickness of beams but only through experience can a hunter judge this characteristic. Finally, the head must have good symmetry—that smazz-ma-tazz which lends uniformity to a typical head. Non-typical antlers are somewhat easier to evaluate. However, with both types one can never say with certainty where a particular muley head will place in the book while still attached to the living critter.

Only when the antlers have been taped can the score be determined. Antlers on live deer generally appear much better—larger—than when measured after death.

THE SEARCH FOR TROPHY MULEYS

The question, "Where do I have a reasonable chance of collecting a record book mule deer head?" I've attempted to answer 39,000 times. During the late 1930's and early 40's we could have hunted in perhaps a dozen localities and had a good chance of collecting a book trophy. The task is much more difficult today. First, because of the tremendous decrease of muley populations; and second, because minimum totals are now skyhigh: 195 for typical heads and 240 for non-typicals.

Perhaps an examination of the 1964 record book will supply a partial answer. The book lists 420 typical muley heads. Of these, 153 were killed in Colorado; 38 in New Mexico; 45 in Wyoming; 33 in Arizona; 30 in Montana; and 24 in Utah. Ten of the top 20 were taken in Colorado. Of the 216 non-typical heads in the book, Colorado again leads with 52; Wyoming has 21; Arizona, 21; Idaho, 19; Montana, 16; Utah, 16. Canada has four of the top 20 non-typical heads; Colorado and Arizona, three each. It's my opinion that the above statistics are misleading. Colorado and Wyoming have a number of record heads in the book because of little publicized factors. Colorado, for instance, has enjoyed for many years a high plateau of interest in trophy hunting. The Colorado Fish & Game Department has encouraged trophy hunting; official measurers have been active; and the famous taxidermy firm, Coleman Bros., has been located for a long time in Denver. The Wyoming Game & Fish Department annually sends a group of official measurers to key locations in the state to evaluate trophy heads. Considerable newspaper publicity precedes the measuring, and awards are given for best trophy in each species category. By comparison, I believe that equally as many trophy muleys are collected in Utah as Colorado, but interest in trophy hunting has only recently begun to develop in the Beehive state. A friend and I have measured many of the Utah heads and have aroused much of the present, somewhat low-key, interest. Pay our salaries for two months, and the heads we'll uncover in pool halls, beer joints, service stations, on barn doors, etc., will place Utah in contention with Colorado. Same can probably be said of several other western states.

Someone wrote an article about 30 years ago in which he suggested that large, trophy heads are the product of areas where soil is predominantly limestone. "Experts" have been echoing this theory ever since, and a few years back another outdoor author suggested that trophy hunters buy a geologic map which would surely be a clue to locating good heads. Deer antlers test 39 per cent animal matter, 52.3 per cent prosphate of lime, and 8.7 per cent carbonate of lime. Consequently, a buck fortunate enough to live in limestone country, it is generally believed, may grow tremendous antlers. Julian S. Huxley writes that the average number of points among deer killed on a limestone park in England was 20, compared with 14 in a sandstone park. In addition, body weight was approximately 25 per cent greater on the lime district. Red deer, transplanted to New Zealand from England, were found to grow considerably larger there—chiefly, it is believed, because their New Zealand home was in a limestone region. As I recall, I've measured equally as many good heads from standstone, igneous, etc., formations as from limestone districts. An abundant source of good browse, especially during winter, I believe is the important key to large muley heads. That, and the fact that deer must have an opportunity to live long enough to produce trophy antlers.

Heredity? Without question it has been scientifically proved that various physical traits among animals are inherited, and there is no reason to believe otherwise in the case of mule deer. I'm sure this explains, at least partly, the presence of large heads in particular localities year after year.

A top, record book mule deer is truly a wonderful trophy. It's an extreme rarity—perhaps only one out of 100,000 animals. And, that's the way it should be. Generally, a lifetime of chasing the muley rainbow is required to appreciate an excellent head. Certainly antlers which are procured with great difficulty make the best trophies. What does a person have hanging on the den wall, anyway? Only memories!

Several friends and I are avid trophy hunters. We've hunted long and diligently—often in far-distant places, the primitive areas. We've tried the most productive method of all to secure trophy muleys: late season hunts when November and December snows drive the ridge-runners, the old, gray-faced veterans from inaccessible places. The Red Gods have allotted us our share of good trophies, but spectacular, magnificent antlers have so far eluded our rifles. Luck, I'm convinced, is *the* important factor. Very frequently it's the beginner or Mr. Average Sportsman who pauses at my doorstep with a super, wonderful head.

The number of dedicated trophy hunters in muley country is increasing. A group of us once paused briefly at an ancient, run-down ranch in Butch Cassidy's Brown's Hole and listened to a whiskered rancher tell of the increasing parade of trophy hunters who were passing through his ranch gates on their way into a portion of the Uinta Mountains seeking large muley heads. Still, unfortunately, the woods are full of men who shoot at the first deer that appears, doe or buck.

The lucky hunter who collects a record muley head should be proud. James L. Clark, of the American Museum of Natural History and big game hunter of Africa, Asia and the Americas, writes: "I have hunted hard for big bucks and have seen them, but they always got away. They are difficult to get, and there is no finer head for beauty than that of a fine mule deer."

PREPARATIONS AFIELD

Nothing serves to recall the vivid memories of a wonderful hunt as well as a mounted trophy, even if it's not a record head. Most muley hunters for reasons of time or inclination do not mount their trophies themselves. They believe that a taxidermist can prepare a head in a more likelife manner. This is true, for an amateur cannot hope to mount a head and achieve the same excellence as a professional. A taxidermist, however, cannot follow you, the hunter, into the woods and mountains. Therefore, you must ensure that the scalp, or cape, as the skin covering the neck and head is called, is removed with least possible damage.

Whether a taxidermist mounts the head, or you do the job, there are a few essential chores that must be done at site of kill. Note color and sketch shape of the eyes. Tape circumference of the neck directly behind the ears and again immediately in front of the shoulders. Next, record distances from center of nose to the following points: base of each antler, the tips of the most forward prongs and also the front corners of the eyes. If possible, photograph the muley from both profile and full-face positions. When feasible, cape the head where the animal fell. As indicated previously, dragging, carrying—even excessive turning—loosens and dislodges hair which can never be replaced. If one guts the animal before caping, carefully keep the scalp as free of blood and filth as possible. This is difficult when a deer is hung western style, head down.

Many hunters make the mistake of leaving insufficient skin for a good trophy. Therefore, decide upon type of mount and then extend the length of skin needed by several inches. A majority of individuals want a long neck mount. But the best type includes part of the shoulders, paricularly if the rack is huge. Another regrettable mistake sometimes made by amateurs is cutting a deer's throat. As pointed out elsewhere, this accomplishes very little and also destroys the cape.

If a cape is ruined by bullet wounds, another cape can be procured from a friend who has chosen not to mount his trophy, or a taxidermist can usually supply a substitute. However, while it may mean nothing to some individuals that a cape has come from an animal killed by someone else; to me, it is incongruous. When you accidentally shoot a trophy through the head or neck, mount only the antlers on a plaque, or postpone mounting until you've collected another deer.

Caping the Head

First, encircle the base of the neck or the withers and brisket with an initial cut, depending upon type of mount desired. Then, working from the rear, insert a knife, preferably small and very sharp, beneath the skin on the crest of the neck and slit the skin forward in a straight line to a point slightly to the rear but between the ears. Then continue cutting diagonally to the base of each antler. Because the thick hide clings tenaciously to the bones and muscles of the head and neck, it's generally necessary to cut and pry the skin away. When the ears are reached, carefully detach them at the base, but leave their skinning until the scalp has been removed from the skull. The antlers are encountered next. With a dull screwdriver pry the skin away from beneath the base of each antler burr. Then continue skinning with a knife until you reach the eyes. Exercise extreme care to avoid cutting the eyelids. Thrust a finger into the eye opening, lift the lid up and out and sever tissues connecting them to the bone. At the corner of each eye tough cartilage joins skin and bone; cut through the skin or pry it loose. Right in front of the eyes are tear ducts into which the skin is recessed. With the tip of a small, pointed knife continue skinning into these openings as far as possible. After the rear molars are reached, lift the lips up and cut them away from the bone, following the procedure already outlined for the eyes. Next, sever the nostrils at a point about 2 inches or so behind point of the nose. A casual inspection of the scalp shows pieces of tissues adhering to the skin, but these will be removed later.

Whatever trouble it may entail, transport the scalp to camp with as little damage as possible. In a burlap bag or wrapped in a roll of canvas and carried behind a saddle or in a back-pack, it will reach camp in excellent condition. Lacking these conveniences, place the cape into a sack or tie it into a roll, and then hand-carry it this way.

Lack of time, impending darkness, bad weather or various other circumstances occasionally alter one's plans, and a hunter may find it impossible to remove the cape soon after making a kill. Approaching darkness or a heavy storm may force one to leave the animal after the viscera has been removed and the carcass hung from a tree or propped off the ground. In fact, several days may elapse before the huntsman can return.

Upon reaching camp, spread the cape-skin, hair side up, on a clean surface and with cool water wash those portions soiled with blood and dirt. Use soap if necessary. If the scalp and skull can be placed into a taxidermist's hands within 24 hours, you need not concern yourself further. However, when a delay of several days on a pack-trail or in camp is imminent, especially if weather is warm, you must take additional steps to ensure that the scalp doesn't decay.

When packing space is a problem, remove the antlers from the skull with a saw (an axe is a poor substitute). Leave a generous piece of skull attached to the antlers, for a strong bridge of bone adds strength—prevents it from splitting. The additional bone also affords a good bite for a saw when the final cut is made to fit the mannequin. If packing space is extremely limited, as sometimes occurs on long pack trips, the skull plate can be broken and the antlers conveniently tied to the top of the gear. A taxidermist can restore them to their original position, but do not expect to enter such a head in the Boone & Crockett competition, for broken skulls are automatically disqualified. If for some reason you plan to bring the entire skull home, remove the brain because, unless temperature is low, this tissue soon decays—and smells. Enlarge the hole at the rear of the brain cavity and remove contents with a small spoon.

Next, skin the ears, a chore requiring utmost care and patience. Commence at the base of the ears with a knife and cut away islands of fat and muscle. However, after reaching the cartilage, separate the skin with tips of the fingers or a spoon, using a knife or small scissors to sever "strings" which will be encountered here and there. Upon completion, the ears are left inside out.

Now lay the scalp with hair-side down on a flat surface and remove all large pieces of muscle and slice the thick tissues around the eyes, lips and nostrils a number of times. Be careful not to cut through the skin. Then rub several handfuls of finely ground salt into the scalp, particularly around the lips, nose and eyes. Next, fold the cape—flesh against flesh—and roll, tie loosely and store in a safe, cool place. Remember: porcupines are made for salt, and camp dogs and miscellaneous rodents may also nibble your precious hide if it is left unprotected.

The following day a reddish fluid will begin to trickle from the skin, an indication that the hide is curing. Unroll the scalp and suspend from a convenient object until the juices have drained away. Resalt and reroll. One or two pounds of common table salt is sufficient to cure one large cape. By the second day most of the fat, muscle and cartilage adhering to the skin will have hardened and can now be removed by scraping with a large, rather dull knife. However, if necessary, slit again the tissues around the eyes, lips and nostrils and rub in additional salt. After scraping, cutting and salting on several successive days, the scalp will be completely fleshed. In this state it should remain in good condition for months. But the best practice is to begin immediately with tanning and mounting; after having been dried, a scalp never seems to become as pliable as one desires.

What to do with the remainder of the deer's skin? Many years ago wandering groups of Ute Indians annually camped on a little stream about a mile from our horse corral, and they always knocked on our door, offering to exchange gloves, moccasins, etc. for muley pelts and/or dollars. However, these same Indians and their descendants are now content to remain on the reservation. In a way this is regrettable, for I still recall the softness and ecstatic cedar-smoke fragrance of those buckskin gloves and moccasins. These days most muley hunters sell their skins, or take them to tanneries which turn them into wonderful buckskin products.

MOUNTING YOUR TROPHY

Many sportsmen fail to consider mounting their trophies themselves because they believe the job to be messy and troublesome, but also because they believe preparation of a deer head is a combination of secret ritual and magic. Actually, the job is quite simple, merely the ability to follow directions. In fact, there are few hobbies that hold so much satisfaction for a beginner since a novice can expect his first mount to be a good one. I mounted my first deer head when only 12 and was told by our troop scoutmaster, a professional taxidermist, that it was a commendable job.

Tanning the Cape

The cape from the first deer I mounted was tanned in a pickle-bath made by stirring two pounds of alum and as much common salt as would dissolve into approximately five gallons of boiling water. After the pickling liquid had cooled, the skin was immersed. When the scalp had turned from bluish to a grayish-white, it was removed, washed thoroughly, shaved thin by scraping and sewed over a mannequin. Years later a better method of "curing" a scalp was developed—tanning in a salt and sulphuric acid liquid prepared in the following way. Into an earthen-ware jar pour four gallons of boiling water. Dissolve about five quarts of common salt, and then slowly pour and stir five ounces (volume) of commercial sulphuric acid into the solution. Immerse the scalp in the cooled liquid, move it around until all portions are in contact with the liquid, and weight with a block of wood. Examine the scalp occasionally and dunk it down a few times to make certain that the tanning liquid is continuing to bathe the entire skin. Then, after the cape is completely tanned (two weeks should be sufficient—or when the skin color has become grayish-white), remove the scalp from the liquid, drain and soak for an hour in water to which a pint of washing soda has been added. Then suspend the skin until water has almost stopped dripping from the hair. Now place it, skin side up, over a fleshing-board (made from a two-by-six piece of soft pine by rounding with a drawknife or plane), and shave with the fleshing knife until the hide is thin and pliable. Special attention must be given to the lips, nostrils, ears and hide which snuggles around the base of the antlers. If these portions are not pared down, they will surely pull away when dry and give a grotesque appearance to the head. Do not shave the skin completely to the hairline, where the hair is anchored, for an obvious reason.

Preparations and First Steps

While waiting for the scalp to tan, secure a head-form from a local taxidermist or one of several supply houses whose advertisements appear in sporting and nature magazines. From your measurements which were taken at time of kill, these people will ship a mannequin that closely approximates the shape of your trophy. The head-form should be slightly smaller than the original head and neck. Although buckskin is elastic, it contracts upon hardening. Consequently, if the head-form is too large, the stitches may open on the back of the neck, and the skin may also pull away from base of the antlers, eyes and mouth. Choose a head-form with a flat rather than a notched crown, for you'll find it much simpler to attach the antlers. Make certain also that the mannequin has a back-board, an antler brace and block. This type is slightly more expensive but purchase no other kind. There are several types of head-forms: neck and shoulder; upright and sneaks in straight, right or left turns of the head. You will remember that a muley's head, while alive, is usually turned. Consider the position a trophy will occupy in a room. A head whose eyes appear to gaze at the individual as he enters a doorway is most desirable.

Other miscellaneous items that must be ordered from a taxidermy supply house are a fleshing knife; two skin needles; two ear liners with bases; a plaque plus a hanger; one to two pounds of papier-mâché; 10 feet of waxed linen thread and two eyes. Eyes give life to a trophy, so buy the best.

Now either attach a two-by-two board about two feet long by means of long wood screws to the back-plate of the head-form which in turn can be placed into a vice to hold the head firmly, or bore a hole through the top of the back-plate so that the hole can be slipped over a large screw or nail driven into a wall. Next, place the head alongside the mannequin and determine where a saw-cut should be made through the top of the skull. Generally, this cut passes through the upper third of the eyes and leaves approximately 4-4½ inches of forehead skull and 2½-3 inches behind the antlers. A slight miscabobble can be repaired with a wood rasp. This is the time, also, to cleanse the antlers of dirt, flecks of wood bark, remnants of velvet, etc. with a brush and warm, soapy water.

Place the antlers atop the head-form; and, after checking to make certain that measurements from nose to antler bases are correct, bore three holes through the skull plate: two through the forehead just in front of each antler and approximately one inch from the crinkly line running toward the nose, and one behind the antlers about 2 inches on a mid-line to the rear. Counter-sink these holes a little so that heads of the screws used to anchor the antlers to the mannequin won't form obvious bumps. Three additional holes, considerably smaller in diameter than the screws, should be drilled into the top of the head-form corresponding with the holes previously made in the skull plate. These holes prevent the block of wood in the top of the mannequin from splitting when the long screws are anchored. Four other holes should also be drilled through the skull plate one-quarter inch out from the base of each antler. Small brass nails will be driven into these holes to keep the skin from drawing away from the antlers.

Now place the antlers into position and loosely insert the screws. Measure from end of nose to the most forward antler prongs, and, if these distances vary from those made in the field, adjust with wood shims. Whatever the difficulty, make certain that the antlers are positioned correctly. Finally, anchor the skull plate firmly to the mannequin by turning the screws completely down into the recesses in the skull. Mix a small amount of papier-mâché according to directions on the package and fill all gaps between the skull plate and head-form. Shellac the entire head, including the ear liners, to prevent absorption of water by the papier-mâché head-form. Let dry.

Immerse the cape in warm, soapy water, move up and down a number of times and then follow with a soaking in clear, warm water. Hang to drain. Were it not for pesky moths and larval beetles the following step would be unnecessary. To ensure that these pests do not ravage your trophy, prepare a borax bath, by dissolving about four ounces of borax in one gallon of boiling water. After soaking the cape in this cold solution for about 6 hours, the hair and skin will remain moth- and beetle-proof for many years.

Mounting the Trophy

Select a day to complete the mounting when several hours are available. Once the scalp has been set on the mannequin, the skin must be placed in its final position, the eyes set and the skin sewed around the head-form.

All set? Place the two-by-two board that is attached to the backboard of the mannequin in a vise, or hang the head on a wall roughly waist high. After the scalp has drained for approximately 10 minutes, open the ears with your fingers and push the ear liners into position. Usually liners need trimming, and this can be done with scissors or shears. When satisfied with fit, paint the insides of ear pockets and the ear liners with glue or a clay-paste (both obtainable from a supply house) and slide the liners into place. Then press the liners and skin together. Some taxidermists sew liners and skin together with loose stitches, but others use clamps.

Now spread with your fingers a thick application of clay-paste, or brush on glue, over the entire mannequin. This holds the cape in place during drying. Place the scalp over the mannequin and secure loosely in position with heavy string. If the ear liners have built-up bases, it may be only necessary to trim them slightly to make them conform to general contour of the head. If not, prepare a small amount of papier-mâché and fill in around the ears until they fit the general shape of the head.

Arrange the cape so it's roughly in position on the mannequin. Now thread the two skin needles and begin sewing with the triangular points of skin near an antler by pushing the needles upward from the flesh side. Pull the thread through to the end and tie it in a square knot. Using the baseball stitch (crossing over with each stitch) spaced at one-half inch intervals, close one prong of the "Y," tie into a square knot and cut. Repeat with the other wing of the "Y" and continue about two inches down the neck. Then push the ears against the head, adding or removing papier-mâché until the ears appear natural. Continue sewing down the neck to the back-board. However, don't tie off and cut the thread—yet.

Slide the cape around on the head-form until eyes and mouth fit the mannequin. Position the ears into an alert or listening attitude and anchor with string to the antlers. Cut pieces of cardboard and shape to fit inside the ears, to hold them in the correct shape until dry. Tuck the lips into position and set temporarily with pins along the edges, or push into slits cut through the mouth of the mannequin. (An alternate method: sew the lips together before the scalp is set on the head-form.) Push the nose skin deep into the nostrils with the eraser end of a pencil. If there is too much skin to fit neatly, trim the excess. Secure the nostril skin in place with two pins.

Setting the eyes is probably the most important step in the mounting process, for it is the eyes that give the illusion of life. Place a small portion of papier-mâché or modeling clay into each eye socket and smooth with the fingertips. Then spread the eyelids and push the glass eyes into the sockets. If you will now refer to your notes and sketches made beside the dead buck, you will have no trouble positioning the eyes correctly. Pupils should be nearly horizontal, perhaps tipped slightly at the inside edge. Now step back several paces and check the appearance. Adjust until they are 100 per cent right. A common fault of many mounted heads is a popeyed, frightened expression, caused when skin draws away from the eyes while drying. Therefore, pull the lids over the eyes until the deer squints. Two or three weeks later the eyelids will have returned to their natural position.

Push the skin into the tear ducts with any instrument which fits these recesses. If there is an excess of skin, cut it off. Drive a tiny brass nail into the base of the tear ducts. This nail remains permanently in the mount so set it firmly against the skin. Also drive heavy pins through the skin at the corners of the eyes, pins that will prevent the skin from pulling away. With palm of hand, pat the skin of the face until it has made contact with the glue or paste previously brushed over the mannequin. To remove wrinkles, lift the skin with a large needle while the skin is being moved over the head-form. For an obvious reason, do not lift the skin by pulling on the hair. Tie the thread and cut. Trim away extra cape at the rear, leaving about one inch to lap and secure with flat-headed brass tacks at three-fourth inch intervals behind the edge of the form. With small scissors clip the hair from the skin which has been lapped behind the back-board.

Do you remember drilling four holes near the base of each antler? Drive brass nails through the skin into these holes, and then arrange hair over the heads to conceal them. Likewise, drive brass nails on each side of the cut down the back of the neck, spacing them one inch apart. Time and pressure may eventually cause the linen thread to break, but the nails will keep the skin in place.

Has the head become soiled here and there? If so, sponge with warm water and then brush and comb the hair until smooth. Hang the mount in a place where circulating air can dry all parts at approximately the same time. After the head has dried, it will feel rather hard to the touch. Remove all temporary pins from the mouth and eyes and the cardboard and string from the ears. Restore natural color to the nostrils, lips, tear ducts and skin near the eyes with a paste-mixture of petroleum wax and benzine to which a small amount of burnt umber has been added. Apply a small amount of this wax with an artist's brush. Color some wax paste with black oil color and paint the nose. After the wax has dried, buff the nose with a soft cloth and varnish. Antlers, however, should never be varnished. And don't use paint; it gives them an unnatural gloss. Just brush a few drops of a mixture of turpentine and linseed oil on the antlers and rub vigorously with a soft cloth.

A final step remains—attaching the head to a plaque. Selection of shape and kind of wood is a matter of individual taste. Generally, a large head appears best on a large panel. Maple, walnut, cedar, cherry and similar woods are all beautiful. To attach a head, position the mount on the plaque, preferably with another's assistance, and drill four holes (slightly smaller than the 2½-inch screws used for attachment) through the panel and into the back-board. Attach the hanger iron to the plaque and suspend the head on a wall. If the hair appears rough in spots, moisten with a damp cloth. Finally, comb and brush the entire head to arrange the hair neatly and smoothly.

Having followed instructions, you now have a trophy of which you can be proud. In fact, there is no valid reason why this head cannot occupy a prominent place in your home—on the living, den or rumpus room wall. Womenfolk need have no fear that it will attract insects, and it can be easily dusted with a brush attachment on a vacuum cleaner or a cloth. When time appears to have soiled the head, washing with mild soapy water will refreshen the mount.

If fees charged by taxidermists appear excessive, or details of mounting too complicated, there is yet another method of mounting that rack which is neither expensive nor detailed. In fact, the entire job can be completed within a couple of hours. The cost: a dollar or so.

Saw the antlers from the skull, as described previously, and clean the bone thoroughly, preferably by immersing in boiling water to which a smidgen of hydrogen peroxide has been added. Scrape all flesh away. Thereafter carefully avoid touching the skull with soiled, oily fingers.

Cut from suitable wood a plaque to which the skull plate is attached with three round-headed wood screws, just as the skull was attached to the mannequin. The plaque can be stained and varnished, merely varnished or finished in one of several other ways. Some individuals paint the skull plate or cover with felt, plaster of paris, or the original hair. I prefer to print date of kill, locality, owner, etc., with black ink on the bone between and below the antlers—and then cover with two coats of clear varnish.

Here, then, hangs the finished trophy, a fitting climax to a hunt, an object which for many years will recall details of a memorable experience.

10

Horse Sense And Leather

Omission of a few remarks about horses in a book of mule deer hunting would be equivalent to a vacation in Cairo without climbing a pyramid. I've "been around" horses all my life, but don't profess to be an equine expert. However, I've learned a few details through the years, usually in the College of Hard Knocks, and writing about some of them may be helpful to others.

I've recently learned never to wander around camp at night in white thermal underwear and unlaced boots. Old Doll, leg-tethered near camp, must have thought I was a wicked sort of ghost as I neared. She snorted, broke her tether rope and disappeared downriver. Furthermore, she threw a shoe which somewhat delayed the start of a week's ride through primitive, Yellowstone Park back-country. Horses shy from many objects: flushing grouse, pieces of automobile chrome, snakes, a fluttering candy wrapper. Shouting, arm-waving humans frightens horses also. Once a particularly lovable mare which I had ridden frequently was among a group of horses being herded into a corral for the night. When they failed to break sharply through the gate, a friend ran toward them, yelling, gesturing. The mare slipped on a patch of ice and broke her right, rear leg. A long time was required to swallow the lump after she was led away, limping through the conifers, to be shot, and to be eaten later by bears.

Many horses, you'll discover, have a few mean tricks. However, this is no excuse to mistreat a horse. Let him know right away that you intend to be kind, but firm. A horse can make your trip miserable if he gains the upper hand. He may not comprehend excellent English, but let him know by the inflection of your voice what you expect. If profanity is necessary—the louder the better.

A horse "sizes you up" when introduced. Walk toward his head slowly, but unafraid; a horse can smell the nervous sweat of a frightened man. Some sportsmen are so timid when near horses that they can't relax and enjoy the experience. Keep the chatter flowing constantly when handling a horse, and use his name frequently. Ask any outfitter what particular tidbit your horse prefers: oats, carrots, candy, tobacco—and feed the animal occasionally—from the flat of your hand, not from the fingertips, for an obvious reason. After he's accepted your gift, pat him gently on the neck, still speaking softly. If you are afraid of horses, the hired help will saddle and bridle your mount. Some packers want it that way and prefer that dudes stand aside until called to mount up. However, caring for one's own horse is part and parcel of a safari experience so, if given permission, care for your own mount. Be as self-reliant as possible; learn to depend on your own resourcefulness.

Stirrup length must be adjusted to each individual. First, place each stirrup under your armpit and extend the arm and hand along the stirrup leather. Your fingertips should reach to where the stirrup leather is attached to the saddle. Next, mount and check for comfortable length. Most individuals are satisfied when, standing in the stirrups, they can pass a fist between their bottoms and the saddle.

When the packer calls for everyone to mount, proceed as taught by your friend, the wrangler. Grasp both reins in your left hand, adjust their length to reach the horn and latch onto the horn with your left hand. Keep a running chatter going with your horse. Then thrust your left foot into the left stirrup, while propelling your weight from the ground with your right leg. A right hand on the horn or cantle assists materially in reaching the saddle. Once aboard, immediately thrust your right foot into the stirrup. A thoroughly trained horse remains standing until a rider is seated and is given a go-ahead signal. Commonly, however, animals begin to travel when your right foot clears the ground. Many ranch horses so react and their owners consider this an admirable trait—an indication of git-up-and-go. Occasionally, you'll be assigned a horse that is quite anxious to be off and traveling, and he may foot-dance or turn as you mount. Tight reins and a little profanity usually prevent repetition of such discourtesy. However, if the horse persists, particularly if you are inexperienced, ask one of the guides to hold the critter's head while you climb aboard. Did the wrangler tell you that it's an excellent practice to lead a horse a short distance before mounting, especially on cold mornings?

The packer or one of his assistants usually heads the column of animals on the trail, and you will be assigned a general station. Maintain this position at least for a day or so—and leave worries to the person in charge. Be alert. Keep 10 feet behind the horse immediately in front to position you and your mount beyond kicking range. Check the near animals occasionally for loose ropes, unbalanced packs, etc. Guides and wranglers can't watch all horses all of the time.

Ride in an erect, upright position, neither to one side nor leaning backward against the cantle. Balls of the feet should rest in the bottom of the stirrups—especially when on a strange horse. In case of trouble, your feet can easily be extracted. A shoe locked in a stirrup may mean real trouble. It's also an excellent practice for amateurs to keep one hand on the horn as often as possible. I do. Hold both reins in one hand; cowboys generally grasp them in the left. Never release reins to dangle over the horse's neck. It's surprising how quickly a very old, supposedly docile nag can react to what she believes is danger. She can quickly jump and easily throw an inexperienced rider before he can regain control. Ride with "comfortable" reins unless the horse wants to travel too fast. Early in the morning Paint may tend to move too rapidly, but most animals "settle down" after about 15 minutes on the trail. On a strange horse don't "knot" the reins. Then, if trouble develops, the reins fall to the ground, which often stops a horse.

Western horses are taught to "neck rein"; so don't confuse them by pulling on the reins to guide them—unless they're cantankerous and about to take off for parts unknown. A very lazy horse may require spurs, or a stick; a good horse requires neither. Horses you ride when muley hunting move out when one "clucks" his tongue in conjunction with pressing knees against his shoulders or urging him gently in the ribs with your heels. He'll stop when you gently pull back on the reins and say "whoa." Stop your horse when a companion is attempting to mount. Rest your horse occasionally—allow him to "blow" for two to three minutes on a steep trail. Most horses voluntarily stop when winded, although some nags attempt to trick a beginner.

An experienced mountain horse senses dangerous situations; so, if he refuses to proceed through a bog, over a very steep or rocky area, etc., dismount and inspect the place. A few horses bluff, however; they want to return to the ranch. Never permit a horse to "con" you. When confronted with an obviously critical place on the trail, lead the horse. At least, loosen the reins somewhat and permit him to "pick his own way." When following other horses, there is no particular need to guide him anyway. Cross bridges and streams carefully. Some horses jump narrow streams and obstructions, so, be alert when obstacles appear. When the day's ride is long or over rough ups and downs, dismount and walk for 10 minutes of each hour. It loosens cramped muscles and permits Old Raisins to relax a bit, too. Allow your animal to drink when he chooses, but don't let him consume excessive quantities when sweating-hot.

At least once during the day the trail boss will call a longer rest stop —for lunch, toilet call, etc. The wrangler will show you how to tie a horse so that about 3 feet of rope extends from his nose to a hefty branch or tree. Attaching the rope at least nose-high insures that your mount can't step over the rope and flounder. Always tie-up with the halter or neck rope, never with the reins. During longer stops remove your rifle, camera, etc. from the horse. It's unlikely that he will roll when tied as instructed, but he may break your precious equipment when scratching his pelt against the tether-tree. If the stop is to be long, perhaps to hunt, remove the saddle and bridle; otherwise they stay on the horse. Check the cinch before resuming the ride.

Be reasonable with your horse. Don't force him to continue at an excessive pace, particularly on rough-tough terrain and with spurs. At the first opportunity he'll likely react to your shabby treatment. However, don't be excessively permissive—such as allowing him to loiter or graze promiscuously along the trail. I've never seen the horse which didn't need some "handling."

Horse-hunting for big game has many advantages. A good horse carries a hunter to where the game is located—sometimes many miles from the end of the road or base camp; assists in finding the deer; and packs the carcass to camp. He may even untangle a dude when lost and return him safely. Type of terrain dictates how a horse should be used to hunt mule deer. In semi-open, easily negotiated country a hunter may remain almost continuously in the saddle from daylight until dark. Elevated, he can frequently see for miles. However, I prefer to ride a horse to where I expect to find deer and then spook around on foot. Deer nowadays are often located in rather rugged terrain, where a horse can't easily go. Some individuals lead their horses as they wander around. A horse walks rather noisily, but most deer have seen men and horses together and may remain around longer than were the man alone. If you leave your horse to stalk or follow wounded game, tie him securely; then remember where you left him. Ridges and canyons in muley country often appear very much alike. When unable to locate Old Smoky, ask a companion to ride his horse through the terrain where you supposedly anchored him. A single horse soon becomes lonesome and, when another horse approaches, he'll nicker.

Don't shoot from the back of your horse. It's difficult to aim properly from such a fidgety platform. Besides, the rifle report and muzzle blast frighten even the most gentle, docile nag. As a matter of fact, don't fire a large caliber weapon anywhere near a horse, particularly one whose acquaintance you have only recently made. A further bit of advice: an experienced hunting horse senses when action is about to commence. In all likelihood he's seen the deer; and, if you dismount hurriedly, snatch the weapon past his head, he'll suspect there's to be some blasting—and he may shy or break and run. A horse may snort and shy when he sees a bear. But, when it's a standing muley or one slowly climbing up a nearby ridge, he'll stop, stiffen and crank his ears forward. When lost, don't argue with the horse over correct direction to camp. Admit to him that you're confused and he'll prove he's right, every time.

Want to please your packer—which usually means a return invitation the following autumn? Ride horses several times at home before reporting to his ranch. He has more important problems than listening to how sore your prat is after the first long day in the saddle. Arrive with your possessions in suitable containers that stow easily into panniers or atop a horse's back. Don't bring unnecessary junk-luxury items. During correspondence with the outfitter, he'll enclose a list of needed equipment. Make increasingly longer walks at home—for two weeks before the dream hunt. It's surprising how much hiking a person does on a horse safari.

Most outfitters do not furnish a rifle scabbard; or, when they do, the leather leaks water and gathers branches, is too short for your rifle, etc. So, for these and several other reasons which needn't be enumerated here, you should own a scabbard. Experiment—try all positions—and learn to your satisfaction the best method of suspending your rifle in its scabbard, from your saddle on your horse. You'll soon discover that suspending a weapon so that the scope hangs downward and supports much of the weight, is no-go. The result is the same when a scope is jammed against leather in an all-fitting scabbard: a rifle whose point of impact may be askiddle because of a bent scope or loose mounts. Flat action weapons are simple to scabbard, but few use such firearms anymore. Here, we're talking chiefly about bolt actions.

A friend hangs his rifle on the starboard (right) side of his horse, recoil pad to the rear. He's a long-armed gent and, when he dismounts, he merely reaches rearward with his right hand, grabs his thunder stick and the rifle moves smoothly off with him. However, I dislike this position; it places the bulk of the weight of the weapon on the rear of the saddle, where there is insufficient support. Consequently, even though there is a second cinch, the saddle often shifts to the right. If mounted rather high, the stock may interfere with mounting and dismounting. Too, when traveling uphill with the rifle hanging fairly low, it may tip out of the scabbard or be pulled out by a snag, particularly when wearing a sling. One distinct advantage is that the rifle forearm and barrel raise only a minor bump under the rider's leg. Most big game hunters suspend their scabbards on the left side, recoil pad to the rear. This position is wrong for most of the reasons advanced for mounting in the same position on the right side of the horse. One important advantage, however, is that the rifle is readily available the moment a hunter reaches the ground. If you prefer this position, remove or tuck the sling into the scabbard. I usually attach a scabbard to the port side of Old Red with the butt plate forward and high enough to permit free movement of the horse's head. Reasons: weapon is where I can watch it constantly; can't easily be extracted by a branch; is hanging from the side from which I usually dismount; and weight is on the main cinch. The several disadvantages of this position were previously enumerated. To suspend a scabbard in this position, run the hanger-straps on the butt end of your scabbard through the neck of the saddle and the other through the upper, rear cinch ring. Adjust and position to satisfy individual whims. Ordinary saddle straps aren't hefty enough to support a scabbarded rifle. Eventually they break and your favorite rifle tumbles to the ground, perhaps to be walked upon by a trailing horse.

Ideal situation is to own a scabbard for each type of weapon, but this involves considerable expense. So, most big-game hunters own but one scabbard. My scabbard accommodates bolt-action rifles with barrels from 20 to 26 inches. For shorter barrels an appropriate length of cylindrical wood is inserted in the forward end of the scabbard. This scabbard is 48 inches long (but telescopes out several inches for longer weapons); has a mouth width of 8½ inches; and the hood measures 14 inches. The hanger-straps are 48 inches long and the scabbard is made from heavy, saddle leather. Such an outfit costs approximately $75. However, it's cheap at twice the price. Some of the stocks I've made for my rifles are each worth several hundred dollars. Left unprotected on a pack trip through rugged country, one of these stocks could easily be battered and scratched into a $10 hunk of near nothingness.

You'll be more than satisfied with a hooded scabbard, particularly on a long pack trip. Some sportsmen prefer hoods which fold back, zipper shut or close with a snap fastener. My scabbard closes by means of two buckled straps, and I've never found a good reason to regret this choice. Don't be tricked into purchasing a scabbard lined with sheepskin. Sometime, somehow, the wool will become wet. How can you dry it? Continued use over several days in a wet condition eventually means a new blue job and stock finish. It's also important not to place a ready-to-fire rifle into a scabbard.

A good pair of saddlebags also helps one become a happy, contented muley hunter. Few packers furnish good ones; so purchase a pair. A considerable portion of the hundred or so items you take on a mule deer safari can be stowed in these bags so that they remain handy for almost instant use. The pair I have, handcrafted and roomy, were purchased by a friend a number of years ago in Mexico for $5. Unfortunately, comparable bags now cost approximately $50. These bags measure 11 inches wide, 10 inches deep and accordion out to 3 inches.

To enter primitive and wilderness areas, a hunter must travel on his feet or by horse. Elsewhere, a horse can transport a person where motor vehicles can't possibly go; where a foot-hunter hasn't the strength and time to reach; into the back-country where most of the trophies live. For me, the odors of horses and saddle leather are among the most delightful on earth.